MICHAEL M. HARMON

RESPONSIBILITY AS PARADOX

A Critique of
Rational Discourse
on Government

 Advances in Public Administration

Foreword by Bayard L. Catron, *George Washington University*

Sponsored by the **Public Administration Theory Network**
and supported by **Lewis and Clark College**

SAGE Publications
International Educational and Professional Publisher
Thousand Oaks   London   New Delhi

Copyright © 1995 by Sage Publications, Inc.

For information address:

SAGE Publications, Inc.
2455 Teller Road
Thousand Oaks, California 91320

SAGE Publications Ltd.
6 Bonhill Street
London EC2A 4PU
United Kingdom

SAGE Publications India Pvt. Ltd.
M-32 Market
Greater Kailash I
New Delhi 110048 India

Printed in the United States of America

Library of Congress Cataloging-in-Publication Data

Harmon, Michael M, 1941-
    Responsibility as paradox : a critique of rational discourse on
government / Michael M. Harmon.
        p. cm.—(Advances in public administration)
    Includes bibliographical references and index.
        ISBN 0-8039-7007-2 (hardcover: alk. paper).—ISBN 0-8039-7008-0 (pbk.:
alk. paper)
        1. Public administration. 2. Responsibility. 3. Political
obligation. I. Title. II. Series.
JF1411. H363 1995
350—dc20   95-7683

This book is printed on acid-free paper.

95 96 97 98 10 9 8 7 6 5 4 3 2 1

Sage Production Editor: Diana E. Axelsen

To my parents,
Judd and Helen Harmon,
who are responsible

Contents

List of Figures

Foreword

◆ The responsibility of a foreword writer seems clear enough, but the role is not without its tensions. The writer is expected to make favorable comments about the book and yet avoid the appearance of being the author's publicist. It would be irresponsible not to describe the book briefly, but equally irresponsible to oversimplify it or steal its punch—which are real dangers with brief comments about complex subjects.

In our current political culture, accountability requires full disclosure of possible conflicts of interest. To be responsible in that sense, I should reveal that I am a long-time friend and colleague of the author. Yet I would not want the reader to discount my opinions of the book for that reason. So to insure credibility, perhaps I should use superlatives sparingly and demonstrate my critical faculties (if not indulge in being critical). But on the other hand, if I fail to express fully my admiration for the book, perhaps I will not satisfy my responsibility to its author, or even to myself.

If a relatively simple role like that of foreword-writer is subject to such ruminations about how to fill it responsibly, how much more so are complex roles like those filled by public officials, in which one of the distinctive marks is multiple and conflicting responsibilities. This book helps to sort out the linguistic tangle surrounding the concept of responsibility. In an imaginative leap, Harmon makes a virtue of the conceptual ambiguity of the term, persuasively demonstrating through careful argumentation that it is inherently paradoxical. The work is a model of clarity without reductionism that we might wish other social theorists emulated.

Responsibility as Paradox provides perhaps the first original treatment of the subject of responsibility in government in more than half a century, offering a new framework for an old debate in political theory. The recent Anglo-American literature on the subject has been an elaboration of the issues and terms set by Herman Finer and Carl Friedrich in 1940. Harmon is the first, I think, to claim that the similarities between the "hard-core" (Finer et al.) and "soft-core" (Friedrich et al.) rationalists are greater than their differences. He critiques both types alike for their impoverished view of reason.

With exemplary linguistic sensitivity, Harmon identifies and preserves paradox as a way of capturing the poignancy and complexity of the concept of responsibility. Paradox, he says, is the crucible within which we wage the struggle to confront the opposing aspects of our responsibility. Rather than treat paradox as a nuisance to be avoided or neutralized, as the rationalists do, Harmon argues that it is the source of much of the richness and power of concepts like responsibility. Thus, this is not only a work on responsibility in government but a work in philosophy and social theory as well.

The architecture of the work is impressive, manifesting an aesthetic only rarely achieved in works of social theory. Each of the three meanings of responsibility—agency, obligation, and accountability—is subjected to exegesis as a paradox. Each is reframed in relation to the others so that the tensions and complementarity are revealed. By systematically considering two types of paradox and showing how to convert the pathological sort into healthy paradox, Harmon avoids the trap of defending one connotation of responsibility over the others.

Harmon exposes the pathology of the current trend in our society toward greater and greater accountability of public officials through edict, rule, and law. In the process, he shows us a way to reinstate the idea of personal responsibility to its rightful place in the moral discourse on government. As he addresses these themes, Harmon illuminates current political issues like "reinventing government," and discusses the complementary deficiencies of liberal and conservative approaches to topics like affirmative action. However, Harmon does not present a program (such as a "way to make government officials more responsible"); to do so would violate his own thesis. Instead, he calls for public servants and citizens alike to struggle honestly with the moral uncertainty that inevitably accompanies public action.

Let me speak plainly: I very much admire this book; I wish I had written it myself. It is beautifully designed, lucidly argued, and refreshingly original. It is a mature work of a first-class mind. It breaks new ground on an important topic, and I hope it receives the attention it deserves.

Bayard L. Catron
George Washington University

Series Editor's Introduction

THE RATIONALE for this series lies in the ongoing need to reexamine and enrich thinking in the field of public administration. It can be argued that few fields need efforts of this sort more urgently. Twenty years ago, Vincent Ostrom declared that an "intellectual crisis" existed in public administration. Significantly, that crisis has continued unabated into the 1990s. Meanwhile, the public's faith in the administrative state has declined precipitously and, in the words of Herbert Kaufman, bureaucrat bashing has become "pandemic."

Intellectually, this crisis lies in the discrepancy between the field's 19th-century roots and the postmodern realities we must face at the turn of the 20th century. Despite 20 years of intellectual foment by academics, most practitioners still adhere to a model of public administration shaped in a world that no longer exists. The Progressive era that gave birth to modern American public administration was an age that believed in universal technical/rational solutions to political, social, and even moral problems. It was a time in which strong Western nation-states and their empires were commonly viewed as the anointed agents of progress and civilization. Most of all, it was a period in which government was beginning to be seen as part of the answer, rather than part of the problem.

Virtually none of these views holds in the contemporary world, yet public administration and its literature have been indelibly marked by these roots. As a result, it remains grounded in the classic model of the centralized nation-state at a time when a global economy is a reality, Western empires disintegrate, and a new feudalism based upon warring ethnic and racial communities seems emergent. Its literature still takes a largely technical/rational view of the world, though the practice of public administration increasingly requires decidedly *nontechnical* ethical and political decisions. Even more troubling, although a thorough reevaluation of first principles and assumptions is in order, the literature, like the field itself, too often retreats into bureaucratic defensiveness or formulaic "solutions" to problems.

It can be argued, then, that public administration badly needs new literature that reexamines its basic premises. There is little question that the materials for this reexamination are present. Certainly they exist in disciplines such as history, philosophy, the humanities, and the social sciences. They range backward and forward in time. Some present a vision of existence in a disordered, fragmented, but exciting postmodern world. Some reach backward to apply traditional philosophic thought to current issues. Others suggest radically new ways to view human thought and action. Still others depict an environmentally centered world in which people are no longer masters but stewards of the world in which they live.

Because public administration often is referred to as an interdisciplinary study, it seems reasonable to expect it to break out of its traditional paradigm and use this body of knowledge to advantage. Two factors seem to prevent this, however. First, to the degree public administration has drawn on other disciplines, it has chosen to rely upon those that fit most easily into its universalistic and rational tradition. Thus, modern economics, analytic philosophy, systems analysis, and behavioral science all have had far more impact on the field than history, contemporary social philosophy, humanities, or qualitative social science research.

Second, to the degree that scholars have developed alternative conceptual rather than technical approaches to public administration, they are more frequently the subject of debate among academics than grist for the professional mill. Academic movements in public administration calling attention to constitutional history, critical theory, Jungian psychology, and postmodern thought have had surprisingly little impact outside scholarly journals. The reasons for this are severalfold. Until recently, the intellectual crisis in the field has not been clearly tied to what might be called the operational crisis in public administration. The traditional paradigms of public administration might be questioned intellectually, but at the level of practice, the general philosophy was "If it's not broken, don't fix it."

In addition, it can be extremely difficult to relate philosophic and social theory to practice in a manner that is readily accessible to students and practitioners. It is inherently difficult to frame much of this thought clearly and cogently enough to speak to individuals who have little background in fields such as history or philosophy. It is even more of a challenge to show how such theories relate to practice in concrete ways, and, conversely, to criticize the applicability of these theories in terms of the experience gained from using them in practice. Yet, unless these two tasks can be accomplished, a firm linkage between theory and practice rarely is achieved.

However, it can be argued that public administration has reached the point at which this situation is ripe for change. In this country, political gridlock, fiscal deficit, administrative scandal, and the sheer inability of government to deal with human needs ranging from health care to disaster relief have caused people to question the viability of the American administrative state as never before. In short, it is harder and harder for thoughtful practitioners and students to dismiss the crisis in public administration as merely "intellectual."

Advances in Public Administration is an occasional, open-ended series designed both to encourage and to contribute to the vital process of rethinking public administration in the light of the issues just discussed. To this end, the editorial board has sought works that meet the following set of criteria as far as possible. Each volume will seek to reconceptualize some aspects of the field in an insightful manner that goes well beyond traditional approaches to the subject. Specific goals will include accomplishing the following:

- Stimulate students and practitioners to reflect critically on the practice of public administration
- Utilize cutting-edge conceptual materials drawn from a variety of disciplines especially those which have had less impact on the study and practice of public administration
- Apply theory to practice and conversely use practice to evaluate theory
- Set forth complex theoretical concepts in an understandable manner without unduly sacrificing their meaning or content
- Provide adequate background material for those readers unfamiliar with the disciplines upon which the work draws
- Be of potential use as classroom material in graduate and/or upper division courses in public administration

The series will consist of monographs, texts, closely edited collections and an occasional reissue of a valuable out-of-print work. Although the works will vary in topic, they will be unified by the editorial selection criteria just outlined.

As Coordinating Editor of **Advances in Public Administration,** I wish to take this opportunity to thank the members of the series Editorial Board, the Public Administration Theory Network, and Lewis and Clark College for their generous sponsorship of this project. Finally, I would be extremely remiss if I did not recognize the efforts of my Associate Editors Camilla Stivers and Guy Adams and those of Carrie Mullen of Sage Publications and my colleague Dr. Douglas Morgan for the unfailing support and encouragement they have given me in launching the series.

Henry D. Kass
Coordinating Editor
Lake Oswego, Oregon

Acknowledgments

◆ AFTER THANKING colleagues, friends, and family for their support and guidance, it is customary for a book's author to absolve them of responsibility for the final product. This granting of absolution evidently assumes that responsibility, at least the sort implied by the custom, is something that those who helped would gladly be rid of, or that the author believes they ought to be. Although I certainly do not hold any of the people mentioned here blameworthy for whatever shortcomings this volume may still have, they as well as I—we—nevertheless share responsibility for it from the standpoint of other salient meanings of the word. The reasons for this should become clearer as the reader proceeds through the pages that follow—for the subject of the book is responsibility, a word whose richness and power, especially during the twentieth century, stem in large measure from the ambiguity and the contradictions embedded in it.

I am especially grateful to my friend and colleague of more than twenty years, Bayard Catron, who served as my personal editor as the manuscript neared completion. Always respecting my aspirations for the book and never imposing his own, Bayard was the

perfect critic, providing both invaluable substantive insights drawn
from his knowledge of philosophy and social theory and a keen
sense of what the structure of the book's argument demanded in
order to sustain its integrity and coherence.

Henry D. Kass, coordinating editor of Sage's series, **Advances
in Public Administration**, not only saw fit to include the book in
the series, but also contributed greatly to its readability both by
offering, and by reminding me of the need for, real-life examples
to animate the intricacies of the argument. Thanks also to Carrie
Mullen, Diana Axelsen, and Jackie Tasch, of Sage Publications, for
their close attention to the details of the book's production and
their prompt responses to my many questions.

The contributions of Cynthia McSwain and Orion White, both
through their writings and our continuing conversation during the
past decade and a half, pervade this book. This can be seen in the
many references to their work in at least three of the chapters; but
a surer measure of the weight of their influence is how often my
private self-congratulation for coming up with an original idea was
soon followed by a recollection of something very similar they had
said or written.

The middle chapters of the book were written in Sydney,
Australia, where the magnificent view of Sydney Harbour, the
bridge, and the opera house, as seen from my flat, alternately
inspired and distracted me from my work. Michael W. Jackson, of
the University of Sydney, and Hal Colebatch, Pieter Degeling, and
Lex Donaldson, all from the University of New South Wales,
provided me with helpful criticisms and stimulating discussion. I
should also thank Anne Crawford, Richard Dunford, Peter Larmour,
and Adrienne and John Wells for their kind hospitality during my
stay.

Camilla Stivers served as the series editorial board's anony-
mous reviewer, offering both encouragement and useful suggestions for the project overall, as well as insights from her own work
on feminist theory and public administration, thereby providing a
partial antidote to the book's essentially masculine (or so I have
been told) frame of reference.

In view of his formidable background in political philosophy,
M. Judd Harmon showed great restraint (no doubt prompted by

parental solicitude) in criticizing the substance of the argument, limiting his comments mainly to lapses in the manuscript's style and composition. He was always right.

Mark Bigelow, Tracy Smith Hall, Melissa Price, and Alecia Ward helped with the final preparation of the manuscript, finding typographical errors, assisting with the index, and (usually) winning arguments about word usage and composition. Milena Baptista and Katy Hayden showed more patience than I deserved by printing out countless drafts of the book's chapters and rescuing me from my general incompetence with computers.

I am especially grateful for the financial support that enabled me to take time off from teaching in order to write this book. Summer research grants from The George Washington University's facilitating fund and GWU's School of Business and Public Management supplemented my sabbatical leave during the 1992-1993 academic year.

Finally, my thanks to all of my colleagues in the Department of Public Administration at George Washington for reasons that are too numerous to list.

Introduction

In the 1964 Broadway production of *Beyond the Fringe*, Peter Cook and Alan Bennett performed the roles of a television reporter and a dim-witted Scotland Yard police inspector heading the investigation of what the media had termed the "great train robbery." Early in their interview the inspector explains that "When you speak of a train robbery this in fact involves no loss of train. It's merely what I like to call the *contents* of the train that were pilfered." After further, and hilariously superfluous, elaboration of this point, the interview continues:

> *Reporter:* Who do you think may have perpetrated this awful crime?
>
> *Inspector:* We believe this to be the work of thieves. . . . The whole pattern is extremely reminiscent of past robberies where we have found thieves to be involved—the tell-tale loss of property, the snatching away of the money substance. It all points to thieves.
>
> *Reporter:* You say you feel that thieves are responsible.
>
> *Inspector:* Good heavens, no! I feel that thieves are totally *ir*responsible, ghastly people who go around snatching your money.

◈ ODD FACTS and random bits of humor first heard or read long ago periodically resurface in our consciousness for no reason at all, or so it initially appears. It is often possible upon further reflection, however, to ferret out some connection between these seemingly trivial recollections and later events in our lives or personal issues that have long-standing salience for us. During the past twenty-five years I have written and lectured frequently about the responsible administration of government and have used the episode from *The Great Train Robbery* (which I first heard as a graduate student) as introductory material to lighten what readers and listeners probably regard, with good reason, as an exceedingly ponderous subject. More recently, however, that episode has provided more than simply a respite from the subject's undeniable seriousness. It has upon further reflection helped to crystallize for me an insight about the significance of responsibility's dual meaning that is conspicuously absent in the mainstream literature about responsible government. Specifically, the double entendre in the comical interview involving the reporter and the police inspector does not simply reflect a linguistic irony rooted in *responsibility's* tangled etymology. Rather, each of responsibility's dual, indeed opposing, meanings is logically necessary for comprehending the other. That is, the belief that people's actions *cause* events to occur (for example, that people can be responsible for robbing a train) is a precondition for their *answerability* to others for those actions.

The power and influence of responsibility, especially during the twentieth century, are attributable in great degree to the very confusion and contradictions that the word evokes. This is simply another way of saying that responsibility is a paradoxical word, a fact unappreciated by the mainstream, or what I shall call the "rationalist," discourse on government, which assumes that responsibility is synonymous with ethical correctness and the conformity of action with authoritative ends. At this writing, for example, the federal government, under the leadership of Vice President Al Gore, is in the midst of a massive administrative reform effort aimed at "reinventing" government. *Creating Government That Works Better and Costs Less: The Report of the National*

Performance Review (NPR) (Gore, 1993), which bears the vice president's imprimatur, recommends as the guiding philosophy of that reinvention that government agencies be charged with articulating clearer, more ambitious, and more measurable goals, which they will then be held accountable for achieving. At the same time the report advises the continual resetting of those goals ("higher and higher" ones), administrative flexibility and creativity, worker participation, and freedom from the shackles of overregulation and micromanagement by the Congress.

All this may be achievable, but in reading the report one wonders if its authors fully comprehend that embodied in their recommendations are paradoxical pieces of advice. Whatever may be its virtues, goal clarity, for example, is frequently achieved at the *expense* of flexibility; employee participation often increases the difficulty of "pinpointing" responsibility; the threat of being held accountable is as likely to inspire scapegoating and buckpassing as creativity; and one person's micromanagement is the next person's vigilant oversight. Like its predecessor reform initiatives, the reinventing government movement runs the risk of forgetting that what appears to be rational from the reformer's lofty perch is frequently irrational from the worm's-eye perspective of those charged with implementing reforms. Moreover, the view from the perch is not necessarily better than the one on the ground. Thus a more sensible approach to reform is not necessarily to adjust the latter to the former in the rational interest of administrative purity, but to regard reform instead as the intelligent management of the contradictory motives and forces that constitute political and organizational life. Attempts to eradicate these paradoxes, or to pretend they do not exist, will inevitably backfire.

The recent history of governmental reform in the United States can plausibly be written as a history of rationalism's failures and, at best, qualified successes. The recommendations and general tenor of the NPR report sound strikingly similar to those of earlier reform efforts such as Program, Planning, Budgeting Systems (PPBS) during the administration of President Lyndon Johnson, Management by Objectives (MBO) during the Nixon administration, Zero-Base Budgeting (ZBB) of the Carter years, and many of the Grace

Commission's recommendations during Ronald Reagan's presidency—all of which delivered far short of their promises to enhance appreciably government's effectiveness, efficiency, and responsiveness. One implication of the arguments developed in this book is that insofar as the government's current reinvention continues to rely on rationalism's equation of reform with effectiveness, efficiency, and even responsiveness, as it is usually defined, we have little realistic hope for its success. Lasting reform cannot be limited to these instrumental objectives but must address the problem of responsibility in its varied and conflicting meanings. Such reform, should we continue to use the word, must in other words take satisfactory account of the paradoxes of responsibility.

For more than half a century the principal terms of the American debate about responsible government have remained largely unaltered; they are characterized by tacit, hidden agreements that outweigh in importance the chief points of disagreement within that debate. It is the points of agreement between what I term the hard-core and soft-core factions of the rationalist discourse that present the most formidable barriers, both practical and moral, to the genuine realization of responsible government. The principal belief shared by rationalists of both camps is that responsible action is synonymous with morally or legally *correct* action, and that the purpose of moral discourse on government and of laws and other guidelines regulating administrative action is to preserve or restore a state of moral innocence.

Rationalists regard paradox as a problem of logic that begs neat solution, or better yet should simply be avoided inasmuch as its continued presence endangers the possibility of moral innocence. As Peter French (1992) observes, however, innocence is less akin to moral purity than to moral virginity. Once initiated, there is no possibility of returning to the safety and comfort of innocence, notwithstanding the tempting promises, as well as the warnings, of moral and official pronouncements to the contrary. Paradox describes the condition of innocence lost irretrievably with the dawning of consciousness. Since that signal event in human evolution, paradox has formed the crucible within which we wage, although we may often seek to evade, the struggle to confront the opposing aspects of our responsibility. The struggle for and against responsibility plays out both consciously and unconsciously in our inner lives, in intimate relations with others, and in social institutions that enable and regulate public conduct. Moreover, the struggle may be expressed in a variety of vocabularies: spiritual (sin and redemption); psychological (guilt, shame, and individuation); moral (blame and obligation); and institutional (accountability and, especially recently, empowerment). Although these vocabularies might seem to depict distinctive domains of our public and private life, the domains are themselves merely the sediment of language. Thus the boundaries that we erect between them distinguish only our modes of speaking rather than hermetically separate spheres of our experience. Of these vocabularies rationalism has been by far the least successful in enabling a comprehension of the paradoxical character of responsibility and by implication the most prone to abet futile efforts to recapture lost innocence. A chief reason for the failure of rationalist discourse, or so I intend to argue, arises from its misplaced insistence on dividing categorically issues of public conduct from those of private life, of collective obligation from personal development.

In the following chapters I challenge the essential point of agreement in the rationalist discourse by showing that the idea of responsibility connotes multiple and conflicting meanings that render it inherently paradoxical. Theologian H. Richard Niebuhr's (1963) depiction of the "responsible self" as embodying two opposing images—"man the maker" and "man the answerer"—is used throughout the latter portion of the book to frame the paradoxes generated by the rationalist conception of responsibility. Because of responsibility's paradoxical nature, the rationalist equation of responsibility with correctness is necessarily flawed in a most fundamental way. Only through an appreciation of responsibility's paradoxical nature can the idea of personal responsibility be reinstated to its rightful place in the moral discourse on government.

An Outline of the Argument

Responsibility as Paradox explains the continuing crisis of responsible government and administration by showing why demands for greater accountability of public servants to authoritative edicts almost invariably fail to achieve their intended results, namely, the satisfaction of public wants and the orderly and efficient attainment of authoritative ends. The first two chapters are devoted to a critique of the rationalist conception of responsibility. Following this introductory chapter, Chapter 2 begins the critique with a brief history of the idea of responsibility, tracing it back to its early Greek, English, French, and German origins and noting some of the early controversies and ambiguities that the word evoked. Three contemporary meanings of responsibility are extracted from this discussion:

Agency, the idea that freedom of the will makes people, in Jean-Paul Sartre's (1956, p. 553) phrase, the "incontestable authors" of their actions

Accountability, the idea that people are answerable to higher, usually institutional, authority for their actions

Obligation, the notion that moral action is determined by its correspondence to principles and standards deriving from sources external to the agent

Eleven statements showing how *responsibility* is variously used in everyday speech are presented, followed by an explanation of how the statements' differing and often contradictory uses of the word are deducible from various combinations and nuances of its three core meanings.

Chapter 3 is introduced by a consideration of why rationalist responsibility is a uniquely modern concept, which, in addition to being grounded within sometimes competing philosophical traditions of the modern era, is also a product of that era's signature institutions: market capitalism and bureaucratic organization. This is followed by a summary of the principal elements of the rationalist conception of responsibility, including the points of dispute between rival factions of rationalist thought. Chief among these is the extent to which, indeed whether, the allowing of discretionary judgments by nonelected public servants is compatible with the responsible administration of democratic governments. Three debates about this subject within the rationalist discourse are considered, pitting advocates of the hard-core faction (represented by Herbert A. Simon, Herman Finer, and John P. Burke) against the soft-core faction (represented by Dwight W. Waldo, Carl J. Friedrich, and Terry L. Cooper). The discussion is critical of both factions for, among other reasons, failing to comprehend the inevitably subjective character of responsible action that inheres in the notion of moral agency.

Chapter 4 explains why the idea of responsibility is paradoxical in the sense that it embodies opposing principles and terms, namely, subjective and objective, personal and institutional, moral agency and moral answerability. Rationalism's inability to comprehend the paradoxical character of responsibility necessarily leads to its neglect of the concept of personal responsibility. Personal responsibility is rooted in the idea of subjectivity, which from the rationalist standpoint is merely an inferior approximation of objectivity. In order to reinstate personal responsibility to a position of deserved prominence, however, it is necessary to probe the various meanings of paradox itself. Paradox has both positive and negative connotations, despite the fact that both the "good" ones and the "bad" ones embody the notion of opposition between polar ideas. The former are termed antinomial paradoxes, in which opposing ideas or principles are maintained in necessary and creative tension with one another—for example, freedom and responsibility, liberty and order. The latter, designated as schismogenic paradoxes, occur when one of two opposing principles is neglected in favor of the other, thus producing predictable pathologies.

Rationalist responsibility is criticized for neglecting the idea of moral agency, and thus the concept of personal responsibility, in favor of the related ideas of obligation and accountability. Niebuhr's image of man the maker is subordinated to the opposing image of man the answerer, with the result that the idea of moral agency is lost. Drawing from two episodes in the fictitious saga of Horatio Hornblower, the chapter defines personal responsibility as incorporating two opposing ideas—self-reflective awareness and commitment to the other as a person—and then explains how the idea of personal responsibility is required in order to avoid the pathologies that inevitably result from the rationalists' exclusive emphasis on institutional accountability and obligation.

The next three chapters focus on three paradoxes generated by the rationalist conception of responsibility: the paradox of obligation, the paradox of blame, and the paradox of accountability. For each paradox the conceptual task is to reframe the relation of each of the three core meanings of responsibility to an opposing or counterpart principle, which rationalist responsibility has permitted to atrophy.

Chapter 5, "The Paradox of Obligation," considers the rationalist view that public officials have a moral as well as a legal obligation to fulfill authoritative edicts and to achieve authoritative ends. In freely entering into contractual agreements that define those obligations, the rationalist view contends, public servants voluntarily sacrifice many of the freedoms enjoyed by ordinary citizens to influence the content of those ends. Rationalism, however, construes the meaning and relation of obligation and freedom in a way that radically splits off each principle from the other, thus creating the paradox of obligation:

> **If people are free to choose but at the same time are obliged to act only as others authoritatively choose for them, then they are not, for all practical purposes, free. If, on the other hand, people do choose freely, their actions may violate authoritative obligations, in which case their exercise of free choice is irresponsible.**

Drawing from philosopher Carole Pateman's (1985) *The Problem of Political Obligation*, the chapter argues that the contractarian political theories of Thomas Hobbes and John Locke, which provide the philosophical grounding for the rationalist conception of obligation, depict a radically privatized individual whose personal aspirations and commitments have become split off from his or her public life. From this view freedom, obligation's opposing principle, has no public or social meaning, being instead the mere expression of private and therefore selfish interests. If this is the case, then freedom is necessarily antithetical to the responsible fulfillment of obligations and is expressed institutionally in bureaucratic opportunism.

The problem of opportunism, however, is an insoluble one for rationalism, which has no plausible answer to the question of why, other than out of fear of punishment, public servants should take their obligations seriously and act from motives other than opportunism. Opportunism can only be ameliorated, although never fully eradicated, by the ongoing participation by public servants in the free, but nevertheless institutionally constrained, creation and even transcendence of their official obligations. The rationalists' schismogenic paradox of obligation, in other words, may be transformed into an antinomial one by altering our understanding of freedom from a purely private and self-interested activity to one of active participation in the mutual creation of interests and obligations.

In Chapter 6, "The Paradox of Agency," I argue that blaming someone else, that is, holding another individual accountable, necessarily constitutes a tacit and usually unconscious declaration of the blamer's innocence. The futile struggle to establish moral innocence by both individuals and collectivities lies at the heart of the schismogenic paradox of agency. By overasserting the individual's guilt or innocence and neglecting the role of collectivities, moral and institutional attributions of blame by conservative rationalists obscure the necessarily shared or relational nature of the concept, thereby producing the predictable pathologies of buckpassing and scapegoating. Conversely, when entitlement liberals, who are rationalists in their own right, hold collectivities solely responsible for the conduct of individuals—for example, through paternalistic policies and the dispensing of entitlements based on past victimization—the individual's sense of personal power and responsibility atrophies as claims of "victim rights" take precedence. The concluding section of the chapter argues that both paradoxes of agency, those deriving from contemporary conservatism's overassertion of the individual and entitlement liberalism's overassertion of the collectivity, result from a failure to see responsibility's dual images of personal agency and moral answerability as being in dialectical relation with one another. What is needed in order to establish that relation is a reframed understanding of the vital role of authority in public institutions.

Chapter 7, "The Paradox of Accountability," completes the series of chapters devoted to the paradoxes embedded in the three core meanings of responsibility. The first section considers the differences between hard-core and soft-core rationalism concerning the legitimacy of public servants' participation in the definition of public purposes. Their long-standing disagreement has produced an unresolvable dilemma in which soft-core rationalists are unable to respond satisfactorily to the charge that their expanded vision of the public servant's role poses a dangerous threat to political authority in democratic government. And hard-core rationalists, by attempting to prevent such participation, reduce that role to one of a compliant technocrat who bears no personal responsibility for the purposes he or she is supposed to achieve.

The next two sections challenge some of the key empirical assumptions shared by both rationalist factions. The first assumption holds that purposes may be understood as consciously rational decisions about ends or goals made independently of and prior to the social processes within which action is taken. Alternatively, purposes are depicted as emerging from social processes characterized by a continuous interaction of thinking (deciding) and acting. A second assumption of rationalism, that accountability for the effective implementation of public purposes may be achieved through bureaucratic control, is criticized for failing to comprehend the inherent limits on the predictability of human action. The idea of control, moreover, depends upon an acceptance of three spurious dichotomies—between means and ends, thought and action, and politics and administration—that have created the paradox of accountability in the first place.

Using the critique of rationalism's empirical assumptions as a starting point, the paradox of accountability is then reframed from the standpoint of philosopher Alasdair MacIntyre's discussion of practice, in which moral "goods," roughly equivalent to ends or purposes, are conceived as internal to social processes. The idea of internal moral goods enables the unification of the opposing principles that rationalism splits apart as dichotomies, thereby making tractable the pathologies of rationalist accountability, namely, the atrophy of personal responsibility and political authority. The chapter concludes with a redefinition of the functional relation between politics and administration that, while honoring the legitimate constraints imposed by the former on the latter, combines the authoritative aspects traditionally associated with the public servant's role with that of facilitating practices of citizens and fellow public servants.

The concluding chapter anticipates the most likely objection to viewing responsibility as paradoxical, namely relativism, which the anxious assert against the quite reasonable belief that moral problems do not permit algorithmic solutions. Rationalist reformers and ethicists characteristically advocate technical fixes and rules for enforcing stricter accountability under the presumption that such algorithms are possible. Responsible government, or so they contend, means "getting it right." The paradoxes elaborated in prior chapters, however, reveal the futility of that belief on both empirical and moral grounds, which combine to show that rationalist responsibility is, above all, impractical. Although I proffer no advice, I do spell out some of the practical implications of viewing responsibility paradoxically. Chief among these is that governing responsibly requires strengthening the social fabric of government institutions so that, together, public servants and citizens might struggle honestly with the moral uncertainty that inevitably attends government's work. By refusing to honor that uncertainty, rationalist responsibility merely generates yet another paradox: the paradox of courage.

2

Three Meanings of Responsibility

Agency, Accountability, and Obligation

Responsibility has three related dimensions. It has an external dimension in legal and political analysis in which the state imposes penalties on individual actions and in which officials and governments are held accountable for policy and action. It has an internal dimension in moral and ethical analysis in which the individual takes into account the consequences of his actions and the criteria which bear on his choices. It has a comprehensive or reciprocal dimension in social and cultural analysis in which values are ordered in the autonomy of an individual character and the structure of a civilization.

—Richard McKeon
(1957, p. 5)[1]

The symbol of responsibility contains, as it were, hidden references, allusions, and similes which are in the depths of our mind as we grope for understanding of ourselves and toward definition of ourselves in action. . . . Our task . . . is to try with the aid of this symbol to further the double purpose of ethics: to obey the ancient and perennial commandment "*Gnothi seauton*," "Know thyself"; and to seek guidance for our activity as we decide, choose, commit ourselves, and otherwise bear the burden of our necessary human freedom.

—H. Richard Niebuhr
(1963, p. 48)

◈ MANY TWENTIETH-CENTURY Western philosophers have remarked upon the idea of responsibility at one time or another, and very often in ways that match its casual everyday usages—confusing and contradictory as they may be. Those few who have analyzed the idea systematically during the past several decades, however, generally regard responsibility as a symbol that, if understood with the rigor they think it deserves, might provide a morally secure guide for judgment and action. Although much of the formal literature on the subject is both negative in its tone—owing to its preoccupation with blame and punishment— and essentially regulative in its intent (McSwain, 1985), its view of responsibility nevertheless echoes a distinctively modernist and optimistic commitment to the idea of progress. However its particular content and direction might be envisioned, progress, which Gunther Stent (1978) calls "that prominent Bicentennial feature of the (Western) human condition" (p. xi), symbolizes our collective hope for a better future, one that is both in principle knowable and, abetted by rational thought and stern vigilance, attainable through willful action. Responsibility has served as one of the century's favored comprehensive moral symbols to which we have anchored our belief in the goodness and necessity of progress, notwithstanding our anxieties about the likelihood of achieving it.

The rigor and precision of the mainstream discourse on responsibility exacts a cost, chiefly in the neglect of the "hidden references, allusions, and similes" that H. Richard Niebuhr, in the second of this chapter's introductory quotations, says that the term contains. By contrast, Richard McKeon's brief paragraph is far more representative of the mainstream literature on responsibility, and it will provide the basis for this chapter's effort at "unpacking" in a rather straightforward fashion three formal meanings embedded in the word. Although Niebuhr figures more prominently in Chapter 4's consideration of the paradoxical character of responsibility, his commentary on the word's historical antecedents is, along with McKeon's, essential to a preliminary understanding of responsibility's role in contemporary moral and political thought.

A Brief History of Responsibility

McKeon, whose brief article in 1957 is still the best available history of the idea of responsibility, traces the first appearance of the word, both in English and in French, back to 1787: Murray's *Oxford English Dictionary* cites Alexander Hamilton's use of *responsibility* in the *Federalist,* paper 64; also, the *Dictionnaire Etymologique de la Langue Française* includes the noun *responsabilité* and the privative adjective *irresponsable,* followed four years later, in 1791, by the noun *irresponsabilité* (p. 8).[2] In English, the adjective *responsible* preceded its noun derivative by nearly two hundred years, being

> used by Ben Johnson in 1599 in the sense of "correspondent" or answering to something; it was used in the sense of accountable or liable to be called to account (i.e., responsible to kingdom or Parliament) in 1643, in the sense of answerable to a charge in 1650, in the sense of "trustworthy" or capable of fulfilling an obligation in 1691 by John Locke. (p. 8)

In view of the relative recency of responsibility's appearance and of its multiple meanings, it should come as no surprise that the word currently subsumes and in some cases has replaced more ancient philosophical terms. Causality (imputation) and punishment (accountability), prominent concerns of Greek philosophers beginning with Plato and Aristotle, are now included among responsibility's contemporary meanings, as well as in the modern philosophical debates about the concept, revealing the word's historical connection with—typically its subordination to—the political notion of justice. Or perhaps more literally of *in*justice, because for the Greeks "the problem of accountability turns on the interpretation of the operation of the punishments, penalties, and indemnities imposed by a community to rectify or prevent injuries arising from crime, misdemeanor, breach of contract, or negligence" (McKeon, 1957, p. 11). Similarly, various Latin and Greek terms for the imputation of blame or praise as well as sin—especially the Greek *hamartia,* which means "missing the mark" or guilt—have also entered into responsibility's newer, expanded meaning. This generally negative connotation of responsibility has carried over virtually intact to the present day. Peter A. French (1991), for example, notes that when we ascribe responsibility to a person, we are asserting that he or she has caused harm to another and cannot provide an acceptable justification or excuse for doing so.

In the latter half of the nineteenth century the introduction of responsibility into the lexicon of respectable philosophical discourse was itself a subject of controversy, having been dismissed as vacuous by some philosophers and hopelessly ambiguous by others. In the 1860s, Alexander Bain called it "a figurative expression" (cited in McKeon, 1957, p. 6), preferring instead the more literal term *punishability* on the ground that "a man can never be said to be responsible, if you are not prepared to punish him when he cannot satisfactorily answer the charges made against him" (p. 7). At about the same time John Stuart Mill took essentially the same stance by declaring that "Responsibility means punishment" (p. 6), although not necessarily in the sense of an expectation of actual punishment by God or by our fellow men, but as the awareness of deserving it. As a utilitarian Mill equated the two words mainly in order to sidestep the endless and, to him, futile metaphysical debates over freedom and necessity waged by the Kantians and others who attempted to embed responsibility in the vocabulary of a science of morals. Mill claimed that in discussing responsibility,

> There is no need to postulate any theory respecting the nature or criterion of moral distinctions. It matters not, for this purpose, whether the right and wrong of actions depends on the consequences they tend to produce, or on an inherent quality of the actions themselves. It is indifferent whether we are utilitarians or anti-utilitarians; whether our ethics rest on intuition or experience. It is sufficient if we believe that there is a difference between right and wrong, and a natural reason for preferring the former. (quoted in McKeon, 1957, pp. 20-21)

Mill was in turn criticized by L. Lévy-Bruhl (McKeon, 1957, pp. 5-6), who, in 1884, published the first comprehensive philosophical treatise on responsibility, entitled *L'Idée de Responsabilité.*

Lévy-Bruhl argued that Mill's equation of responsibility with punishment revealed only one of the two significant meanings of
responsibility, namely the political/legal notion of accountability.
The second meaning, imputability—strictly speaking, "the ascrip-
tion of an act to an agent" (p. 13)—regards responsibility as essential to understanding the moral nature of people as agents. Imputability assumes the presence of "a reasonable free being . . .
generalized beyond reference to a kingdom of ends or a noumenal
world" (p. 22).

Despite Lévy-Bruhl's and others' insistence on viewing responsibility as a moral concept, its political meaning predates both its
moral and cultural meanings in the historical development of the
idea. As McKeon notes:

> The idea of *moral* responsibility originated and developed in the
> context of the evolution of political and cultural responsibility.
> There was no moral responsibility until there were communities in
> which men were held accountable for their actions and in which
> actions were imputed to individual men. There were no moral
> individuals prior to the development and recognition of moral
> responsibility. (p. 28)

The distinction between the political (including the legal) and
the moral meanings of responsibility parallels other distinctions
made by philosophers who began the discourse on the subject. Its
political meaning suggests that responsibility is "objective" in the
sense that it refers to a reality that is external to the individual,
whereas "the notion of moral responsibility . . . is purely subjective and empty of concrete content" (McKeon, 1957, p. 21). The
former meaning not only took historical precedence over the latter,
but it was also consistent with the idea that responsibility chiefly
involved the identification of nonarbitrary (or objective) criteria
for making judgments about appropriate blame and punishment.
Responsibility's unavoidably subjective dimension, however, was
evident by the self-understanding of the acting subject—that is,
self-awareness of the motives of one's actions—stipulated as a
necessary condition for blameworthiness and the legitimate re-
ceipt of punishment.

I should note here that this account of the objective and sub-jective dimensions of responsibility is not the only way in which the distinction between them may be drawn. The preceding para-graphs leave the impression that objectivity has priority over subjectivity because responsibility, and indeed the whole enter-prise of moral philosophy beginning with Immanuel Kant, should involve the systematic attempt to resolve moral questions accord-ing to transpersonal and even ahistorical principles. On this view subjectivity means simply that agents, although imperfectly, learn those principles, which then "internally" motivate their actions, in contrast to the idea that actions, especially compliant actions, are "externally" determined by the objective prospect of social disapprobation or actual punishment. *Objective* and *external* are thus regarded as virtual synonyms for one another, as are *subjective* and *internal.*

We shall see later in this chapter, and more fully beginning with Chapter 4, however, that within alternative philosophical tradi-tions subjectivity connotes something quite different from simply the imperfect approximation of objectivity. Beginning with Sören Kierkegaard (1844/1957) and extending through existentialist, prag-matist, and postmodernist philosophers, subjectivity has been radicalized and elevated to primary status both in philosophical analysis generally and in the discourse about responsibility in particular. The radically subjectivist view of responsibility re-verses the priority of the objective and the subjective by disputing the contention that social reality exists either independently of or prior to the interpretations made by agents (subjects). Instead of explaining how people internalize norms and principles of a preex-isting, objective social world, the subjectivists are more concerned with the means by which people externalize and then treat as objective a prior and more fundamental subjective reality.

As the discourse about responsibility has unfolded during the present century, the chief tension within in it may be seen as involving a tacit contest between the objectivists and subjectivists. Although McKeon is correct to say that the idea of responsibility provides "a way to discuss moral problems of individual action, political problems of common action, and cultural problems of

mutual understanding, without commitment to a single philosophy or to the expression of values traditional in a single culture"
(pp. 29-30), that virtue may in fact obscure submerged epistemological differences between competing conceptions of responsibility that are found within particular (especially Western) cultures.
Because the objectivists, with a few notable exceptions, have
dominated the formal writing about responsibility, the term's
apparent philosophical neutrality is thus misleading.

The objectivists' dominance has not only excluded from wider
view alternative philosophical conceptions of responsibility, but
has also frequently failed to take into account important everyday
meanings that the word represents. On the belief that such meanings should be duly accounted for and indeed respected, I shall
begin the discussion of responsibility's formal meanings by listing
several examples of the word's highly variable use, both in conversation and in public pronouncements:

1. The secretary of state is directly responsible to the president for
   the conduct of the nation's foreign policy.
2. Over the objections of the men in the homicide squad, Detective Chief
   Inspector Jane Tennison was given the responsibility for directing the
   investigation of a series of apparently related murders.
3. Faced with the prospect of having to fire several employees because of recent cuts in the county's Department of Social Services
   budget, the office manager felt a deep personal responsibility for
   the welfare of her staff.
4. Adolf Eichmann disclaimed responsibility for his role in the mass
   execution of millions of Jews on the ground that he was just
   following orders.
5. For Jean-Paul Sartre (1956), the French existentialist, responsibility is the "consciousness of being the incontestable author of an
   event or an object" (p. 553). That is, people cannot shift the moral
   onus—by denying personal authorship—of their actions to anyone
   or anything else.
6. In *Habits of the Heart* (1985) and *The Good Society* (1991), sociolo-
   gist Robert Bellah and his associates describe America's failure to
   develop a sense of communal responsibility as a chief reason for
   its moral disintegration.
7. Mary Parker Follett (1924), management theorist and ardent prag-
   matist, wrote more than a half century ago that "Empty will can no

longer masquerade as a spiritual force. We can rely neither on facts
nor . . . on our 'strong will,' but only on full acceptance of all the
responsibility involved in our part in that unfolding life which is
making both 'facts' and ourselves" (p. 150).

8. The Palestine Liberation Organization claimed responsibility for a
   recent wave of car bombings in Beirut.

9. People who are judged insane are not, at least in the same way that
   sane people are, legally responsible for their actions.

10. People who repeatedly offer excuses or look for scapegoats are
    simply avoiding responsibility for their actions.

11. In firing H. R. Haldeman and John Ehrlichman, Richard Nixon
    explained in a televised address that although he felt that he had
    no choice but to relieve his trusted aides of their duties, he, as
    President, ultimately bore responsibility for their actions.

Responsibility as Agency, Accountability, and Obligation

These eleven examples, which variously attribute, acknowledge, disclaim, avoid, obfuscate, and confuse the meaning of
responsibility, incorporate several combinations of three distinct
meanings of the word: agency, accountability, and obligation. Each
of these meanings, in turn, has both an individual and a collective
or institutional aspect, which as we shall see later introduces
elements of tension as well as confusion into the discourse on
responsibility. Following the explanation of the three meanings
provided in this section, I will return to the eleven examples,
examining each in terms of the combinations and nuances of
responsibility's generic meanings.

Agency. To qualify for status as an agent, one is first assumed to
possess the power to cause events to happen through the voluntary
exercise of one's will. Agency embodies the ancient symbolism of
"man the maker" (Niebuhr, 1963, p. 49), one who is in charge of
his own actions and mistress of her own fate. These actions are not
only purposeful in the sense that they are directed toward ends,
but they are also the formative material from which agents shape,
and continually reshape, themselves. The second aspect of agency,

symbolized by what Niebuhr calls the image of "man the answerer" (p. 56), holds that agents are accountable for their actions to other members of their communities, limited only by the stipulation that the agent is "a normal adult intentional agent, that is, an intentional agent who is not insane or retarded and has received and absorbed a moral education" (Baier, 1986, p. 193). It is this second aspect that transforms agency from a merely descriptive concept into an explicitly moral one.

The idea of agency, by virtue of terms such as *voluntary, causality,* and *intention* that are used to define it, has become entangled in ancient philosophical controversies, including most particularly the debate over free will versus determinism. With only a few prominent exceptions, contemporary philosophers who write about responsibility regard agency as evidence of free will (or something nearly like it) and thus view arguments for determinism as compromising the notion of responsibility. Gerald Dworkin (1970) summarizes the standard argument against determinism as follows:

1. A necessary condition for holding a person responsible, blaming, or punishing him for an act, A, is that the person did A freely.
2. If determinism is true, nobody ever acts freely.
3. Therefore, if determinism is true, no one is ever responsible, blameworthy, or punishable.
4. At least sometimes agents are responsible, blameworthy, or punishable for what they do.
5. Therefore, determinism is false. (p. 8)

Dworkin, of course, realizes that this is not the whole story, even setting aside objections by that minority who might quarrel with the correctness of the fourth item or who, like David Hume and G. E. Moore, tried to show that free will and determinism are not necessarily incompatible. The concepts of voluntarism, causality, and intention are also sufficiently ambiguous and problematic that mainstream writers have felt obliged to qualify what agency can reasonably mean in the context of their theories of responsibility. Although most would generally agree with Aristotle, for example, that a significant portion of people's actions *are* voluntary, many of their actions are not. Moreover, the dividing line between voluntary and involuntary is often a hard one to draw, both as a theoretical and a practical matter, and which kinds of harmful voluntary actions ought to be exempted from liability for blame and punishment is a subject of continuing dispute.[3] Does my not knowing the gun was loaded, for example, properly excuse my killing my neighbor if I voluntarily pulled the trigger?

On the general issue of the relation between ignorance and responsibility, Aristotle (1962), in Book Three of *Nicomachean Ethics*, observed that:

> Even ignorance is in itself no protection against punishment if a person is thought to be responsible for his ignorance. For example, the penalty is twice as high if the offender acted in a state of drunkenness, because the initiative is his own: he had the power not to get drunk, and drunkenness was responsible for his ignorance. (pp. 65-66)

Even Aristotle, however, could not have anticipated all of the contemporary ramifications of his position in the light of the continuing legal dispute surrounding the Alaskan oil spill caused in 1989 by the tanker *Exxon Valdez*.

*   *   *   *   *

In the immediate aftermath of the spill, Exxon officials testified before two congressional subcommittees that the captain of the *Valdez*, Joseph J. Hazelwood, had been drinking shortly before the ship ran aground on Bligh Reef, and at the precise moment of the incident (and in violation of company regulations) had been away from the ship's bridge. If true, the charges of drunkenness would serve to mitigate, or so it seemed at the time, the company's liability for damages by locating responsibility for the event squarely on Captain Hazelwood's shoulders. A year later, however, Hazelwood was acquitted of the charges of drunkenness, although he *was* convicted of negligence for being absent from the bridge.

What subsequently came into dispute was whether the company knew of Hazelwood's drinking habits during the years immediately preceding the incident. In 1985, Hazelwood was treated for alcohol abuse, a fact known to his superiors at Exxon, who warned him that his first drink following the rehabilitation period would be grounds for his immediate dismissal. In a lawsuit against Exxon brought by 12,000 Alaskan natives, fishermen, businessmen, and landowners, the plaintiffs alleged that the company had acted recklessly because its officials knew that Hazelwood had begun drinking again shortly after treatment for alcoholism but still permitted him to serve as captain of its tankers. The company's officials later claimed, on the basis of new evidence (and in *agreement* with Hazelwood), that alcohol had nothing to do with the oil spill and that Exxon had carefully monitored Hazelwood ever since his rehabilitation period.[4]

*   *   *   *   *

The implication of Exxon's revised position, of course, is that if the company's officials had in fact known of any drinking by Hazelwood after 1985, their claim of ignorance would be compromised, and so too would their claim of exemption from responsibility for the oil spill. In the absence of any such knowledge, or in the event of clear evidence showing that Hazelwood had in fact *not* been drinking, Exxon's claim of exemption from responsibility would be easier to sustain, because it is clearly unreasonable to expect that its officials could know or anticipate that Hazelwood would be absent from the bridge of the *Valdez* during those critical moments. Under such a circumstance ignorance by the company would be a satisfactory excuse.

Although *cause* and *determine*, in ordinary usage, are typically used interchangeably, various meanings of the former do not necessarily imply a deterministic philosophical outlook. French (1991, p. 133), for example, distinguishes between two kinds of causality: *Regular event causality* explains events in terms of the antecedent physical motions, and also presumably the social conditions, that caused an event to occur ("Guns kill people"), whereas *agent causality* refers to the power of intentional agents to cause their own actions ("People kill people"). Kurt Baier (1986) draws a similar distinction between *thing-responsibility* and *agent-responsibility:* "In . . . ascribing thing-responsibility, the central idea is to identify the thing, suitable control or manipulation of which would prevent the undesirable or produce the desirable result" (p. 188). In ascribing agent-responsibility, we impute to an agent the power intentionally to cause events to occur, including the activation of thing-responsibility, for which the agent is then morally liable.

Intentionality is central to virtually all descriptions of morally responsible agents. The modern baseline for these descriptions is J. L. Mackie's (1977) so-called *straight rule of responsibility*, which holds that "an agent is responsible for all and only [its] intentional actions" (p. 208). Although later authors have amended Mackie's rule to allow for excuses based on mitigating circumstances, the idea of intentionality has been essentially preserved. Even though by *some* true accounts a particular event may be explained deterministically—that is, in terms of regular event causality (French) or thing-responsibility (Baier)—so long as the event may in at least one other account be correctly described through reference to someone's intentions, then he or she qualifies as a morally responsible agent.

A strict determinist, of course, would argue that intentions are nothing more than artifacts of physical or mechanistic causes (that is, agent-responsibility is merely thing-responsibility in disguise), which if true would seriously undermine the notion of agency. An influential opponent of this view is Donald Davidson (1980), who has argued that "there are no strict laws at all on the basis of which we can predict and explain mental phenomena" (p. 117). The basis for this claim rests on Davidson's argument that the languages used to describe physical as opposed to mental events are radically incommensurable, despite the fact that mental events cannot occur in the absence of physical events. The idea that mental events are explainable in terms of physically deterministic laws is impossible because such laws can only be expressed in a physical vocabulary. Such a vocabulary is necessarily inadequate for judging the truth of sentences regarding intentions or indeed any other mental event.[5] As Davidson explains,

> There are no strict psychophysical laws because of the disparate commitments of the mental and physical schemes. It is a feature of physical reality that physical change can be explained by laws that connect it with other changes and conditions physically described. It is a feature of the mental that the attribution of mental phenomena must be responsible to the background of reasons, beliefs and intentions of the individual. (p. 116)

The idea of a "Davidsonian agent"—that is, someone whose actions may, according to at least one of the agent's own true accounts, be described or redescribed as intentional—preserves the general meaning of Mackie's rule, but broadens it to include negligent actions. The idea of negligence assumes a distinction between, on the one hand, action that is willed and, on the other hand, particular consequences of that action that might not be what the agent says was intended. Negligent actions are in a strict sense defined as those of a Davidsonian agent, although most philosophers would probably agree with French (1991, p. 138) that excuses in the form of mitigating circumstances may nevertheless be considered.

As this emphasis on the consequences of action suggests, intentionality is a prerequisite for moral agency, but it is the fact that something has gone awry that instigates our concern about it. "We determine first that something went wrong. Then we find out whose action produced it. That person is morally responsible, but if it were not the person's intention to do that action, mitigating or exculpating excuses are entertained" (French, 1991, p. 135). This summarizes what French calls the *extended principle of accountability* (EPA), to which he then adds a corollary notion called the *principle of responsive adjustment* (PRA).

> In effect moral responsibility may be assigned specifically because the perpetrator subsequent to the event failed to respond to its

occurrence with an appropriate modification of his behavior or habits that had as an outcome the unwanted or harmful event. . . .

PRA captures the idea that, after an untoward event has happened, the person(s) who contributed to its occurrence is (are) expected to adopt certain courses of future action that will have the effect in his (their) future conduct of preventing repetitions. (p. 138)

In combination the extended principle of accountability and the principle of responsive adjustment link the two chief images— maker and answerer—that Niebuhr says underwrite the notion of personal agency. The discussion thus far marks only the beginning of our consideration of agency, however, which as I shall explain in later chapters has complex psychological and institutional as well as moral dimensions that render it far more complicated than it may at first appear.

Both accountability and obligation, the subjects of the next two sections, presuppose the idea of agency as it has thus far been presented. Indeed it has been impossible to define agency without reference to these two latter ideas. Each, however, requires some additional explication in order to complete this preliminary discussion of responsibility's basic ingredients.

Accountability. In its simplest form, accountability refers to an authoritative relationship in which one person is formally entitled to demand that another answer for—that is, provide an account of—his or her actions; rewards or punishments may be meted out to the latter depending on whether those actions conform to the former's wishes. To say that someone is accountable, in other words, is to say that he or she is liable for sanctions according to an authoritative rule, decision, or criterion enforceable by someone else (Kelman & Hamilton, 1989, p. 195). Accountability assumes that the agent of whom such answerability is demanded is both self-aware and in possession of the necessary means to cause an event or action to occur. Accountability also assumes, in keeping with what is conventionally termed the *principle of alternate possibilities*, that the agent could have acted otherwise.[6] Because of the promise or threat of rewards and punishments that are

typically associated with it, accountability tends to be individualized (or pinpointed) because, among other reasons, authoritative
favors and rebukes are difficult, although not impossible, to dis-
pense en masse.

Obligation. Obligation introduces an explicitly moral meaning of
responsibility by suggesting that one should, or should not, perform a particular action. When responsibility is followed by the
preposition *for*, the meaning of obligation is combined with that of
agency, although it should be mentioned, following Sartre, that
personal agency may also be understood, both as a moral and a
psychological concept, independently of obligation and therefore
without the syntactical requirement that responsibility be followed by any preposition at all. When it is followed by the preposition *to*, the "obligatory" meaning of responsibility is linked to
accountability, although the latter word also may be construed as
morally neutral, simply describing the factual conditions of an
authoritative relationship.[7]

Although obligation and accountability assume that action is
undertaken by willful agents, it is possible to speak of moral
obligations independently of the authoritative contexts that the
notion of accountability presupposes. With or without its authoritative trappings, however, obligation has what Baier (1986), in discussing the idea of agent-responsibility, terms a forward-looking
dimension, in addition to the backward-looking dimension implied by ascriptions of responsibility to an agent for having already
caused an event to happen. It is this forward-looking sense of
responsibility that enables us to speak of a duty or obligation to
bring about a desired future state of affairs. It should be noted,
however, that the negative characterization of responsibility[8] is
still preserved, because the subject is typically brought to our
attention as a consequence of someone's failure "*to discharge a
moral requirement*" (p. 190).

Obligation and personal agency represent the two opposing
moral meanings of responsibility. Obligation implies that morality
derives from sources external to people such as law, formal authority, and moral principle, whereas agency suggests that the moral

nature of responsibility is intrinsic to the human psyche or soul. Those who hold that personal agency supersedes obligation are in turn divided over whether people's moral nature is located a priori in the individual or produced through the individual's experience in social relationships. Whatever their stance on this latter question, moral agency theorists are more likely than their obligation counterparts to regard feeling or affect, as opposed to simply thought and logic, as vital ingredients of responsible action.

The Combinations of Responsibility's Meanings in Everyday Usage

The preceding section does not capture fully the richness of responsibility's varied connotations, but for the present it is sufficient for examining important differences in the meaning of the word implied by the eleven examples presented earlier.

1. The secretary of state is responsible to the president for the conduct of foreign policy.
2. Detective Chief Inspector Tennison was given the responsibility for directing the investigation of a series of apparently related murders.

These first two examples depict the reciprocal relation of accountability and institutional agency. As accountable *to* the president, the secretary by implication has been delegated the institutional means *for* carrying out the president's, and by extension the public's, authoritative will. Conversely, Tennison, having been granted the institutional means *for* directing the murder investigation, is in turn accountable *to* her superior by virtue of the reward or punishment she may receive, depending on whether she and her fellow officers catch the murderer. Although these examples chiefly describe the factual conditions of authoritative relationships, in order to be sustained they typically take on an overlay of moral obligation. Doing what is factually required by authority is simultaneously regarded as the morally right thing to do.

3. Faced with the prospect of having to fire several employees because of recent budget cuts, the office manager felt a deep personal responsibility for the welfare of her staff.

The reciprocal relation of accountability and institutional agency form the authoritative backdrop against which the office manager in the third example must decide which of her employees she must fire. Her *feeling* of responsibility for their welfare, however, accents a combination of moral obligation and caring that transcends and is in tension with the authoritative requirements of her role. The manager is likely to regard her accountability to her political superiors chiefly as a constraint—although probably a morally legitimate one in her eyes—within which she must act, rather than as the moral impetus for her action. Whereas the conditions enabling her to act upon her feeling of responsibility derive from her authoritative role, her expression of that feeling is possible only insofar as she is able to distance herself at least partially from that role.

4. Adolf Eichmann disclaimed responsibility for his role in the mass execution of millions of Jews on the grounds that he was just following orders.
5. For Jean-Paul Sartre responsibility is the "consciousness of being the incontestable author of an event or an object."

Eichmann was incapable of distancing himself from his official role because he could not discern the crucial distinction between personal and institutional agency, notwithstanding his possibly genuine expressions of sorrow for the fate of his victims. Eichmann's grotesque denial of his responsibility provides a vivid counterpoint to Sartre's insistence that people cannot escape personal responsibility for their actions. His claim presupposes not only a radical separation of personal and institutional agency, but also the conviction that the former is the exclusive province of the moral. To imbue institutional agency, in combination with accountability, with moral status is tantamount to denying the responsibility that inheres in personal agency. Indeed obligation itself, with or without these institutional trappings, is a morally dubious notion for Sartre because it locates responsibility outside the individual and by implication denies the moral character of the individual's personal agency.

> 6. Robert Bellah and his associates describe America's failure to develop a sense of communal responsibility as a chief reason for its moral disintegration.

Bellah's concern for the absence of communal responsibility provides the social counterpart to Sartre's individualized conception of personal agency. Communitarians believe that Sartre's responsible individual requires the presence of stable and caring relationships that enable the individual to develop a *sense* of responsibility. Responsible people, in other words, are made rather than born. Moreover, obligations are not at odds with personal agency so long as those obligations emerge from and serve to promote social relationships that enable individual development. Obligations can serve this function, however, when they are internal to the social processes that promote such development, but not when they are invoked as impersonal and ahistorical principles.

> 7. Mary Parker Follett wrote that "Empty will can no longer masquerade as a spiritual force. We can rely neither on facts nor . . . our 'strong will,' but only on full acceptance of all the responsibility involved in our part in that unfolding life which is making both 'facts' and ourselves."

In speaking of responsibility Follett is referring to agency as the reflective awareness of our participation in the flow of social processes rather than to the more common view of agency as the individual expression of conscious will. To Follett responsibility describes the sense of personal efficacy and self-discovery produced by moral and psychological investment in cooperative activity. Responsibility is both an active and a social creation; and people's obligations, although Follett seldom uses the word, are properly seen as deriving from the "law of the situation." Thus, authority is construed as collective moral *authorship* that inheres in cooperative relationships, rather than as the enforcement of hierarchical edicts.

8. The Palestine Liberation Organization claimed responsibility for a recent wave of car bombings in Beirut.

In claiming responsibility for the car bombings its spokesman not only asserted that the PLO caused (was the agent of) the bombings, but also that it was morally justified in its actions. That justification implies a repudiation of the structures of accountability to which the agents of similar actions are legally bound. The claim may be defended either on the ground that the PLO felt obliged to obey a higher authority, such as the will of God or a moral principle, or by asserting that the existing structures of accountability are themselves illegitimate. Had the claim that the PLO perpetrated the bombings been made by representatives or defenders of those structures, then responsibility would be taken to mean not only that the PLO caused the bombings, but that it was also both legally and morally blamable for them.

9. People who are judged insane are not, at least in the same way that sane people are, legally responsible for their actions.
10. People who look for scapegoats are simply avoiding responsibility for their actions.

Whereas the PLO acknowledges itself as a self-aware agent of its actions, representatives for the legally insane seek to limit or avoid altogether the force of accountability structures, not by questioning their moral or legal legitimacy, but by denying or qualifying their clients' status as self-aware agents. Sanity, a designation that defines the extent and nature of a person's legal accountability, has a curious affinity with the scapegoaters mentioned in the next example. As a legal designation, sanity reduces to a question of either/or, whereas scapegoating may be seen as a question of the degree of self-awareness possessed by the agent. Those who are concerned about scapegoating and other means by which people seek to avoid or deny responsibility for their actions might well accept Sartre's notion of personal agency as a moral and philosophical ideal, but would regard it as psychologically problematic. Because none of us, as psychologists ever since Freud have commented, are fully rational beings, our sanity in the broader sense of the word is always contingent on our ability to comprehend realistically the possibilities and limits of our personal agency and therefore of our responsibility.

> 11. In firing H. R. Haldeman and John Ehrlichman, Richard Nixon explained that although he had no choice but to relieve his trusted aides of their duties, he, as president, ultimately bore responsibility for their actions.

The example involving President Nixon, as well as the investigator of the train robbery introduced in Chapter 1, reveals how the ambiguity of responsibility may produce confusing conversations about it. I shall forbear further dissection of the train robbery on what I trust is a safe assumption that most readers are not, in Dave Barry's phrase, humor impaired. The President's announcement, which shows how an acknowledgment of responsibility may obfuscate the meaning of responsibility by simultaneously admitting and denying it, does beg further explanation.

Acknowledging responsibility usually means an admission of self-aware personal agency—an owning up to one's actions—in causing an event to happen, with the implication that the acknowledger stands ready to suffer whatever consequences might result from that acknowledgment. If sincere, such admissions serve a redemptive function whereby the agent's personal development is enhanced either through recognition of heretofore unrecognized motives or simply through the confession of sin. When made publicly, these acknowledgments may be seen as ennobling (and, as with President Nixon, are often *intended* to be seen as such), especially when they are accompanied by acts of public atonement such as resigning from office. Nixon, of course, did not resign until nearly a year after he fired Haldeman and Ehrlichman, and he disavowed in his announcement any prior knowledge of or complicity in Watergate. Thus his acknowledgment, in which he tried to convey the appearance of an ennobling, even redemptive, admission of personal agency, simply noted the contextually irrelevant, not to mention "perfectly clear," fact of the institutional agency inherent in his role as president.

Conclusion

The discussion of the eleven illustrative statements about responsibility has introduced several issues and nuances of meaning
that were not fully anticipated by the preliminary summary of
agency, accountability, and obligation. By virtue of its primary
concern with identifying criteria by which individuals are properly liable for causing harmful actions, the standard view of responsibility leaves unaddressed a host of questions that will occupy
our attention later. These questions include: whether responsibility
may extend beyond individuals to include collectivities (May &
Hoffman, 1991); whether the search for transpersonal, objective
criteria of responsible action might create more problems, both
practical and moral, than it can solve; and whether the standard
view's preoccupation with blame might conceal more positive
meanings of responsibility. Also ignored or mentioned only in
passing by that summary are several other important concepts,
such as justice, freedom, and individual rights, without consideration of which the standard philosophical conception of responsibility is rendered barren and overly technical (Kaufman, 1967).

Finally, the eleven responsibility statements provide some preliminary hints concerning the ambiguity of the word and of the
contradictory meanings and moral lessons implied by it. These
contradictory meanings, however, are not solely a consequence of
the paradoxical relationships among the three core meanings of
responsibility, but also of the internally paradoxical character of
each meaning taken separately. As we shall see in Chapters 5 through
7, obligation, agency, and accountability each generates its own
paradox in the context of the standard view of responsibility. Further
discussion of these matters, however, will have to be deferred until
after Chapter 3, which examines how the standard view has influenced the mainstream literature on democratic government.

Notes

1. This quotation and others from McKeon, 1957, are reprinted by permission of
Revue Internationale de Philosophie, where they were originally published.

2. McKeon (1957) notes that

> Heinrich Heine was the first author to use "Verantwortlichkeit" according to the Grimms' *Deutsches Wörterbuch*, but whereas in English "responsibility" moves into the place of "accountability" and is then related to the broader term "imputation," in German the discussion of "Verantwortlichkeit" is superimposed on a preceding discussion of "Zurechnung" or imputation. In each language the adjective was used earlier: as early as the 13th century in French, in the last year of the 16th century in English, and in the middle of the 17th century in German. (p. 8)

3. Although the word *voluntary* originated as a synonym for "freely made" actions, its derivative noun form, *voluntarism*, is now commonly used as a pejorative term by social scientists to describe the naiveté of accounts of action that ignore the "determinants" of it that are embedded in social or psychological structures.

4. Based on a *Washington Post* article by Nancy Phillips (1994a). On June 13, 1994, a federal jury in Anchorage decided that Exxon Corp. had been reckless, paving the way for an award of $15 billion in punitive damages to the plaintiffs. At this writing, a decision regarding Exxon's liability for an additional $1.5 billion in compensatory damages is still pending (Phillips, 1994b, p. A3).

5. As Jennifer Trusted (1984) has noted, Davidson's position suggests that

> The difficulty in reducing the mental to the physical (neurological) is analogous to the difficulty behaviourists have in reducing inner experiences to observable behaviour and the difficulty phenomenalists have in reducing all talk about physical objects to talk about actual or possible sense experiences. Such difficulties cannot be overcome. Davidson says that the existence of law-like statements in physical science depends on concepts that are intelligible only within a framework of beliefs about physical objects: for example, laws involving the length of objects depend on our concept of length, a concept which presupposes notions of the properties of visible, more or less rigid, physical objects. (p. 112)

6. Although the principle of alternate possibilities is generally accepted in one form or another, its precise definition is still controversial. For a summary of the current debate about it, as well as an extended argument as to its falsity, see Frankfurt, 1991.

7. The plural form of the noun, *responsibilities*, is virtually always synonymous with *obligations*, unlike agency and accountability, which, as alternative synonyms for responsibility, are only used in their singular form.

8. A balanced view of responsibility, however, should accentuate its positive as well as its negative connotations. In addition to its negative characterization of blameworthiness, responsibility also implies the virtue of trustworthiness, without which responsibility's paradoxical nature would be incomprehensible.

3

The Rationalist Conception
of Responsible Government

◈ THE PRACTICAL MEANING of any idea deeply woven into the social fabric seldom results directly and never results exclusively from what philosophers have said about it, a rule to which the notion of responsibility is most certainly no exception. The dominant, or rationalist, view of responsibility that has emerged in Western democratic governments during the past two centuries is more broadly understandable in terms of institutional requirements and historical contingencies than of literal adherence by public servants to philosophers' precepts. And philosophers themselves, despite their commonly avowed quest for ahistorical truths, are as much the products of history and institutions as anyone else.

This chapter reviews the main features of the rationalist discourse on responsibility, focusing on its philosophical lineage, the historical conditions that gave rise to it, and the controversies that are embedded within it. I begin with a summary of the rationalist view as it incorporates the generic meanings of responsibility—agency, accountability, and obligation—discussed in Chapter 2. The unique manner in which rationalism combines and interprets these three meanings is then traced to its origin in the competing philosophical traditions of the modern era and its association with modernism's signature institutions: market capitalism and bureaucratic organization. The major portion of the chapter discusses three debates over the proper meaning of responsible government and administration—the first two occurring a half century ago, the third more contemporary—that have arisen *within* the rationalist tradition. I intend to show that despite their disagreements, rationalism's opposing factions share more in common with one another than their stated disagreements suggest, and that it is their points of agreement that are most problematic.

Rationalist Responsibility in Summary

Rationalist responsibility combines aspects of all three generic meanings of responsibility discussed in Chapter 2. First, as agents, public servants are presumed to be self-aware, by virtue of which they are free to choose from among alternative courses of action. In other words, their actions are determined by forces neither totally beyond their personal control nor outside their scope of cognition. Second, through their institutional roles, these officials are invested with the authoritative means to act, to require others to act, or otherwise to cause events to happen. Because they act on behalf of institutions rather than on the basis of personal preferences, public servants are legally accountable to institutional authority. That is, they are subject to authoritative rewards or punishments corresponding to their degree of success or failure in achieving desired results, or according to whether their actions obey the dictates of higher authority. Third, because it is unreasonable to hold people accountable without granting them sufficient authority and resources to hold *others* accountable, authority should be commensurate with accountability. As adherents to the rationalist view concede, the ideal of commensurability is seldom attainable in practice, although it should be approximated insofar as possible. Finally, the obedience to authority implied by the notion of accountability constitutes the chief source of public servants' moral obligations. Although these obligations may later be personalized, their origin is institutional or otherwise external to public servants as persons.

Although it predates by more than a century what Deborah Stone (1988) calls the "rationality project" of contemporary policy analysis, the rationalist view of responsibility effectively serves as the normative ground for sanctions against those who violate its tenets. According to the model typically associated with the rationality project, decisions are made in the following sequence:

1. Identify objectives.
2. Identify alternative courses of action for achieving objectives.
3. Predict and evaluate the possible consequences of each alternative.
4. Select the alternative that maximizes the attainment of objectives.
   (p. 5)

In the rational decision model, responsibility refers to the means by which implementors of policy decisions are held accountable not only for whether their actions obey authoritative edicts, but, consistent with the maximizing assumption in Step 4, for whether they do so effectively and efficiently. Thus, extending the rational model further, Step 5 would require that someone other than the authoritative selector of the maximizing alternative implement the decision. Finally, Step 6 would involve allocating rewards and punishments to assure the accountability of the implementor for not just the dutiful, but also the maximal, attainment of the objectives.

To anyone familiar with the workings of contemporary government there should be little in this summary of rationalist responsibility that seems novel, surprising, or arguable. It is a view that most of us take for granted as a prescription for how public officials should behave, even if they fall short of that ideal. When gaps appear between the actual and the morally ideal, the former may be adjusted to the latter provided only that the ideal does not strain our credulity about what is factually possible. In critically examining rationalist responsibility, therefore, we must assess not only its moral adequacy, as philosophers who write about responsibility typically do, but also whether its account of the facts of social life can withstand scrutiny. The latter is probably more difficult inasmuch as the "social facts" generated by modernism's 200-year hegemony over Western consciousness may make any alternative accounting of them seem wrongheaded and even bizarre.

The Modernist Heritage of Rationalist Responsibility

In *After Virtue,* philosopher Alasdair MacIntyre (1984) portrays the modern individual as having to choose between two apparently competing, but in the final analysis converging, grounds for making moral judgments. These define by implication the meaning of responsible action taken on the basis of those judgments. The first of these grounds is rational or principled argument, in which moral judgments are logically deduced from universal and ahistorical principles rather than made on the basis of selfish interest or personal gain. Among the chief difficulties associated with this approach is that philosophers and laity alike often disagree about which principle among the many available should take precedence. The resulting debates are quite literally interminable owing to the incommensurability of opposing premises. Thus,

> premises which invoke justice and innocence are at odds with premises which invoke success and survival; . . . premises which invoke rights are at odds with those which invoke universalizability; . . . the claim of equality . . . is matched against that of liberty. It is precisely because there is in our society no established way of deciding between these claims that moral argument appears to be necessarily interminable. From our rival conclusions we can argue back to our rival premises; but when we do arrive at our premises argument ceases and the invocation of one premise against another becomes a matter of pure assertion and counter-assertion. Hence perhaps the slightly shrill tone of so much moral debate. (p. 8)[1]

The second ground for moral judgment is emotivism, the belief that all moral judgments are nothing but subjective, feeling-based,

and therefore irrational preferences. Individual preferences and
moral judgments are equivalent, which by implication means that
the arguments among the rational (principled) moralists are futile.
To stem the chaos that would otherwise result when individuals
act on the basis of their naturally differing preferences, people
need to be regulated by institutions that are by intent and design
impersonal. Markets, although MacIntyre devotes little attention
to them, more or less perform this function in private economic
affairs, whereas bureaucracies do this when large-scale collective
action is required. Bureaucracies, and to a lesser extent markets,
are thus the institutional regulators of anarchy.

The debate between the rationalists and emotivists has been
the chief source of tension, indeed the main topic of conversation
and analysis, in Western moral and political philosophy ever since
the late eighteenth century. The chief philosophical antagonists
are, on the side of the rationalists, the followers of the Kantian
tradition, whereas emotivism is represented by various brands of
utilitarianism. In the technical argot of the philosopher's trade, the
former are called *deontologists* and the latter *teleologists.*

As is so often the fate of long-standing philosophical arguments, progress is achieved not by one side winning out over the
other nor through the emergence of a synthesis of or compromise
between them, but instead through an imaginative reformulation
of the problem that initially caused the deadlock. Typically these
reformulations begin by exposing either hidden or taken-for-granted
assumptions on which the currently opposing factions *agree*, but
which themselves turn out to be disputable. This is what MacIntyre
has shown to be the case in the modernist debate between the
rationalists and emotivists. Rationalists and emotivists share a
common belief that the moral aspects of public life are *not* in any
fundamental sense personal matters. To rationalists, the universal-
ity of principles also implies the concomitant attribute of imper-
sonality; principles by definition cannot be person-specific. Although rationalists may develop strong feelings about their moral
principles, the public defense of them requires laying aside such
"merely" personal, idiosyncratic investments. The rationalists
thus share an ironic affinity with the emotivists with whom they
profess disagreement. They believe (as in John Rawls's [1971]

influential notion of the "veil of ignorance," behind which rational individuals suspend their selfish interests in order to comprehend and embrace universal principles of justice) that the moral principles used to adjudicate public disagreements are necessary precisely in order to shield society from the emotivist expressions of our private selves that would otherwise infect public discourse.

The rationalists fear and seek to protect against emotivism in public life mainly through enacting principles in the form of policies, which in turn are implemented and enforced by bureaucratic means. The emotivists reach the same bureaucratic conclusion, but do so by relying on the marketlike process of pluralistic competition rather than principled argument to mediate as well as mitigate the effects of rampant emotivism. Rationalism thus conceals a latent emotivism, while emotivism resorts to a rationalist fix to save itself from its own excesses. Both sides in practice are rationalists. Because each radically separates private life from public life—the rationalists by means of principles, the emotivists by pluralistic competition, and both ultimately through bureaucracy—the role of the personal, because it is limited to purely private activities, can play no legitimate role in public life. Public morality is reduced to a synonym for obligation to something impersonal, external to oneself, whether to principles, bureaucratic authority, or a combination of the two. By extension, obligation is institutionalized through legal and organizational structures of accountability in order to regulate public conduct. Accountability becomes the only permissible operational meaning of responsibility. Personal responsibility in any meaningful sense is excluded by the terms of the discourse on which the participants in the modernist debate tacitly agree.

If MacIntyre is right in arguing that bureaucracy is congenial to both rationalism and emotivism, it is easy to see how proponents of the rationalist conception of responsibility have been able to sidestep debate over the proper meaning of justice. Although Arnold S. Kaufman (1967) is correct in saying that "a theory of justice is the essential foundation for a theory of moral responsibility" (p. 188), rationalist responsibility is not incompatible with theories of justice deriving from either the philosophical rationalism of Kant or the emotivism of utilitarianism. Both depend upon bureaucracy to buffer public servants from the full weight of their moral responsibility by divorcing the concept of responsibility itself from a moral concern with ends, viewing it instead as merely the technical equivalent of accountability. Effectiveness and efficiency, the twin criteria that serve as the rational decision model's instrumental redefinition of duty and moral obligation, are and must be neutral about ends and therefore silent about justice. Transformed into an essentially technical idea, rationalist responsibility forsakes any vital connection with justice by declaring in effect that the latter is someone else's department.

The Internal Debates
Within the Rationalist Perspective

Despite its apparent neutrality on the matter of justice, the rationalist conception of responsibility contains important internal disagreements that parallel those found in modernist moral philosophy. Rationalism's disagreements, however, mask an underlying unity of the assumptions shared by its opposing factions. To illustrate this, I shall review three debates in the public administration literature bearing on the problem of responsible government. In each debate the antagonists are divided according to whether they represent "hard-core" or "soft-core" variants of rationalist responsibility. Hard-core rationalists are those who cleave more strictly to the assumptions of rationalism, whereas soft-core rationalists relax those assumptions without abandoning them altogether in order to subsume a wider range of opinion or, in the interest of flexibility, to account for practical difficulties in applying them in real-world situations. In particular, the chief point of contention revealed by the three debates is whether, to what extent, and on what moral grounds public servants should be permitted or even encouraged to exercise discretion in the interpretation of policies and the application of administrative rules.

The first debate (presented here out of chronological order) involves two of the leading figures in American public administration, Herbert A. Simon and Dwight W. Waldo, who quarreled in the early 1950s over the role of political philosophy in clarifying the nature of responsible government; the meaning and limitations of science for administrative study; and the analytical separation of values and facts, policy and administration. Simon's writings, as reflected both in his confrontation with Waldo and in his earlier *Administrative Behavior* (1947/1976), provide public administration's classic expression of hard-core rationalism, whereas Waldo's side of the argument, as well as his previously published *The Administrative State* (1948/1984), represents its soft-core variant. As I hope to make clear in the review of their debate, the label of rationalism is appropriate in only a limited sense when applied to Waldo's position. Waldo challenges Simon's rationalism on many important counts, but he leaves intact some of Simon's central assumptions, which lie at the core of rationalism's worldview. Although the subject of responsibility is not the principal point of dispute between Simon and Waldo, their disagreements concerning both the empirical and the normative character of public administration nonetheless have an important bearing on how problems of responsible government are defined.

The second debate, between Herman Finer and Carl J. Friedrich in 1940, grapples with the question of whether administrative discretion in implementing public policy is legitimate in view of the departure from strict legal-political accountability that it represents. Finer presents a hard-core defense of strict accountability, whereas Friedrich, although sharing Finer's overall sentiments concerning the subordination of administration to politics, defends the soft-core alternative, which relaxes strict demands for accountability in the interest of flexibility.

The third "debate" is actually a comparison of two contemporary writers, John P. Burke and Terry L. Cooper, who, although not commenting directly on each other's positions, offer contrasting views about whether responsible administration requires in all cases the threat of external sanctions of legal and bureaucratic authority, or alternatively whether responsible action might also be guided by internally held personal and professional values. Burke extends the hard-core tradition of Finer, whereas Cooper's position is a refinement of the soft-core tradition begun by Friedrich.

Simon Versus Waldo[2]

In 1952, the *American Political Science Review* (APSR) published the most memorable and acrimonious debate in the intellectual
history of American public administration. Herbert Simon and
Dwight Waldo, arguably the two chief antagonists in the discipline
during the past half-century, squared off in a public confrontation
involving polar extremes of both philosophical orientation and
intellectual style. The exchange between the two men in the APSR
was provoked by a footnote in Waldo's lengthy essay, "Development
of Theory of Democratic Administration" (1952a), which appeared in
the same journal earlier that year. Late in his essay, Waldo asserted
that a chief obstacle to a fuller development of democratic theory in
public administration was the belief in "efficiency as the central
concept in our 'science' " (p. 97). Waldo held that efficiency was not
a value-neutral concept and that its acceptance as a primary value
encouraged us merely to "tolerate a certain amount of democracy
because we 'believe' in it," which in the end "commits one's self to
nihilism" (p. 97). Waldo's target was clearly Simon (who had already
attained notoriety with the publication of *Administrative Behavior*
a few years earlier), although this was made explicit only in a
footnote that abruptly injected Simon's name into the discussion:

> In this contention, the present "weight of authority" is against me.
> But I believe that there is no realm of "factual decisions" from which
> values are excluded. To decide is to choose between alternatives;
> to choose between alternatives is to introduce values. Herbert
> Simon has patently made outstanding contributions to administra-
> tive study. These contributions have been made, however, when he
> has worked free of the methodology [logical positivism] he has
> asserted. (p. 97)

To appreciate fully what lay behind Waldo's reference to Simon, it is instructive to contrast selected aspects of their positions
presented about five years earlier in Waldo's *The Administrative
State* and Simon's *Administrative Behavior.*

The Administrative State. In Chapter 9 of *The Administrative State,*
"Principles, Theory of Organization and Scientific Method," Waldo

(1948/1984) traces the history of "science" in public administration from its naive association with principles of moral necessity and discusses the linkage of these scientific-moral principles with reformism in public administration, which was followed by the rejection of them by the pragmatists. He ends with a critique of the "principles" approach to administration. Waldo's intent in this chapter is to sharpen the distinctions between science and common sense in the study of public administration. In support of his separation of science and common sense Waldo approvingly cites Simon's (1946) "interesting essay" on "The Proverbs of Administration,"[3] noting that "on the analytical side Simon's essay is corroborative of many of the points made in this discussion" (p. 185).

That Simon's essay should meet with Waldo's approval is understandable in view of the criticisms made by both writers of the naive scientism that had pervaded much of the public administration literature up to that time. The two men extended their criticisms in different directions, however, and toward altogether different ends. The point of Waldo's (1948/1984) critique was to demarcate science, which deals with questions of what is the case, from administration, which involves questions of what is to be done (p. 171). In asserting a commonsense distinction between *is* and *ought*, Waldo seems at first glance to be not very far apart from the dichotomy between facts and values that Simon asserted in *Administrative Behavior*. However, while Waldo invoked the fact/value dichotomy to separate administration from *science*, Simon used it to separate administration from *policy*. For Waldo both policy and administration belong on the value or "ought" side of the equation (with science on the fact or "is" side), whereas Simon's version puts policy and administration on opposite sides (with science the servant of the latter).

Waldo says that administrative study is concerned with thinking and valuing. "Valuing implies morality, conceptions of right and wrong. *It is submitted that the established techniques of science are inapplicable to thinking and valuing human beings*" (p. 171). Furthermore, "questions of value are not amenable to scientific treatment" (p. 171). Simon could well have endorsed Waldo's last sentence, but most assuredly not the conclusions that he adduced from it. Waldo's project was, after all, to warn of the limits of science in administrative affairs, whereas Simon's was to inform us of its power.

Administrative Behavior. The pivotal section of *Administrative Behavior* (Simon, 1947/1976) for the APSR exchange was Chapter 3, "Fact and Value in Decision-Making." Much has been said by Waldo and other commentators about the influence of logical positivism on Simon's distinction between factual and value "elements" in decisions, as well as about the connection of that distinction with the dichotomy between administration and politics. Simon does not actually defend the philosophical basis of his theory, saying that to do so would require a treatise even longer than his own volume. Thus absolved, he simply states that "the conclusions reached by a particular school of modern philosophy —logical positivism—*will be accepted* [italics added] as a starting point, and their implications for the theory of decisions examined" (p. 45). Offhandedly, Simon shifts the onus of philosophical argument to would-be dissenters by suggesting that "the reader who is interested in examining the reasoning on which these doctrines are based will find references to the literature in the footnotes to this chapter" (p. 45).[4]

Despite some ambiguities in Simon's explanation of facts and values, it would be a caricature of his position to say that value judgments are relevant to policy making and factual judgments are relevant to administration—and leave it at that. Although Simon's intent is to use the fact/value dichotomy to establish an analytical distinction between administration and policy, he is also acutely aware of the difference between analytical and real-world distinctions, as well as the difficulties of adhering to them in practice. For example, Simon grants that although the dividing line between value judgments and factual judgments is often blurred, that does not logically force the rejection of the analytical distinction between them. Indeed, such a distinction is necessary to ensure some semblance of administrative responsibility in democratic government, which is possible only when some *functional* distinction between the roles of legislators and administrators is maintained. Some general guidelines for that distinction are deducible from the analytical distinction between factual and ethical (value) questions:

1. Responsibility to democratic institutions for value determination can be strengthened by the invention of procedural devices permitting a more effective separation of the factual and ethical elements in decisions.
2. The allocation of a question to legislators or administrators for decision should depend on the relative importance of the factual and ethical issues involved, and the degree to which the former are controversial.
3. Since the legislative body must of necessity make many factual judgments, it must have ready access to information and advice.
4. Since the administrative agency must of necessity make many value judgments, it must be responsive to community values, far beyond those that are explicitly enacted into law. (pp. 57-58)

The APSR Exchange. In "Development of Theory of Democratic Administration," Waldo (1952a) sought to demonstrate the historical role of democratic theory in the study of administration and "to comment upon the prospects and problems of the further development of theory of democratic administration" (p. 82). Among the encouraging trends that "have cleared the ground and laid the foundations for major development of democratic administrative theory" (p. 87), Waldo noted, first, the virtual abandonment of the belief that policy and administration are exclusive categories and, second, the "increasingly critical treatment, and even occasional rejection, of efficiency as the central concept in administration study" (p. 87).

Simon's discussion of efficiency, it should be remembered, depends directly upon his *analytical* separation of policy from administration and value from fact. But Waldo (1952a) notes that despite the close logical linkage between these two issues the rejection of efficiency

> is not nearly so clear and equivocal as is that of the separation of politics and administration. . . . In fact, Herbert Simon's recent *Administrative Behavior* presents a closely reasoned defense of the notion of an abstract science of administration centered on efficiency.

> The general trend, however, is clear; it is to deemphasize, to broaden and "socialize," even to reject the concept of efficiency. (pp. 87-88)

Waldo's tone is more pessimistic, however, later in his essay when he says that the belief in efficiency as a value-neutral concept is a major obstacle to the development of democratic administration.

Simon is clear throughout Chapter 3 of *Administrative Behavior* that factual and value elements are involved in both administrative and policy decisions and that he is simply drawing an analytical distinction between them. This distinction is necessary not only to make sense of the concept of efficiency, but also to establish a logical basis for the accountability of administrators to their political superiors. Both efficiency and accountability depend upon a distinction between facts and values (means and ends), which at a purely analytical level Waldo does not dispute.

More generally, Simon is critical of Waldo's article as yet another example of "the kind of prose I encounter in writing on policy, [which is] decorated with assertion, invective and metaphor" (p. 494). He concludes his stinging attack with this parting shot:

> Quite apart from whether Mr. Waldo's premises are right or wrong, I do not see how we can progress in political philosophy if we continue to think and write in the loose, literary, metaphorical style that he and most other political theorists adopt. The standard of unrigor that is tolerated in political theory would not receive a passing grade in an elementary course in logic, Aristotelian or symbolic. (p. 495)

After his own rhetorical salvo, including a mock apology to Simon for "profaning the sacred places of Logical Positivism" (Waldo, 1952b, p. 501), Waldo takes aim at Simon's contention that democratic institutions are principally justified as means for validating value judgments. Waldo notes that this is Simon's first mention of democracy in *Administrative Behavior* and that in the context of his argument " 'democratic' loses any significance . . . because *all* political institutions exist to validate value judgments" (p.

502), and even then only provided that we accept the loose and unexplained sense in which Simon uses the word *validate*. Waldo argues that stating a value is not the same as validating it, leaving unresolved the question of how political values are legitimated.

Simon was probably guilty, however, of little more than imprecise language in saying that values are "validated by human fiat." The phrase is surely intended ironically to mean that values, with the possible exception of the "intermediate" value of efficiency, cannot be validated. Ultimate or final values are simply to be taken as given, but in the interests of responsibility and efficiency ought to be separated insofar as possible from questions of fact. Simon's occasional references to democracy, therefore, are irrelevant to his broader argument because his views on administrative responsibility would logically apply to *any* political system professing a hierarchical distinction between policy and administration. At bottom, Waldo's disagreement stems from his belief that democratic theory, which Simon regards as peripheral to the study of public administration, is in fact the central issue for it.

Although democratic theory's proper relation to the theory of responsible administration is still a vital issue, the meaning of democracy itself remains ambiguous. In *The Administrative State* Waldo did little to reduce that ambiguity in his otherwise astute survey of its diverse philosophical roots, thus preventing him from developing a satisfactory foundation for a theory of responsibility. In view of the compelling arguments that Waldo himself made both for and against the various contenders for democracy's proper justification, his readers may be left to wonder if choosing from among them must ultimately be on emotivist grounds, just as Simon asserts that choices about values more generally are and must be.

Finer Versus Friedrich

For more than a half-century, controversy surrounding the meaning of administrative responsibility has consisted chiefly of replays of a confrontation, in 1940, between political scientists Herman Finer and Carl J. Friedrich. Although I shall devote greater

attention to a contemporary version of their debate in the next
section, a brief summary of the original encounter is helpful in
setting the stage for that later analysis. Finer and Friedrich each
believed that responsible government required that public administrators be held accountable for serving the public interest. Both
men considered themselves democrats, but they harbored differing
views about the preferred practical role of administration in real-
izing democratic aims. To clarify their differences concerning that
role, Friedrich's soft-core position will be summarized first, because he initiated the debate; this will be followed by a summary
of Finer's hard-core stance, which was written shortly afterward
as a rebuttal to Friedrich.

Friedrich on the Need for Administrative Discretion. Friedrich (1940)
begins his critique by noting that even under the best of institutional arrangements, a considerable amount of irresponsibility is
inevitable in democratic governments. The possibility of responsibility, he says, assumes some agreement between an agent[5] (an
administrator) and a principal (an elected official or body of
elected officials) to whom the agent is accountable. Owing to the
complexity of modern government, however, the degree to which
that agreement can be achieved is necessarily partial, leading
Friedrich to conclude that all institutional safeguards for enforcing
accountability represent "only loose approximations" (p. 235).
Later, however, he concedes that the weakness of those safeguards
is due mainly to "contradictory and ill-defined policy, as embodied
in faulty legislation" (p. 223) and "the intrusion of party politics"
(p. 235).
    At various points in his essay, Friedrich characterizes the "will
of the state" (p. 225), the idea upon which the principle of strict
accountability is predicated, as "pious," "arbitrary," "abstruse,"
and even fascist, but in any event unnecessary for effective and
responsible administration. In democratic governments, public policy "is a continuous process, the formation of which is inseparable
from its execution. Public policy is being formed as it is being
executed, and it is likewise being executed as it is being formed"
(p. 225). His observation is in pointed opposition to not only
Finer's earlier writings, but more particularly Frank Goodnow's

(1900) influential advocacy forty years earlier of a strict distinction between policy and administration. The blurring of that distinction, Friedrich held, required that administrators be creative solvers of novel and complex problems. Although "it is the function of the administrator to make every conceivable effort toward the enforcement of the law which he is called upon to administer" (p. 237), considerable latitude and discretion are needed to perform that function effectively. Friedrich remained sanguine, however, about the prospects of responsible administration so long as it exhibited a

> proper regard to the existing sum of human knowledge concerning the technical issues involved . . . [and a] proper regard for existing preferences in the community, and more particularly its prevailing majority. Consequently, the responsible administrator is one who is responsive to these two dominant factors: technical knowledge and popular sentiment. Any policy which violates either standard, or which fails to crystallize in spite of their urgent imperatives, renders the official responsible for it liable to the charge of irresponsibility. (p. 232)

Friedrich's optimism that this relaxed conception of responsibility would satisfy democratic tenets stemmed from his belief that in relying upon the latest advances in technical knowledge, administrators would subject themselves "to thorough scrutiny by their colleagues in what is known as the 'fellowship of science' " (p. 233). And in calling upon administrators to exercise discretion in interpreting prevailing public opinion, he makes a virtue of necessity by suggesting that responsible administrative action is mainly "elicited," rather than "enforced" through strict mechanisms of accountability, which in any case can never work as effectively as the traditionalists claim that they should.

Finer on the Perils of Discretion. In defending the traditional view against Friedrich's permissiveness, Finer (1940) forthrightly insists upon administrative "subservience, for I still am of the belief with Rousseau that the people can be unwise but cannot be wrong" (p. 255). If the will of the people is, as Friedrich claims, often distorted by faulty institutions and legislation, the remedies for irresponsible administration surely consist in eliminating those imperfections rather than acceding to them. However difficult the accomplishment of such reforms, the fact remains that responsible administration in democratic government requires that public servants be held accountable to the will of the people via their elected representatives. Mindful of the tyranny resulting from unchecked government power in Nazi Germany and the Soviet Union, Finer construes administrative responsibility in democracies as subservience to the popular will enforced by "an arrangement of correction and punishment even up to dismissal both of politicians and officials" (p. 248). "The servants of the public," he argues, "are not to decide their own course, . . . [but are] to be responsible to elected representatives of the public, and these are to determine the course of action of the public servants to the most minute degree that is technically feasible" (p. 249).

Although Finer does not reject outright Friedrich's moral interpretation of responsibility as including a sense of responsibility based on adherence to professional standards and technical knowledge, he regards moral responsibility as merely an "auxiliary" to the more basic principle of political accountability. Moral responsibility, he says,

> is likely to operate in direct proportion to the strictness and effi-
> ciency of political responsibility, and to fall away into all sorts of
> perversions when the latter is weakly enforced. While professional
> standards, duty to the public, and pursuit of technological effi-
> ciency are factors in sound administrative operation, they are but
> ingredients, and not continuously motivating factors, of sound
> policy, and they require public and political control and direction.
> (p. 275)

Especially offensive to Finer is Friedrich's naive faith in administrators' accountability to the "fellowship of science" in their roles as technical experts and creative problem solvers. "What," Finer asks rhetorically, "is the force of the phrase 'have to account for their action'? Exactly to whom? By what compulsion?" (p. 269). Rather than promoting genuine responsibility, "the result to be feared is the enhancement of official conceit and what has come to be known as 'the new despotism' " (p. 257).

Some Similarities Between Finer and Friedrich. Friedrich was among the first writers to distinguish between objective (external) and subjective (internal) responsibility. Both he and Finer agree that institutional controls and professional codes of ethics are objective, although Finer is more pessimistic than Friedrich about their adequacy for ensuring responsible conduct. Professional standards, moral and political values, and assessments of public sentiment appear to fall on the subjective side, as does a vaguely defined "psychological factor which supplements 'objective' responsibility" (Friedrich, 1935, p. 38).

However, Finer and Friedrich share some common assumptions and beliefs. Despite his more serious reservations, Finer agrees with Friedrich in conceding an important role for the subjective aspects of responsibility, demanding only more stringent standards than Friedrich for justifying departures from the legal-institutional view. And Friedrich does not reject the legal-institutional view advocated by Finer as providing the moral foundation for a theory of responsible government. The two men also implicitly agree that the subjective is the imperfect approximation of the objective. Both writers, that is, believe that the moral basis for action derives from sources *external* to public servants, for example, from law, authoritative edicts, or moral values that are learned and internalized. Finer and Friedrich differ chiefly, therefore, in their answers to the practical questions of how closely the hard-core rationalist view can be adhered to and how effectively administrators can internalize moral principles, apply technical knowledge, and discern public sentiment.

Burke and Cooper

A comparison of two representative contemporary views of administrative responsibility by John P. Burke and Terry L. Cooper reveals more than anything else how little the contours of the discourse have changed since the days of the Finer-Friedrich debate. Because both of these two more recent authors have written book-length treatises rather than brief articles, it is not surprising that Burke's and Cooper's efforts are richer in detail and more thorough in their justifications than those of their predecessors. Like Finer and Friedrich, however, Burke and Cooper differ from one another mainly in the tone of their presentation; on close examination the substance of their proposals is strikingly similar.

Burke's Hard-Core Rationalism. In *Bureaucratic Responsibility* John Burke (1986)[6] elaborates the hard-core variant of rationalist responsibility by drawing not only from Finer but also from the traditions of Max Weber and Woodrow Wilson. Burke's starting point is Weber's (1946) classic essay on "Politics as a Vocation," in which Weber urges that an "ethic of responsibility"—consisting of the qualities of "passion, a feeling of responsibility, and a sense of proportion" (quoted in Burke, p. ix)—is better suited for contending with the realities of political life than an "ethic of ultimate ends." Weber held that in "conduct that follows the maxim of an ethic of responsibility, . . . one has to give an account of the foreseeable results of one's action" (p. 120), rather than, in Burke's words, depend upon "great religious traditions or grand ideological visions for easy solutions" (p. ix). But where Weber says that the art of politics requires committed but sober participation in the rough-and-tumble of compromise and an appreciation of the paradoxes of politics, Burke sets his own sights more narrowly by focusing upon the more encapsulated and prosaic world of bureaucracy. If Burke is a Weberian, therefore, it is only in the limited sense of deducing from Weber's description of the bureaucratic ideal a conception of administrative responsibility as obedience, with some explicit caveats, to political authority.

In listing the chief ways of thinking about administrators' responsibilities, Burke (1986) distinguishes between "external political control" and an "inner sense of duty," roughly analogous to Friedrich's distinction between objective and subjective sources of responsibility. On the external side are two categories, the first being "formal-legal" responsibility based on a respect for hierarchy that ensures administrators' compliance with legal and other authoritative dictates. The second and less formal external approach has two variants, the first of which is "interest group pluralism, which emphasizes the interaction of and accountability to group pressures"; the other variant is "decentralized participation, which posits the devolution of administrative decision making to local bodies and direct citizen involvement in policy formulation and implementation" (p. 17). On the internal side are also two kinds of responsibility, the first being a reliance on professional norms and values (à la Friedrich), whereas the second draws from principles of justice or from personal moral ideals in order to "1) provide for the common good, 2) fulfill basic needs, . . . [or] 3) maximize individual utility" (p. 31).

Burke cites examples in the literature to show that each way of thinking about responsibility has its own supporters, and then lists the pros and cons of each approach. Following this, he endorses the formal-legal definition of responsibility as the baseline for his theory because it

> takes seriously the dictates of higher political authorities, and it recognizes that bureaucratic office is a domain where politically determined obligations rather than personal preference should prevail. This accords with the logic of democratic and constitutional government, a logic that recognizes the supremacy and legitimacy of higher political authorities, whether Congress, president, or the Supreme Court. (p. 38)

Administrators' discretionary actions informed by any of the other three kinds of responsibility must ultimately be reconciled with the formal-legal baseline. Departures from formal-legal responsibility are sometimes necessary, however, in view of its two major limitations: "1) the overly broad prohibition against exercising discretion; and 2) the strict adherence to obedience to superiors in the organizational hierarchy as the principal means of ensuring responsible conduct" (p. 11).

Under Burke's "democratic alternative," public officials have "a basic duty, other things being equal, to take the dictates of hierarchical authorities seriously" (p. 39). Their consent, however, is not merely to a set of rules imposed by those authorities, but is also (Burke quoting Ronald Dworkin) "to an enterprise that may be said to have a character of its own" (p. 41). That larger enterprise to which administrators owe allegiance permits moving beyond Finer's strict legalism by logically inferring additional responsibilities from the administrators' formal duties. Having granted that the

three kinds of responsibility other than the formal-legal kind
have legitimate roles to play in a democratic conception of
responsibility, Burke's advice about what administrators should
do to resolve conflicts between them—for example when professional judgments or moral commitments collide with direct
orders and rules—is simple and direct: Ask higher political authorities to resolve them. If administrators perceive the existence of
inequities in the treatment of some citizens, for example, "the
general course of action officials should take is . . . to encourage
other relevant authorities and institutions . . . to recognize their
failures and take corrective measures" (p. 70). Or, "a democratic
theory of responsibility presents a more coherent way of resolving . . . tensions among rights and between rights claims and policy goals . . . [by counseling] action that encourages proper political authorities to make the proper determinations" (p. 137). A
permissible exception to the general rule that "substantive" decisions should be pushed up to higher authorities is when those
authorities are not available (p. 218). In view of the deference to
higher authority that forms the core of Burke's theory, it is not
surprising that he regards, as MacIntyre says that rationalists must,
broader questions of justice as beyond the legitimate scope of
administrative concern.

   Although my purpose in this section has been mainly to sum-
marize Burke's theory, it is hard to restrain immediate critical
comment on two aspects of it. The first is his manner of arguing
against the various alternatives to the formal-legal view that he
favors. In criticizing these alternatives he gives the impression that
their advocates are unmindful of or even opposed to formal-legal
accountability by virtue of their *exclusive* reliance on other sources
of responsibility. In criticizing the notion of professional responsibility, for example, Burke cautions that it "can prove problematic
when it is employed in a bureaucratic context as either the exclusive form of responsibility or one that is unmodified by qualifications or the consideration of other relevant factors" (p. 26). Similarly, in discussing the subjective or individual aspects of
responsibility he warns that although a "strong case may be made
for viewing individual responsibility as a necessary instrument for
squaring bureaucracy with democratic rule, . . . [it] can by no

means be regarded as either a wholly sufficient or exclusive means to this end" (p. 224).

Burke fails to mention, however, that none of the advocates of professional or individual responsibility whom he cites, nor those about whom he issues similar warnings, who recommend administrative discretion informed by judgments about justice or the public interest, has ever claimed that these alternatives should be used exclusively, and certainly not to the exclusion of legal requirements for accountability. All of the writers whom Burke discusses, including Herman Finer, whose approach he finds most congenial to his own, differ only in their relative emphasis on one or another approach. Although Burke is right in pointing out the limitations of the various alternatives if carried to extremes, he never identifies anyone who actually proposes the extremes that he fears, nor does he show that serious problems of responsible government have ever resulted from an exclusive or even excessive reliance on them.

What seems to attract Burke to the formal-legal approach is little more than a gut conviction that "control," a word appearing repeatedly throughout his book, is synonymous with responsibility. As Friedrich astutely observed, however, the various alternatives to the formal-legal view are not chiefly means for controlling behavior, but serve instead as bases for reflective judgment when control is impossible. Control represents one meaning of responsibility, whereas professionalism and moral precepts imply quite different meanings of the word.

A second troubling aspect of Burke's theory is the way he tries to resolve problems arising from conflicts between personal conscience and political authority. Commenting on the tensions between personal beliefs about moral duty (which in a revealing choice of words he calls "The Problem of Personal Integrity") and political obligation, Burke recounts an episode that purportedly illustrates why the former should be subservient to the latter. After conceding that "we cannot wholly depersonalize individual choice and action, even in a bureaucratic context" (p. 164), he says that:

> The need for some kind of personal connection or "element" in difficult situations is well illustrated in Freeman Dyson's recollection

of his commanding officer in an RAF bombing group during the Second World War. Dyson, a prominent nuclear physicist and member of the Manhattan Project, was charged with providing technical advice on bombing operations. Dyson found, however, that the commanding officer "did not want to talk about bombers, he talked only about silkworms. Since I was a scientist, he thought I would appreciate the fine points of silkworms. He took me out to his greenhouse, where his silkworms were feeding on carefully tended mulberry trees. . . . I found it shocking that a man who carried the responsibility for the lives and deaths of thousands should be wasting his time on silkworms." Forty years later, Dyson admitted that the commanding officer was "the wisest of the group commanders . . . the cultivation of silkworms helped keep him sane." (pp. 164-165)

Then, in order to show the relevance of this story, Burke explains:

Cultivating silkworms kept Dyson's commander sane by acting as a cushion against the moral jolts and precipices of his difficult job, but it did not serve as a personal substitute for his military judgment. It enabled him to do his work better, but it did not tell him how to do his job. This suggests that the personal does have a role to play in the moral quandaries of officials, but as an aid to psychological balance and well-being and as a source of personal relief and comfort. Dyson's experience also indicates that encouraging a conception of duty, obligation, or responsibility that is not wholly personal does not necessarily separate the individual-as-official from the individual-as-private self. (p. 165)

It is difficult to see, however, what connection Burke is trying to draw between Dyson's silkworms story and conflicts between conscience and authoritative obligations. The silkworms provided a *diversion* from the officer's obligations, not a source of conflict with them. Moreover, his hobby has no evident bearing on a conflict involving personal conscience, unless of course Burke is suggesting that the officer worried (or ought to have worried) that his official duties might prove detrimental to his silkworms' welfare.

Conflicts of conscience and obligation are usually lamented for the terrible personal cost they exact when conscience is denied any legitimate role in fulfilling public responsibilities. Such conflicts, in other words, reflect the interminable struggle to define a proper *relation* of the individual to the collectivity. Yet, for Burke, individual conscience and a feeling of personal responsibility are nothing more than palliative denials of any kind of relation except one of subordination. Burke is thus consistent in his adherence to rationalist precepts; by divorcing bureaucratic obedience from the paradoxes of moral and political life that Weber described, responsibility can only be a synonym for control, in which the exercise of personal conscience is reduced to the moral equivalent of growing silkworms.

Cooper's Soft-Core Alternative. Subtitled *An Approach to Ethics for the Administrative Role,* Terry Cooper's (1990) *The Responsible Administrator* extends the Friedrich tradition by arguing that administrative responsibility entails a balancing of competing obligations. Cooper departs from Finer's and Burke's demand for strict obedience by asserting that the administrator's obligation "for something" is more fundamental than his or her hierarchical accountability "to someone." Obligations, which fit into the category of objective responsibility, may be of four kinds: to organizational superiors, to elected officials, to the citizenry, and to the "public interest," the last of which Cooper acknowledges to be a highly ambiguous concept (p. 69). Consistent with Friedrich, Cooper argues that the "objective responsibility that an administrator experiences from the organizational hierarchy must not be viewed as the strict one-way process exemplified by the strictest interpretation of the Weberian ideal type" (p. 65). He also agrees with Friedrich in recommending a two-way process of consultation and cooperation between administrators and their political superiors (p. 66). On the subjective side are individual feelings as well as "beliefs about loyalty, conscience, and identification . . . [reflecting a] professional ethic developed through personal experience" (p. 71), all of which are acquired through a process of socialization. These beliefs are called values, which in turn "become more or less elaborated as principles [that] connect values to broad criteria of conduct" (pp. 73-74).

Cooper's position on the relation between the objective and the subjective is much the same as Finer's and Burke's. The subjective is derived from and ultimately subordinate to the objective inasmuch as the external obligations of objective responsibility provide the administrator's role with

> a structure, stability, predictability, and continuity that approximate the will of the citizenry. The subjective component consists of a subsystem of values and principles that we construct in the process of responding to those objective obligations and expectations. . . .
>
> We develop a structure of subjective responsibility that is the counterpart of the objective responsibility imposed from outside ourselves. In this way we mesh our own needs and idiosyncratic perspectives with the demands of the role. (pp. 74-75)

Cooper says that administrators may be judged to have acted responsibly if their actions are congruent with their inner codes of professional responsibility. He regards such codes, however, as instruments of control: "To the extent that our codes do not consistently control our behavior, we may be described as irresponsible. A responsible person's conduct [by definition] is not at odds with his or her code for that role" (p. 75). As the chief feature of subjective responsibility, these codes are legitimate insofar as they are "significantly informed by some professional consensus about the responsibility of public administrators" (p. 75). That consensus must agree, however, with the objective requirements of political accountability.

Like Burke, Cooper is cautious about endorsing the "internal controls" that subjective responsibility provides, noting that they "are not completely reliable" (p. 130). The meaning of *reliable* is not explained, however, nor does Cooper clarify why the external controls of objective responsibility are any more reliable than internal controls, nor indeed any less influenced by subjective interpretation. As a rationalist Cooper assumes that the burden of justifying the subjective or internal is always greater than for the objective or external. Thus when he later states that "the critical task is to develop a balance between internal and external controls, as well as a congruence between them" (p. 154), *balance* in the context of his prior argument can only be a euphemism for subordinating the former to the latter. This is inevitable because for

Cooper, just as for John Burke, responsibility always boils down to the *control* of conduct undertaken to perform an official mission.

In view of the priority that Cooper gives to the objective dimension of responsibility, it seems incongruous that he should include, near the end of the book, a chapter on "Safeguarding Ethical Autonomy." Under such a heading, one would anticipate commentary on the existential dilemmas resulting from collisions of conscience with formal authority. Cooper considers the standard cases of the Nuremberg trials and Adolf Eichmann but interprets them as problems of suboptimization rather than as moral dilemmas. That is, conflicts between conscience and authority are simply conflicts between higher-order and lower-order obligations, in which the Nuremberg defendants and Eichmann were guilty for having obeyed the latter.

In his chapter on ethical autonomy, Cooper describes the pathologies—such as group-think, excessive subservience to bureaucratic norms, and capitulation to political pressures—that result from moral passivity and unquestioning obedience to authority. To remedy those pathologies, he recommends that administrators blow the whistle on superiors whose orders conflict with their (the administrators') "ultimate obligations to the public" (p. 188). Throughout the chapter, however, Cooper equates "ethical autonomy" and "personal responsibility" with a higher or more encompassing obligation, an equivalence of meaning to which neither philosophers nor most laymen would ordinarily subscribe.[7] Traditionally such conflicts are seen as involving, not competing obligations, but the paradoxical relation of moral agency—in the Sartrean sense of an "agent" who is aware of his or her incontestable authorship of an event—with the generic idea of obligation itself.

Later Cooper appears to get onto the right track by identifying the problem of oversocialization of civil servants, which then leads into a discussion of Stanley Milgram's (1974) notion of the "agentic shift."

> In the organizational society there are two functional modes: the autonomous, self-directed mode, and the systemic or organizational mode. The transition from autonomous to organizational

functioning is the "agentic shift." It involves an alteration of attitude; we shift from acting out our own purposes to an attitude of acting as an agent who executes the wishes of another person. When an individual views himself in this agentic state [quoting Milgram] "profound alterations occur in his behavior and internal functioning. . . .

"The most far reaching consequence of the agentic shift is that a man feels responsible *to* the authority directing him but feels no responsibility *for* the content of the actions that the authority prescribes." (pp. 198-199)

What, then, are we to adduce from this problem? In a concluding comment Cooper (1990) advises that:

This diminution of personal responsibility for the consequences of one's action or inaction in the agentic state ought to be of major concern in a consideration of administrative ethics. If we worry that so few public servants speak out against destructive authority, if loyalty to superiors tends to override individual conscience and obligations to the citizenry, then Milgram's findings should cause us to inquire further into means of modifying the extent to which individuals in the public service make the agentic shift. (pp. 200-201)

In this passage Cooper seems to assume that "individual conscience" (presumably a synonym for "ethical autonomy" and "personal responsibility") and "obligations to the citizenry" can be regarded as companion moral alternatives to bureaucratic obedience. By most reckonings, however, obligations of any kind are more akin to obedience than they are to conscience,[8] a word that Cooper uses too casually throughout his book for the reader to know what it is or from where it comes. From his earlier depiction of public servants as acquiring their values through processes of socialization, Cooper may intend conscience to mean something like an "internalized aggregation of values" that were originally external.[9] If this is what he means by conscience, however, should we not hope to find more public servants who are *im*perfectly socialized, rather than public servants, such as Eichmann, having a virtually perfect congruence between the objective and subjective requirements of their role responsibilities? Eichmann not only felt bound by *his* conscience to obey orders, but he also believed that his participation in the extermination of the Jews helped to fulfill what in Cooper's terminology could plausibly be called his (Eichmann's) "ultimate obligations" to the German citizenry. Thus there was an almost total compatibility among all the obligations of which he was capable of being aware.

If, on the other hand, Cooper intends conscience to connote truly autonomous moral judgment, then it is not obvious why its exercise is necessarily compatible with "higher" obligations to the citizenry or indeed to anything else. Conscience *may* subsume feelings of obligation, but in common usage it typically refers to other things as well, some of which might lead people to violate their obligations.[10] Finally, Milgram's statement that personal responsibility involves a feeling of responsibility *for* the consequences of one's actions seems far closer in meaning to Sartre's "consciousness of incontestable authorship" than to Cooper's notion of obligation *to* the citizenry.

Moreover, that Cooper should prefer the latter seems to contradict his earlier contention that obligations *for something* are superior to obligations *to someone*. It is unfortunate that Cooper's argument should hinge on a matter as seemingly trivial as the wrong choice of a preposition; but his evident confusion about the proper usage of *to* and *for* has led him into all manner of difficulties. In particular, it provides the clue as to why he misses the point of Milgram's idea of the agentic shift.

The phrase "obligation *for* something" is, in the first place, grammatically incorrect. One may have an obligation (or alternatively, be obliged) *to* someone or something, or have an obligation to *do* something; but one cannot have an obligation *for* something. One can, however, be *responsible for* someone or something, and *also* be responsible *to* someone or something. Responsibility, that is, may be correctly used with either preposition, depending on whether one wishes to connote its meaning of agency (in which case responsibility is combined with *for*) or to connote its meaning of obligation (in which case it is combined with *to*).

This mention of Cooper's incorrect preposition is more than a grammatical quibble, for it bears directly on the coherence of his theory. In particular, it reveals that he has conflated responsibility's two generic—and paradoxically opposed—images of making (agency) and answering (obligation) by reducing the former to the latter. In reading his incongruous phrase, it is not clear whether *obligation* or *for* is the operative word. Cooper probably means *obligation*, but combines it with *for* in order to imply a distinction from *obligation to* that is essentially meaningless. The real distinction to be made is between obligation and moral agency as incontestable authorship, the latter of which is the meaning of agency assumed by Milgram's agentic shift. Cooper appears unable to grasp this idea, however, owing to the compliant, "socialized" conception of individuals on which he bases his theory of responsibility. Such beings, were they to exist, would indeed be incapable of such authorship and therefore ignorant of the power implied by the humble preposition *for*.

Similarities Between Modernism and Rationalist Responsibility

Early in this chapter I briefly reviewed Alasdair MacIntyre's description of the modernist debate in political philosophy between rationalism (or rational idealism) and emotivism. My purpose was to set the stage for examining three debates about administrative responsibility, all of whose participants agree on basic rationalist assumptions. In particular I wanted to show that many of the similarities between hard-core and soft-core rationalism may be explained in terms of the similarity of their assumptions with both branches of modernist philosophy. Although some of the connections between modernism and rationalist responsibility should already be evident from the summary of the three debates, the discussion may still profit from a brief review of the chief similarities between them.

It will be recalled that modernists of either sort agree that:

1. If permitted to act according to their natural emotivist proclivities, people will seek to satisfy, even maximize, their own wants and interests, very possibly at the expense of others.

2. Morality, which derives from sources external to the individual, is thus conceived as a constraining force against the expression of those natural proclivities.

3. Either in conjunction with or in the absence of effective normative constraints (for example, ethical codes and moral principles), bureaucratic authority promotes order and control while at the same time shielding public servants from personal responsibility for the consequences of their official actions.

Of the six authors discussed in the preceding section, only Dwight Waldo resists easy categorization as either a modernist or a rationalist. At least part of the reason is that *The Administrative State* is mainly an historical survey—in which Waldo does not advocate a particular philosophical view—of the diverse and often contradictory strands of political thought that have influenced administrative theory and practice. Although he does not develop a sustained argument in favor of a single philosophical position, his belief that the study of administration, like the study of politics, involves "values" and "conceptions of right and wrong" sets him apart, although somewhat ambiguously, from the modernist position. This is because both branches of modernist philosophy, unlike Waldo, agree that the bureaucratic issues of efficiency and control should be separated from political concerns about justice and the proper ends of the state.

The three hard-core rationalists—Herbert Simon, Herman Finer, and John Burke—may be readily classified as modernists, with each showing a slightly stronger affinity for emotivism than for anything like the rational idealism of Kant. Their emotivism, however, owes little to utilitarianism, which is the principal representative of emotivist philosophy. Were hard-core rationalism to succeed in divorcing politics from administration, political questions about utilitarianism's "good" or idealism's "right" would have little bearing on problems of responsible administration. The emotivism of Finer and Burke is revealed instead by their visceral distrust of public servants if left to their own devices. Finer (writing, it will be recalled, in 1940) feared mainly the totalitarianism produced by the collapse of political accountability in various European regimes, whereas Burke fears that personal avarice and caprice will be the chief motive behind public servants' discretionary judgments. Simon's emotivism, on the other hand, seems to derive less from fear than from his belief that because values and therefore politics are inherently irrational, the goal of rational administration requires that it be isolated from politics to the fullest practical extent.

The linkage of Carl Friedrich and Terry Cooper to either variant of modernist philosophy is slightly harder to demonstrate than that of their hard-core rationalist colleagues. This is especially true of Friedrich, who, owing to his wariness of philosophical abstractions, advocates expanded administrative discretion mainly on grounds of practical necessity. Like Friedrich, Cooper urges a greater degree of administrative discretion than either Finer or Burke; but unlike Friedrich, who blithely concedes the inevitability of substantial "irresponsibility" in modern democratic government, Cooper regards the "structure of subjective responsibility" informed by personal and professional ethical codes as supplementing, although still subordinate to, more formal mechanisms of political control. Although Cooper occasionally invokes idealistic phrases such as "ultimate obligations to the public" in support of his position, his effort to reconcile such language with the primary aim of political and bureaucratic control suggests an emotivist stance as deeply held as Finer's and Burke's. As we shall see in Chapter 7's consideration of the paradox of accountability, the rationalists' alarm over the consequences of rampant emotivism in administration is likely to increase after reading why bureaucratic control of the sort they advocate is largely illusory. It is in Chapter 4, however, that the chief liabilities of rationalism's emotivist view of the self will begin to be fully apparent, namely, in its failure to comprehend the paradoxical relation between human agency and moral answerability.

Conclusion

As the debates between the hard-core and soft-core rationalists have shown, vigorous disagreement persists along lines largely unchanged for more than a half century. Varying answers to three related questions have provided the grounds for that disagreement:

1. To what extent can and should administrative behavior be controlled through the strict enforcement of formal-legal accountability?

2. When maintaining control solely by means of formal-legal accountability proves impossible, what sources of moral obligation might provide adequate substitutes for or supplements to it? Relatedly, when moral obligations conflict either with one another or with an explicit requirement for accountability, which should prevail?

3. Under what conditions should discretionary actions informed by public servants' value judgments be permitted? And, in view of the threat to formal-legal accountability that they represent, how might discretionary actions be controlled or reconciled with the principles of democratic government?

It should come as no surprise that I regard answers to these questions as supplying very limited practical and moral guidance in dealing with problems of responsible governance. In view of the narrow range of disagreement, especially in the Finer-Friedrich and Burke-Cooper debates, it is more profitable to show why the assumptions embedded in the questions impede rather than promote a fruitful understanding of the subject. In later chapters I attempt to show why rationalism's assumptions are not just moral ones having to do with what public servants ought (or ought not) to do. They are also empirical because they portray in a peculiarly restrictive manner the factual context within which public servants define their roles, formulate problems, and decide about appropriate courses of action.

The empirical limitations of rationalist responsibility bear directly upon the reasons for its moral inadequacy. For no matter how skillfully the illusion of rationalist responsibility is sustained, rationalism cannot come to terms with the irreducibly subjective character of individual moral agency and thus of personal responsibility. As I shall explain in Chapter 4, the subjectivity of moral agency, in conjunction with objective requirements for obligation and accountability, means that responsibility is an inherently paradoxical idea. By ignoring paradox, rationalism perpetuates the illusion that the recovery of moral innocence is possible, which is itself an irresponsible masquerade.

Notes

1. Quotations from *After Virtue* by Alasdair MacIntyre, (©) 1984 (second edition), are reprinted by permission of the publisher, University of Notre Dame Press.

2. In slightly revised form, portions of this section were published in Harmon, 1989b.

3. A slightly modified version of this article appeared in *Administrative Behavior* (as Chapter 2) under the less evocative heading "Some Problems of Administrative Theory."

4. Simon probably exaggerated only slightly, however, the space needed for a defense of logical positivism adequate for a philosophical grounding of his theory of decision making. And had he shouldered the burden of offering one, it is doubtful that many public administration academics would have taken the trouble to read his book. More importantly, it is likely that the attractiveness of *Administrative Behavior* to those academics was affected less, if indeed at all, from the presence or absence of a full-blown defense of logical positivism than from the commonsense appeal of the fact-value dichotomy. In its simplest form, the dichotomy between fact and value is identical to the everyday distinction between *is* and *ought*, which most adults understand. Moreover, the practical importance of the ideas that Simon develops in Chapter 3 may be fully appreciated on the basis of their commonsense foundation alone. To the untutored the passing references to logical positivism may well seem gratuitous in view of the absence of a fuller explication of them, whereas some scholarly readers might well object to Simon's entrusting the philosophical defense of this theory to luminaries mentioned in footnotes.

5. *Agent* in this context refers to someone, such as an appointed public administrator, who acts on behalf of—as the agent *for*—someone else rather than to a "moral agent" (as described in the previous chapter) who is the incontestable author of an action or event.

6. Quotations from this work are reprinted by permission of author John P. Burke and The Johns Hopkins University Press.

7. In discussing "self-awareness concerning values, rights, needs, duties, and obligations" (p. 216), Cooper (1990) departs from the standard usage of the term *self-awareness*, which is ordinarily used to describe the capacity for reflective insight concerning our motives and intentions in order that we may avoid deceiving ourselves. Self-awareness connotes psychological flexibility rather than moral rectitude informed by "values, rights, needs, duties, and obligations," which may just as often impede self-awareness as aid it. As with "moral autonomy," "conscience," and "personal responsibility," self-awareness, as Cooper construes it, chiefly serves as a reminder of obligations in whose service behavior must be controlled.

8. This point will be developed more fully in Chapter 5, "The Paradox of Obligation."

9. My interpretation of Cooper on this point is reinforced by his claim that "individual responsibility," evidently a rough synonym for "conscience," is something that "can be inculcated" (p. 205).

10. I shall develop this theme further in Chapter 4's analysis of the case of Horatio Hornblower and his steward, Doughty.

4

Paradox and
Personal Responsibility

In every truth the opposite is equally true. For example, a truth can only be expressed in words if it is one-sided. Everything that is thought and expressed in words is one-sided, only half the truth; it all lacks totality, completeness, unity. When the Illustrious Buddha taught about the world, he had to divide it into Sansara and Nirvana, into illusion and truth, into suffering and salvation. One cannot do otherwise, there is no other method for those who teach. But the world itself, being in and around us, is never one-sided.

Herman Hesse, *Siddhartha* (1957, p. 144)

We stand in a turmoil of contradictions without having the faintest idea how to handle them. . . . Paradox lives and moves in this realm; it is the art of balancing opposites in such a way that they do not cancel each other but shoot sparks of light across their points of polarity.

Mary Morrison (quoted in Smith & Berg, 1990, p. 3)

RATIONALISM DESCRIBES a one-sided world that exists *around* but not *in* us, except as the inner world is both reduced to a mere residue of the outer world and so privatized that it is deemed mainly a contaminant of the public realm (McCollough,

1991, p. 22). The world around us may be thought of as the objective world and the world within as the subjective. To be sure, these two "worlds" imply only a figurative distinction, rather than denoting actual domains or even hard-and-fast analytical categories. Yet the distinction is significant not only for differentiating the objective and the subjective but for reminding us that neither is possible but for the presence of the other.

Rationalism's one-sidedness—its insistence on the primacy of an objective accounting of social life—ignores the importance of the relation between the external world and the world of inner experience for comprehending the subjective, the personal, character of responsibility implied by the idea of moral agency. It is subjectivity that animates H. Richard Niebuhr's (1963) image of "man the maker" to accompany "man the answerer," the latter of which alone dominates rationalism's objectivist conception of responsibility. Although each image is needed for grounding the "sparks of light" that Mary Morrison says shoot across the polarities of the objective and the subjective, the inclusion of both poses a threat to the certitude on which rationalism places so high a premium by revealing the relation of the objective and the subjective as irreducibly paradoxical. Paradox, however, both foils rationalism's logical claims with unpredictable revelations of counterexamples and mocks its moral exhortations with continual reminders of the ambiguity inhering in situations that demand action.

Redemption and the Existential Paradox

As the expression of our status as moral agents, personal responsibility is implicated in the most basic of paradoxes, namely, the spiritual predicament pitting the impulse toward self-creation against the demands for answerability emanating from a world not entirely of our own making. This spiritual predicament, which, following Kierkegaard (1844/1957), is usually called the *existential paradox*, embodies the essential polarities of the human condition. Their depiction is by no means uniform: Otto Rank (1978), for example, distinguishes the creatureliness of our animal nature from the insight enabled by consciousness, which in turn reveals the dual burdens of the fear of life and the fear of death. Rollo May (1991) notes that these polarities are expressed most profoundly in mythology, especially in the myth of Oedipus, noting Freud's contention that civilization "involves the eternal struggle between Eros, the myth of love, and Thanatos, the myth of death" (p. 77). And, in *Answer to Job*, Carl G. Jung (1958) explains why evil, rather than needing eradication in order for good to prevail, is in fact "the shadowy side of God's luminescence" (as paraphrased by Smith & Berg, 1990, p. 26) and is thus indispensable to the existence and comprehension of the good.

Rationalism's failure to comprehend the inevitability and necessity of paradox derives chiefly from its embracing what Niebuhr calls the conventional view of responsibility as obedience, in which *ir*responsibility is therefore construed as sin, or transgression, that is deserving of punishment. Redemption, according to the conventional view, is achieved through sorrow for one's sins, which is to say, through the feeling and acknowledgment of guilt. The conventional view's preoccupation with guilt and obedience, by stressing one-sidedly the image of man the answerer, generates "notorious paradoxes," including the dilemma fostered by the attempt

> to reconcile the requirement of the law to love God with heart, soul, mind, and strength and the neighbor as oneself, with the spontaneity, the unrequired character, of genuine love. To love in obedience to requirement is not to love at all; yet it is required that one love unrequiredly. There is the similar paradox in the reflection that the action of the redeemed must be obedient to the will of another than the self, namely, God, and yet that if redeemed it be done in freedom, namely, in the doing of one's own will. (pp. 130-131)

Missing from the conventional view of redemption is the co-presence of man the maker, with which man the answerer stands in paradoxical tension. Responsibility as obligation and accountability must be balanced by a moral agent, one who is conscious, in Jean-Paul Sartre's (1956, p. 553) phrase, of his or her incontestable authorship of a thing or event. In the absence of an agent (a maker), answering to obligations and authoritative commands reduces the quest for redemption to the recapturing of innocence, with the ironic consequence that personal responsibility is denied in the process.

The essential difference between the rationalist and paradoxical conceptions of responsibility turns on the question of the proper relation between innocence and redemption. For rationalism, redemption consists of the restoration of innocence through the eradication of sin and evil, whose recognition is experienced as sorrow and its acknowledgment as guilt. By implication, redemption is achieved and sustained through obedience, which keeps sin and evil at bay. In opposition is Kierkegaard's account of nearly two centuries ago, which still stands as the paradigmatic statement of the paradoxical view. In *The Concept of Dread* Kierkegaard (1957) equates innocence not with the absence of evil but with ignorance of both evil and good. Innocence produces "peace and repose" (p. 38), but at the same time it kindles a nascent sense of dread experienced subliminally as the dawning possibility of freedom enabled by self-consciousness.[1] Thus God's prohibition to Adam against eating from the tree of knowledge awakens in Adam a dread evoking simultaneously the paradoxical specter of freedom's tantalizing yet still incomprehensible promises and anxiety about the loss of sublime comfort that innocence, as ignorance, affords. For Kierkegaard, redemption cannot be achieved through the recovery of innocence, which after all necessarily entails ignorance of both good and evil. Moreover, acts of obedience undertaken in the misplaced hope of recovering innocence would inevitably produce the "notorious" paradoxes of the sort described earlier by Niebuhr.

If the struggle for responsibility entails a quest for redemption in the paradoxical sense that Kierkegaard describes, then the reasons for Niebuhr's criticism of redemption through obedience— and thus responsibility, exclusively or even primarily, as obligation and accountability—become increasingly clear. Relatedly, sin and therefore irresponsibility should be understood not as guilt but as loss and confusion, or, in Niebuhr's (1963) words, "as *hamartia*, the missing of the mark rather than as transgression of the law" (p. 131). Thus, the task of moral theology and, by extension, that of discourse on responsibility, should be "to uncover the source of confusions and paradoxes" (p. 135) rather than systematically to explicate and defend prescriptions for morally correct action.

The Privatization of the Individual

Rationalism's resistance to such suggestions stems in large measure from the uniquely modernist notion of individuality that accompanied its development. With the emergence of bureaucracy, technology, and the expanded powers of the nation state, individuality has become increasingly privatized (McCollough, 1991, pp. 22-23) in that the subjectivity of personal experience is split off from the larger community that the individual inhabits. The contemporary distinction between objectivity and subjectivity may itself be a product of that division, that is, of the estrangement of the individual from the community. In academic parlance, this split is expressed in the assumption that individuals are chiefly self-interested utility maximizers—in Charles Hampden-Turner's (1982) phrase, "ambulatory cash registers" (p. 32)—which guides the research programs and underlying ideologies of market economics, public (or social) choice theory, and even various brands of psychology, most notably behaviorism.

Rationalism radically privatizes the subjectivity of the individual's inner experience by construing it as diametrically opposed to the "objective reality" of the external world of institutions, communities, and other collectivities, rather than as in dialectical and creative tension with it. The institutions of modern society have fostered the estrangement of the individual from the community; rationalism, the legitimator of modernism's worldview, seals their divorce and prevents their reconciliation. Rationalism thus fears and seeks to protect society from the product—the estranged in dividual—of its own making rather than reconsidering the assumptions and institutional forms that created such an individual.

It is therefore hardly surprising that rationalism necessarily interprets any effort to ground an ethic of *public* conduct in subjectivity as an invitation to chaos and views efforts to ground an ethic of *private* conduct in subjectivity either as irrelevant to the public sphere or as dangerous when it infringes upon it. Unable to think paradoxically, rationalists can conceive only of a forced choice between objectivity and subjectivity, the individual and the collectivity, the public and the private. As Thomas McCollough (1991) has explained, however, such a conception of the choice to be made, as well as the fears that attend it, is rooted in a fundamental misunderstanding of subjectivity and the nature of personal responsibility. To pose ethical questions in personal terms

> is not to give warrant to "individualism" but to locate moral responsibility in the self. A public ethic represents in the first instance the creative and critical product of the reflection of an individual. It is social in context and meaning, but personal in judgment, decision, and responsibility. (p. 24)

Categories of Paradox

The discussion to this point has merely hinted at a comprehensive definition of personal responsibility, focusing instead on its general connection with the notions of subjectivity and paradox. Whereas subjectivity has been a recurring theme of earlier chapters, particularly in relation to objectivity, the notion of paradox has received far briefer treatment, consisting of what some readers may see as cryptic metaphorical allusions and even contradictory signals about the meaning or meanings I intend the word to convey. Thus it now seems appropriate to clarify more precisely what I mean by paradox, not only because Chapters 5 through 7 are devoted to a consideration of three paradoxes generated by the rationalist conception of responsibility, but also because the elaboration of the concept of personal responsibility appearing later in this chapter is itself paradoxical, albeit in a different, nonpejorative sense of the word.

The American Heritage Dictionary of the English Language defines paradox in three ways, all of which refer to the idea of contradiction: "1. A seemingly contradictory statement that may nonetheless be true; 2. A person, situation, or action exhibiting inexplicable or contradictory aspects; 3. An assertion that is essentially self-contradictory, although based on a valid deduction from acceptable premises" (Morris, 1969, p. 950). Together, these definitions point to two sorts of distinctions germane to this analysis.

Paradoxical Statements and Situations. The first distinction has to do with whether paradox refers to a statement (or set of statements) that exhibit contradictory aspects *or* to a situation in which particular actions generate consequences either contrary to what would ordinarily be expected or otherwise inexplicable. In the first category, an example of a single paradoxical statement (that is, a statement that is self-contradictory) is the claim that "I am now lying," which can be a lie only if it is true, and true only if it is a lie. Similarly, an easily grasped illustration of a paradoxical *set* of statements is Smith and Berg's (1990) simplification of Jourdain's paradox:

> The following sentence is false.
> The preceding sentence is true. (p. 13)

The two statements taken together are paradoxical in the sense that although each could be true independently, in relation to one another they are contradictory because each denies the truth of the other. Smith and Berg also provide an excellent illustration of the second category, that of paradoxical situations, by describing three elements of paradox in social groups:

1. an awareness of opposing or contradictory forces
2. an acknowledgement and understanding that these are natural and inevitable forces that attend individual and collective life
3. an assertion . . . that these contradictory and opposing forces are somehow linked or connected (p. 45)

The distinction between paradoxical statements and paradoxical situations is not terribly clear-cut inasmuch as social situations of the sort that Smith and Berg describe, and with which we will be chiefly concerned, typically comprise, among other things, sets of statements. Conversely, all statements presuppose a social situation, either real or imaginable, within which they are or might be uttered. The distinction is a useful one despite the overlap of the two categories in view of the differing kinds of analysis appropriate for them. Paradoxical statements, especially formal statements such as Jourdain's paradox, are typically regarded as the province of logicians and philosophers of language, who apply tests of logical and linguistic analysis in order to reveal contradictions and inconsistencies. Paradoxical situations, by contrast, invite investigation by social scientists and others interested in explicating the real-world consequences of action that appear to be contradictory, ironic, or unexpected. Some overlap in these modes of analysis may be present, because one way to simplify the real world for analytical purposes is to reduce some characteristic aspect of it to an ideal-typical representation embodied in a statement. Moreover, the logical contradiction that defines a statement or set of statements as paradoxical must also in some form or another be present in situations that are properly described as paradoxical. This allows us to distinguish situations that are paradoxical from those characterized merely by irony, ambiguity, or conflict. That is, the contradictory consequences or conflicts that define particular situations as paradoxical must be shown to derive necessarily from the "logic of the situation," having some referent in the logical contradictions found in paradoxical statements. So, although my concern in the present project is chiefly with situations rather than with statements, the requirements of logical analysis required for the latter need to be honored.

Schismogenic and Antinomial Paradoxes. The second distinction implied, although less clearly, by the dictionary definitions has to do with whether paradox should be regarded as a problem to be solved or at least avoided, as opposed to an inevitable feature of human existence that, although often fraught with suffering, provides the context within which the quest for meaning and redemption must and can only occur. As an example of the first category, consider Hughes and Brecht's (1975) formal definition of paradox as "a statement or set of statements that are self-referential and contradictory and that trigger a vicious circle" (as paraphrased in Smith & Berg, 1990, p. 12). Deferring for the moment a discussion of the significance of "self-referential," it is the "vicious" aspect of paradox noted in this definition that probably first attracts our attention and even puzzlement when juxtaposed with Morrison's more hopeful depiction of paradox as shooting "sparks of light across . . . points of polarity," or Jung's paradoxical view of human development, which involves the individual's struggle to unify inner opposites. Similarly, in making a paradoxical *statement* one is usually deemed to be in error, whereas being able to *think* paradoxically redounds to one's credit. There is clearly a significant difference in the tone and emotive content of these examples ("unifying opposites" and "vicious contradictions" can hardly be uttered, except ironically, in the same breath), which, moreover, are quite representative of the wide variation in the literature about paradox. So it seems that, depending on whom one reads, there are both bad paradoxes and good ones; one author's condemnation of paradox as evidence of error appears to contradict another's celebration of its presence.

Rather than write off these apparent contradictions as merely a mildly ironic coincidence likely in any word found in multiple philosophical and literary traditions, we might instead think of the word *paradox* as itself paradoxical. That is, its "good" and "bad" meanings are each possible only in the context of the other. We need, therefore, to find labels suitable for capturing the distinction between them; but more importantly, we need to show how their common denominator, contradiction, is altered in the transformation of the bad to the good or, alternatively, of the good to the bad. I have found the problem of labeling these two kinds of paradox especially vexing, inasmuch as possible candidates drawn from ordinary language, especially pairs of everyday words and terms connoting standard opposition, invariably seem to miss the mark. This reflects in part the fact that the distinction I wish to draw is not between symmetrically opposite types nor between bad and good in any straightforward sense. Furthermore, although the intended distinction is to some extent an invidious one, I want the terms identifying the two categories also to have enough precision and explanatory power to facilitate the analysis that follows.

The two terms I have settled upon are an incongruous pair, having been borrowed from two quite distinct traditions. Using a word coined by Gregory Bateson (1972, pp. 68-72), I shall call the first category of paradoxes, the bad or vicious ones, *schismogenic* and the second category, following Jung, *antinomial.* Schismo-genesis literally means "the creation of schisms," deriving from *schismo,* meaning split or broken, and *genesis,* meaning in the beginning or at the outset. The adjective *schismogenic,* then, may be used to describe sets of opposing or contradictory virtues, values, and principles whose individual elements have become split off from one another, and in which one side or element has been comprehended or chosen to the exclusion of the other, ostensibly in the interest of logical consistency and the pursuit of a purpose. Schismogenic thinking is a rational process characteristic especially of Western societies, and it reflects many of both the virtues and liabilities that rationality and rationalism exhibit. Robert Quinn (1988) has commented on the problems generated by schismogenic thinking's premium on purposiveness, noting its inability to comprehend the inevitability of opposition and contradiction.

> When behaving with a conscious purpose, people tend to act upon the environment, not with it. They seek to impose their wills. . . . This is a useful way of acting, but the assumption, paradigm, or world view that underlies such rational-deductive approaches prevents us from seeing or appreciating the recursive nature of the world or the feedback loops that connect us to the environment we are altering. Contradictions must be circumvented or crushed. Adaptation and transformation are made difficult. (pp. 26-27)

Schismogenic paradoxes shall be defined both as *statements,* singly or in sets, that either lead to self-contradictory conclusions or that contradict one another, and as *situations* in which particular actions produce consequences that are contradictory to those intended, but which on closer examination are predictable and even logically inevitable. Schismogenic paradoxes are thus properly regarded as problematic, and cogent explanation of why particular statements or situations are paradoxical in a schismogenic sense provides the grounds for critical evaluation of them.

Jung (1977) uses *antinomy* to describe the complementarity of inner opposites—for example, of good and evil—in which the struggle for their unification defines the dynamic of the individual's quest for wholeness and individuation.[2] Thus, what I shall term antinomial paradoxes embody the notion that opposition and contradiction are inevitable features of human existence, the paradigmatic example of which is Kierkegaard's existential paradox, including various restatements of it noted earlier. Antinomial paradoxes, therefore, can only be struggled with rather than solved, and attempts to avoid them will inevitably backfire.

The question now needs to be addressed as to the nature of the connection between schismogenic and antinomial paradoxes. In particular, why is it that contradiction is a problem in the former instance but natural and necessary in the latter? My thesis is that schismogenic paradoxes are evidence of something gone awry in our understanding of antinomial ones. Schismogenic paradoxes reflect lapses or failures to see situations as unavoidably involving opposition or contradictory aspects, or the inclination to regard one or another of those contradictory aspects, when it *is* perceived, as inherently pathological. This seems to be what Hampden-Turner (1982) has in mind when he says that such paradoxes may simply reflect an inability to comprehend "recursive systems which operate in patterns of mutual restraint and coordination" (p. 112). Recalling Kierkegaard's existential paradox as the primary exemplar of antinomial paradoxes, we might say that schismogenically paradoxical situations are at least analogous to, if not deeply rooted in, attempts to recapture lost innocence; or, in the language of contemporary psychology, that such situations reveal the existence of "avoidances" or even neurosis.

Although spiritual and psychological vocabularies may provide insights concerning the underlying impulse that generates schismogenically paradoxical situations, those situations may also be explained in more straightforward terms. Schismogenic paradoxes are often simply difficult to see, rendered invisible by ingrained habits of thinking or an inability to shift back and forth between levels of analysis. Some of these paradoxes, in fact, are evidence of precisely such difficulties. In explaining Gregory Bateson's (1972) "theory of logical types," for example, Smith and Berg say that "to describe a class of objects or events we require a concept (or set of concepts) that operate(s) at a different level of abstraction than the concepts appropriate for describing one of the objects or events of which the class is constituted" (1990, p. 54). Thus, in order to comprehend a conflict between, say, two oppos-

need to extract ourselves from the logic internal to each principle, that is, move to a higher level of abstraction, in order to grasp the common denominator that locates them in the same class and enables us to understand the root of their contradictory injunctions.

An example of a situation involving two different types at the same level of abstraction might be a conflict between two administrators, one of whom regards his primary obligations as deriving from the orders of hierarchical superiors, the other of whom feels that her obligation is chiefly to the welfare and interests of her subordinates. The conflict between them may be especially difficult to resolve because what is at stake is probably not so much two different kinds of conscious choices about the proper objects of obligation as two systems of logic and meaning, reflected both in and by those sources of obligation, that produce radically different framings of the context within which the conflict is occurring. A similar conflict may also be played out internally, that is, in the mind of a single administrator ethically torn between competing feelings of obligation and between two mutually exclusive definitions of the action context. In both kinds of conflict, continued deadlock, what Bateson (1972) calls a "double bind," is assured unless the participants are able not only to suspend their current beliefs about what ought to be done in the situation but also to stand outside their current understanding of the reasons for the conflict.

Contradictory injunctions may also result from logical types that are located at differing levels of analysis, which permit explanation of why an action that is rational from the standpoint of a higher level of analysis may be quite irrational at a lower level, and vice versa. The classic example of this involves farmers who as individuals act rationally by growing and selling as much produce as they can, because the more they sell, the more money they will earn. Collectively, however, the more produce that farmers are able to sell, the more that prices will be driven downward owing to the law of supply and demand, thus paradoxically lowering their average individual income. Similarly, introductory management texts warn of the danger of suboptimization, which results when individual organizational units try to maximize the attainment of the subgoals for which they are responsible and in the process undercut the broader objectives of the organization.

When caught in the double bind created by schismogenic paradoxes, the sensible way out is to reframe the problem, beginning with trying to understand why in fact the situation *is* paradoxical. This is difficult because in addition to reasons already mentioned, reframing runs up against what Smith and Berg call the problem of self-reference—the tendency to use a current definition of the problem as the only basis for reflecting on what needs to be redefined or reframed.[3] Managers who struggle to find more effective means to control the behavior of difficult subordinates, for example, will typically be frustrated in their attempts unless they realize that control itself may be a problematic objective, one which prevents a more inventive way of framing their problem. Apart from the fact that it is intellectually difficult to escape the vicious circularity that it produces, self-referencing is also emotionally seductive because it provides a temporary respite from the discomforting experience of paradox; however, the respite is paid for later through unresolvable conflicts with others and anxiety within ourselves.

The Paradoxical Character of Personal Responsibility[4]

The discussion of personal responsibility that takes up virtually the remainder of this chapter explores the antinomial relation of Niebuhr's images of "maker" and "answerer." Relatedly, it attempts to explain some of the reasons for and consequences of splits between these two images. What happens, that is, when the manifestations of one image are either ignored or interpreted as being irreconcilably opposed to the other? Or, in the technical terminology introduced earlier, how does antinomy degenerate into schismogenesis, both in a person's interior life and in relations with others? Three fateful consequences of such splits involving both individual and collective action in institutional settings will be discussed in Chapters 5 through 7. In order to understand the operation of schismogenic paradoxes in these settings and in the public sphere more broadly, however, we need to know more about the connection between the interior experience of personal reflection and the intimate experience of personal relationship that, together, define the individual's status as a morally responsible agent. It is these latter two aspects that in complementary (or antinomial) relation with one another enable a two-sided, paradoxical conception of personal responsibility.

Before elaborating that conception further, however, I need to provide a way to visualize the complementarity of its dual elements, as well as to show how the splitting off of one from the other transforms their complementarity into irreconcilable opposition.[5] The vehicle by which I intend to do that, termed the *countervailing principles framework*, captures two basic ideas. First, for any principle, moral virtue, or image that we might stipulate, it is possible to identify at least one opposing or "countervailing" principle with which the first stands in tension. This notion may be grasped quite easily by recalling an elementary lesson from high school civics, in which democracy is often described as a process of mediating between the opposing principles of liberty and order (or, from a somewhat different perspective, between liberty and equality). The second idea depicted by the framework is the corollary notion that serious harm results from an emphasis on one principle to the exclusion of the other. Each principle may generate its own pathologies unless it is held in tension with its partner. Extending the present example, unless liberty is checked by order, chaos ensues, while order that is not countervailed by liberty results in oppression.

Although I believe that this framework has much commonsense appeal, it is usually grasped only partially, owing to our tendency, evident in conversations that have broken down or stalled, to be oblivious to the pathologies of our own preferred principles, virtues, and images. In addition, by unconsciously projecting our fears onto others, we often interpret the counterparts of our own preferred principles exclusively in terms of their pathological or "shadow" side, thus blocking the possibility of their reconciliation. The advocate of unbridled liberty as a consequence would regard oppression as the sole alternative to *his* preferred virtue, while the champion of order would regard chaos as the only option to *hers*.

The notion of countervailing principles is used here to frame the paradoxical conception of personal responsibility that follows. Personal responsibility, I intend to show, is doubly paradoxical—in the first instance because its two elements, internally within the individual, stand in paradoxical relation to one another, and in the second instance because personal responsibility, as the expression of people's status as moral agents, stands in outward paradoxical relation to the rationalist equation of responsibility with obligation and accountability. Consideration of the second sense in which personal responsibility is paradoxical will be taken up in later chapters; it is the first sense with which we shall be mainly concerned here.

I shall define personal responsibility as referring to action that (a) is informed by self-reflexive understanding and (b) emerges from a context of social relationships wherein personal commitments are regarded as valid bases for moral action. By placing the two elements of this definition—self-reflexivity and personal commitment to another—within the countervailing principles framework, it is possible to depict schematically their complementarity as well as the pathology associated with each element. Figure 4.1 is intended to illustrate only the basic structure of the framework. Later in the chapter, the terms included below are fleshed out (and summarized in Figure 4.2) in order to show how the pathologies of narcissism and confluence are produced by splitting the two principal elements of personal responsibility, as well as how the effects of each pathology may be mitigated by reasserting its opposing, or countervailing, principle.

Principles
Self-Reflexivity ◄─────────► Personal Relation

Narcissism   Confluence
Pathologies

Figure 4.1. Personal Responsibility as Countervailing Principles and Pathologies

*   *   *   *   *

In 1804, with the Peace of Amiens having broken down and war between England and France renewed, Horatio

Hornblower, Commander of H.M. Sloop *Hotspur,* engaged
his small ship in his country's desperate and protracted
blockade of French seaports, thwarting the Emperor
Napoleon's plans for invasion. During an incident near Brest
the *Hotspur* drew heavy fire from a French shore battery while
attempting to rescue survivors from a companion vessel that
had just been sunk. After the rescue, but while the *Hotspur*
was still within enemy range, its main topmast backstay was
parted and fell to the deck with a loud thump not three
yards from Hornblower's feet. The damage had been done
by the impact of a live shell that had yet to explode

> and there on the deck, death, sizzling death, was rolling
> towards him; and, as the ship heaved, death changed its course
> with the canting of the deck, in a blundering curve as the belt
> round the shell deflected its roll. Hornblower saw the tiny thread
> of smoke, the burning fuse one-eighth of an inch long. No time to
> think. He sprang at it, as it wobbled on its belt, and with his
> gloved hand he extinguished the fuse, rubbing at it to make
> sure the spark was out, rubbing at it again unnecessarily
> before he straightened up. (Forester, 1962, p. 283)[6]

Hornblower, whose courage and cunning had already
made him a hero in the eyes of his crew and something of a
legend among others of the British blockade fleet, impatiently
ordered onlooking crewmen back to their duties when, "as if
some Gorgon's head had turned them all into stone" (p. 283),
they gaped at their captain in slack-jawed amazement in the
wake of his seemingly calm, even casual heroics.

With characteristic understatement, Hornblower
reported in the most minimal of terms the *Hotspur's* rescue
operation to his superior, one Captain Chambers. Some
weeks later Chambers's own report to the Admiralty
appeared in the Naval Chronicle, as was then the custom in
such matters, and it would be read widely thereafter by the
British public. Its last sentence read:

> Captain Hornblower informs me that *Hotspur* suffered no
> casualties although she was struck by a five-inch shell which

did considerable damage aloft but which fortunately failed to explode. (p. 286)

On reading Chambers's account, Lieutenant Bush, Hornblower's admiring second-in-command, strenuously protested the omission of any mention of Hornblower's daring action.

> "'Tisn't right, sir. 'Tisn't fair to you, sir, or the ship."
> "Nonsense, Mr. Bush. What d'you think we are? Actresses? Politicians? We're King's officers, Mr. Bush, with a duty to do, and no thought for anything else. Never speak to me again like this, if you please, Mr. Bush." (p. 287)

whereupon Hornblower abruptly dismissed his subordinate.

> It was horrible to see Bush shamble out of the cabin, hurt and depressed. The trouble with Bush was that he had no imagination; he could not envisage the other side. Hornblower could—he could see before his eyes at that moment the words he would have written if Bush had had his way. "The shell fell on the deck and with my own hands I extinguished the fuse when it was about to explode." He could never have written such a sentence. He could never have sought for public esteem by writing it. Moreover, and more important, he would scorn the esteem of a public who could tolerate a man who would write such words. If by some chance his deeds did not speak for themselves he would never speak for them. The very possibility revolted him, and he told himself that this was not a matter of personal taste, but a well-weighed decision based on the good of the service; and in that respect he was displaying no more imagination than Bush.
> Then he caught himself up short. This was all lies, all self-deception, refusal to face the truth. He had just flattered himself that he had more imagination than Bush. More imagination, perhaps—but far less courage. Bush knew nothing of the sick horror, the terrible moment of fear which Hornblower had experienced when that shell dropped. Bush did not know how his admired captain had had a moment's vivid mental picture of being blown into bloody rags by the explosion, how his heart had almost ceased to beat—the heart of a coward. Bush did not know the meaning of fear,

and he could not credit his captain with that knowledge either.
And so Bush would never know why Hornblower had made
so light of the incident of the shell and why he had been so
irascible when it was discussed. But Hornblower knew, and
would know, whenever he could bring himself to face facts.
(pp. 287-88)

*   *   *   *   *

Self-Reflexivity. By permitting us access to Hornblower's inner
struggle to grasp the real motives for his action, the episode of the
live shell illustrates how our understanding of responsibility may
be altered and enriched. In the first of the two paragraphs describing his private reflections after dismissing Lieutenant Bush from
his cabin, we read how Hornblower, the consummate professional,
refuses to allow his sense of duty to degenerate into a craven
attempt to curry favor with his superiors. Although his loyalty to
the service is virtually absolute, Hornblower exhibits an acute
appreciation of how it might have been contaminated by opportunism, had he followed Bush's advice to trumpet his own bravery.
His professionalism is further evident as he defends as being for
"the good of the service," rather than a matter of personal taste, his
conviction that his deeds must speak for themselves. This is not
because Hornblower has a passion for anonymity. Indeed, because
he despairs of languishing for the rest of his career at the middling
rank of commander, Hornblower desperately hopes for the kind of
notoriety that he could so easily have achieved.

So far, Hornblower's internal dialogue neatly encapsulates the
tensions between duty and integrity that characterize the internal
divisions within the rationalist conception of responsibility. But
just when the reader is prepared to bestow accolades on him for
his selfless and professional devotion to duty, Hornblower pro-
nounces himself a coward and his rationalization of his action a
fatuous self-deception. Although Hornblower as usual overstates
the case against himself, he nonetheless instinctively knows that
beneath the noble expression of principle lurk the demons of his
psyche, which only he knows about—and even then only when he
has the courage to "face facts." Although Hornblower no doubt

exaggerated in believing that his prior analysis was "all lies," he would have been right to conclude that it contained only partial truths. Rational discourse can contain only part of the truth, the virtue of which is transformed into the pathology of rationalization unless it is understood, if only incompletely, in the context of one's deeper project of personal development.

Being able to probe the relation between the intellectual content of one's principles and the less visible role they serve in sustaining one's emotional life constitutes the essence of the idea of self-reflexivity. To be personally responsible is to face, however unpleasant the prospect, the facts of our personal authorship so as to avoid self-deception and self-justification. For Hornblower, this reflexive capability is evident in his awareness that his omitting any mention of his valor was as much to conceal from himself his own cowardice as it was a sober expression of his integrity.

In defining responsibility as being conscious of one's personal authorship, Sartre (1956) explicitly warned against taking the presence of consciousness at face value.[7] For while we are all conscious, we are at the same time limited in our ability to comprehend in a reflective way our powers of authorship, which consciousness enables. Man the maker, in other words, also has in addition to his (and her) self-awareness a virtually unlimited capacity for self-deception. Self-reflexivity or some equivalent term is thus needed for drawing attention to this difficulty, inasmuch as the reflective awareness of personal authorship may have less to do with the conscious exertion of moral will than with the psychological courage to probe the depths of one's inner experience.

Self-reflexivity depicts the process by which people monitor the flow of their inner lives so as to be aware of the relation of consciously intended actions to the less visible, deeper projects of the psyche that are reflected in those actions. In Jungian terms, to be self-reflexive is to be aware of the dialectical relation between conscious will and unconscious energy, to realize that knowing the manifest content of action constitutes only a partial understanding of it. Self-reflexivity means that people "retroflectively consider unconscious material as it appears in their actions and otherwise in their lives generally" (White, 1990, p. 216).[8] Because access to the unconscious can never be immediate and direct, self-reflexivity cannot be deliberately willed by asserting shoulds and oughts. It can be prompted, however, by fostering "disinterested curiosity," a "friendly collaboration" (p. 216) between conscious awareness and the unconscious that is marked by an attitude of acceptance rather than denial or judgment toward one's spontaneous acts.

Personal responsibility derives its moral nature from its self-reflexive character. *Moral* in this context does not refer to correctness as measured by adherence to a principle or an objective standard. Rather, the moral nature of personal responsibility inheres in the actor's status as agent of his or her actions, for which responsibility cannot ultimately be lodged externally in, for example, a higher authority or learned principles of conduct, no matter how sincerely they may be felt or persuasive their intellectual justification. This should not be read as an indictment of principled thought but as a caution against believing that principles can be in any decisive sense authoritative. Principles serve instead as valuable yet fallible symbols both for framing the emergent and unique contexts of action and for self-reflexively questioning one's personal, emotional stake in those contexts.

In the absence of such a self-reflexive understanding, the latent pathology of principles is manifested in their reification. This occurs when people overobjectify principles by unconsciously divorcing them from their original, affective source in the psyche or by incorporating them whole as memorized instructions from others. The reification of principles is a profound act of forgetting, in which the project of knowing oneself is truncated in the narrower interest of self-justification. It amounts to a kind of intellectual Eichmannism in which responsibility is projected onto what have come to be regarded as compelling abstractions, reducing morality, as Edward Whitmont (1982, p. 90) has put it, to petrified legalism. Even a passionate belief in principles displays an unauthentic passion when the principles are invoked as compelling explanations or justifications of action rather than as symbols that are used self-reflexively.

The pathology of principles is evident not only in self-justification, but also in self-condemnation, which in a similar manner inhibits self-reflexivity and thus personal responsibility. When we reify our principles, which in truth are usually someone else's, our failure to live up to them leads to a feeling of guilt requiring constant absolution from others, rather than leading to reflective self-understanding. To be self-reflexive about principles entails an attitude of self-acceptance in order to probe the role that principles play in our inner lives, allowing us to see splits between who we wish to be and aspects of ourselves that for the present we deem unacceptable. As Whitmont describes it:

> While unavoidable as a first step in individuation, this split needs bridging over once an ego is established. Only through perceiving one's transgression as "missing the point" (the original meaning of the Hebrew *chato* and the Greek *hamartia* which came to mean "sin") rather than as reprehensible sin, can the individual personality liberate itself from rigidity and continue the course of its evolution. (p. 91)

Personal responsibility is as much a psychological notion rooted in the mysteries of the unconscious as it is a straightforward matter of moral courage that can be consciously willed. When people speak of "taking" or "accepting" personal responsibility for their actions, they are therefore likely to lose sight of its unconscious aspect. *Taking* and *accepting* connote conscious intention rather than self-reflexive awareness. Similarly, being personally responsible should not be confused with acting on the basis of one's personal values. As intellectual constructs, personal values differ little from professional or political values, regardless of how sincerely they may be felt. They are authentic only to the extent that the person self-reflexively understands them in the context of their relation to the psychological purposes they serve. This idea may be grasped intuitively by reflecting on the experience of listening to someone whom we sense is posturing about his values, rather than authentically believing them. That is, we perceive a disjunction or inconsistency between the content of what the speaker is saying and the real reason he is saying it. It is not that we judge the speaker to be deliberately deceptive or hypocritical; rather, we sense that the speaker is unaware that his words and the context in which they are spoken fail to match, that they stand in awkward relation to one another. On these occasions, our feeling typically is not one of anger, which we would feel if we sensed a deliberate attempt to deceive us, but one of embarrassment owing to our sense that the speaker is not fully aware of what he is doing and saying.

*   *   *   *   *

Several weeks after the incident of the live shell, Horatio Hornblower was summoned to the flagship of Admiral Cornwallis, commander of the Channel blockade fleet, to discuss orders, which he would soon thereafter receive formally in writing, to sail alone to the neutral port of Cadiz, in Spain, to deliver dispatches to the British consul there. Upon returning by launch to the *Hotspur,* Hornblower was informed by a chagrined Lieutenant Bush that his steward, Doughty, had been charged with mutiny and thrown into the ship's brig for striking a superior officer.

Doughty, despite his lowly rank of ordinary seaman, had often taken advantage of his position as the captain's steward, regarding himself as exempt from the chain of authority that rigidly enforced discipline aboard ship and to which all officers and men of the *Hotspur,* save Doughty, gave unquestioning obedience. While skilled and dutiful in attending to Hornblower's personal needs, Doughty was ill-suited for life in the British navy, whose stern discipline was coupled with a rough-and-tumble daily existence. His loyalty was to his captain, not to the service, which Hornblower grew grudgingly to appreciate. Himself a product of humble origins and having even now very meager resources, Hornblower was grateful for, though somewhat ashamed of, whatever small luxuries Doughty's employ afforded him. A bond of friendship had implicitly formed between the two men, insofar as their differences in rank permitted it and despite Hornblower's inability to acknowledge the fact even to himself.

During Hornblower's absence to confer with Admiral Cornwallis, Doughty had been assigned to a working party of other seamen to take on stores aboard ship.

> Taking stores on board at sea was a job for all hands, and even
> when they were on board there was still work for all hands,
> distributing the stores through the ship. Doughty, in the
> working party in the waist, had demurred on being given an
> order by a bosun's mate, Mayne by name. Mayne had swung
> his "starter," his length of knotted line that petty officers used
> on every necessary occasion—too frequently, in Hornblower's
> judgment. And then Doughty had struck him. There were
> twenty witnesses, and as if that were not enough, Mayne's lip
> had been cut against his teeth and blood had poured down.
> (Forester, 1962, p. 297)

Hornblower, who knew the Articles of War by heart, was
instantly aware of the consequences of Doughty's act.
Striking a superior officer, even a bully like Mayne who
sadistically abused his authority, was punishable by nothing
less than death upon conviction by a court martial
composed of other ships' captains, several of whom were
aboard ships of the fleet clustered together close by. Within
the hour Doughty would be tried and condemned, and by
morning would hang by the neck from a yardarm of the
Hotspur.

As Hornblower grimly pondered the inevitability of
Doughty's execution, a messenger from Cornwallis's
flagship delivered to the *Hotspur* a packet of sealed orders,
which Hornblower quickly opened. The first sentence read:
"Sir: You are requested and required to proceed
immediately in H.M. Sloop *Hotspur* under your command to
the Port of Cadiz" (p. 298). Hornblower fixed his gaze on the
word *immediately*—a word that would postpone Doughty's
doom—and abruptly gave orders to set sail for the
three-week voyage to Cadiz, out of sight of his fellow
captains who would have served as members of the court
martial. In Cadiz, however, would be other British captains
available for the same purpose.

On reaching Cadiz, Hornblower ordered Doughty's
incompetent replacement, Bailey, to prepare a special
dinner for the consul, who was to join him aboard ship that

evening. When Bailey stumblingly offered some thoroughly
inadequate suggestions (as Hornblower knew he would), in
feigned disgust Hornblower ordered Bailey out of his sight
and testily instructed Bush to bring Doughty out of
confinement to prepare a proper meal. Later, alone with
Doughty in his cabin to discuss the menu and dinner
arrangements, Hornblower idly interspersed comments
about other foreign ships also in port, especially those
carrying flags of nations with which Britain was not at war.
He made particular note of the *U.S.S. Constitution,* which
was anchored a short distance away. Hornblower then
asked, "By the way, Doughty, can you swim?" Doughty did
not raise his head. "Yes, sir," his voice was hardly more
than a whisper. "Thank you, sir' " (p. 308).

Hornblower left his cabin and went to the quarterdeck to
receive his guest, who was just stepping onto the gangway.
Later, at the close of their conference in the chartroom, the
consul regretfully declined Hornblower's invitation for
dinner, urging that the *Hotspur* depart from Cadiz as soon
as possible, while the tide was still high. The consul feared
a one-sided encounter between the *Hotspur* and hostile
Spanish warships in or near Cadiz, in view of recent
intelligence revealing that Spain would soon ally with
France against Britain, if it had not already done so.

As the consul was leaving Bush nervously approached
his captain to report Doughty's escape. After feigning
surprised outrage and then self-condemnation for his own
foolish negligence, Hornblower awkwardly changed the
subject, informing Bush of their imminent danger should
the *Hotspur* remain in port and also of the tantalizing
prospect of gold on Spanish ships out at sea. Thus the
episode of Doughty's escape was almost immediately
forgotten by the ship's crew amid the frantic bustle of
preparations to set sail for the safety of open waters.
Forgotten, that is, by all but Hornblower, who hours
later sat alone in his cabin, consumed in despair and
self-loathing.

He sat with drooping head, deep in depression. He had lost his integrity, and that meant he had lost his self-respect. In his life he had made mistakes, whose memory could still make him writhe, but this time he had done far more. He had committed a breach of duty. He had connived at—he had actually contrived—the escape of a deserter, of a criminal. He had violated his sworn oath, and he had done so from mere personal reasons, out of sheer self-indulgence. Not for the good of the service, but because he was a softhearted sentimentalist. He was ashamed of himself, and the shame was all the more acute when his pitiless self-analysis brought up the conviction that, if he could relive those past hours, he would do the same again. (p. 313)[9]

* * * * *

Personal Commitment to Another. The second relational aspect of personal responsibility derives from its social character. Action takes place in or presupposes a social context, which is to say a context of human relationship. Action is necessarily interaction and is distinguished by its emergent and unpredictable quality rather than, at least principally, its rationally planned quality. The more intimate the relationship, as in, for example, a face-to-face encounter, the more it may be mediated by the unique contingencies of the moment rather than governed by general, impersonal categories of appraisal and principles governing correct behavior. Such categories and principles can and do influence the encounter, but they increasingly seem gratuitous, contrived, and inappropriate as the unpredictable dynamic of the encounter unfolds.

Although appropriate and even necessary in less intimate contexts, principles serve as barriers to authentic relationship by distancing people from one another. In gestalt psychology, the use of principles as barriers to relationship is defined as a form of *introjection,* the "swallowing whole of other people's ideas, judgments, and styles" (Herman & Korenich, 1977, p. 52), which can never be fully assimilated. In social relationships, introjects have the effect of stifling authentic feelings and thus block genuine contact with others by functioning as "screens or walls of alien material blocking a free exchange of ideas and feelings" (p. 54). When this happens, the relationship is regulated rather than allowed to take its natural course. The result is that people calculate their action toward one another so that what was once or might otherwise have become a relationship is transformed into a transaction between self-interested, atomistic selves. Mutual commitment and understanding are replaced by the individual calculation of utility. Although cooperation may occur under such circumstances, it is, as Arendt (1958) draws the distinction linguistically, *in order to* achieve a goal rather than *for the sake of* the relationship itself.

To be personally responsible is to act on the basis of a commitment to—out of a feeling of responsibility for—another person and to recognize, as poor Hornblower could only dimly fathom, that such commitment is a valid basis for moral action. Action based on personal commitment to another does not deny the legitimacy of principled thought, but it does suggest that the latter serves mainly to frame the context within which action occurs, rather than to determine in any final sense its content or outcome. Thus, in view of Hornblower's final and (to him) inexplicable realization, it would be the worst kind of injustice to accept at face value his punishing self-analysis. The Doughty affair does not disclose, as Hornblower supposed, simply a victory of sentiment over duty and integrity. Instead it reveals that Hornblower instinctively knew, even though he could not understand, that the principles he so revered could not have ultimate probative power in guiding his actions, that all action is personal. The source of Hornblower's heroism was also his tragic flaw: his inability to comprehend that he acted better than he thought—while believing to his continuing sorrow and consternation precisely the opposite. Hornblower failed at genuine self-reflexive understanding, but he succeeded in spite of himself in acting on humane instincts—instincts that in his mind he could only equate with irresponsible sentimentalism.

The Countervailing Relation
of Self-Reflexivity and Commitment to the Other

Self-reflexivity and human relationship, the two cardinal elements of personal responsibility, both presuppose the other. Self-

Principles

Self-Reflexivity: ◄──── the reciprocal of ────►	**Personal Relation:**
The reflective self-awareness of personal agency enabled by monitoring the relation between conscious actions and deeper projects of the psyche that are reflected in them	Emerging from a context of social relationships wherein personal commitments are regarded as valid bases for moral action

Narcissism:	**Confluence:**
Posturing about personal values in order to deny the legitimate constraints of authority; narcissism is countervailed institutionally by political authority and personally by the capacity for commitment to and relationship with others	Overpersonalizing decisions in order to justify incompetence or avoid confrontation; confluence is countervailed institutionally by professional standards of objectivity and personally by a self-reflexive capacity for integrity

Pathologies

Figure 4.2. The Antinomial Paradox of Personal Responsibility

reflexivity, wherein people engage in an open and flexible dialogue between their outer and inner worlds, depends fundamentally on the quality of the relationships that bound and provide them a social context. Action takes place in a context of intersubjectivity in which meaning is mutually negotiated, constituted, and revised. In the absence of relationship with others, there could be no action toward which to direct self-reflexive attention. Self-reflexivity is an interiorized form of intersubjectivity that presupposes a prior and ongoing relation with others in order that it may avoid being stranded on the "reef of solipsism," to borrow Sartre's phrase. Not only must others be present, but present in relationships characterized by mutual commitment and caring. Self-reflexivity is fragile, elusive, and at best a partially successful effort at self-understanding. It may easily degenerate into defensiveness and self-justification unless the sincerity and goodwill of one's partner in the relationship are implicitly felt.

Conversely, authentic relationships based on mutual commitment need self-reflexive participants having a strong sense of independence and individuality, to assure that the commitment is not transformed into cloying sentimentalism or collusion in one another's "craziness," to use the current idiom. Mutual commitment requires independent, self-aware agents capable of confronting one another with unpleasant facts or an alternative perspective. Thus self-reflexivity and personal commitment to the other stand in paradoxical relation as countervailing aspects of personal responsibility—each potentially pathological unless complemented by the other.

Narcissism. In the absence of authentic relationship, self-reflexivity is transformed into the pathology of narcissism. Among the characteristics of narcissism that Christopher Lasch (1979, p. 33) identifies is "pseudo self-insight," rooted in the self-absorption of an inflated ego desperately fending off the anxiety of being alone in the world. Narcissism, which Lasch notes derives more from self-hatred than self-admiration, is a ubiquitous feature of the present age in which the bonds of "outmoded" authority have been cut loose, leaving individuals "free" to act on impulse, pursuing instant gratification and happiness.[10] The tragedy of narcissism inheres in its fear of intimacy. In the absence of intimacy, the social context that enables genuine self-reflexivity is denied, and pretensions to it are reduced to mere posturing. Personal values become nothing more than hollow slogans of autistic self-absorption.

It is no coincidence that the narcissistic personality both fears intimacy and at the same time rejects traditions, history, and authority. An appreciation of the past, as well as a concern with the future, presupposes the presence of relationship, whereas narcissistic gratification is atemporal, ahistorical, and oblivious to, even contemptuous of, cultural tradition. Intimate relationship, if not exactly a microcosm of historical and cultural association, is at least a precondition for it. And authority, however it may be abused, plays an essential role in the preservation of a human community and historical continuity.

The pathology of narcissism, which in organizations is expressed in posturing about personal values in order to deny the legitimate constraints of authority, is therefore countervailed externally by the requirements of public accountability and the

assertion of legitimate political authority. Despite their own pathologies, authority and accountability serve as macrolevel ana-
logues to the more intimate level of face-to-face relationship. They
are healthy, even necessary, so long as they embody legitimate
historical commitments and cultural traditions; they are pathological when asserted as objective and incontrovertible truths. By
bringing all authority into disrepute, the narcissist is incapable of
knowing the difference.

Confluence. In the absence of self-reflexivity, authentic relationship degenerates into the pathology of confluence. In gestalt psychology, confluence describes relationships in which people lose
their individual identities, the apparent benefit of which is a sense
of stability, comfort, and predictability. Ironically, the pathology
of overextended confluence is evident in people who, having lost
their sense of individual identity, also lose "their capacity for real
contact with one another" (Herman & Korenich, 1977, p. 74).
Authentic relationship thus has a paradoxical quality simultaneously involving both unity and separation. Rather than sustaining
and enriching the relationship, confluence actually aids in destroying it. In order to retain and revitalize the relationship, "confluence needs to be broken intermittently by differentiation" (p.
74), which means that individuality must be reasserted. This
reassertion requires a self-reflexive awareness of the limitations
and possibilities of relationship insofar as it may affect one's own
development and sense of individuality.

Confluence is the pathological partner of narcissism. While
narcissism sacrifices relationship in order to sustain a false image
of independence, confluence sacrifices the independence enabled
by self-reflexivity to a false sense of relationship. Authentic commitment to the other is reduced to collusion—or, in Jerry Harvey's (1974)
metaphor, a "trip to Abilene." As a result, superficial harmony spu-
riously passes for relationship, and its real purpose is to disguise
the person's anxiety about an autonomous moral existence.

Where public accountability symbolizes the virtue of unity
around a common project, professionalism symbolizes the integrity of one's individuality in the face of pressures to collude in
collective pathologies such as "groupthink." That is, a sense of

responsibility generated by a feeling of professional integrity may be seen as a macrolevel analogue to self-reflexivity at the level of the personal. In this way, professionalism may externally countervail the pathology of confluence, which is evident organizationally in decisions that are inappropriately personalized—for example through dubious claims about wanting to avoid hurting another's feelings—when objectivity or confrontation is really needed.

Conclusion

Thus far the argument against the rationalist conception of responsibility has proceeded along two general lines, the first maintaining that the empirical conditions required for it to work do not and cannot exist, the second claiming that rationalism cannot comprehend and integrate the personal, subjective character of responsibility into its own ideal conception. In the next three chapters I intend to show in a more focused way how these two lines of argument converge. This will be accomplished by examining three schismogenic paradoxes—of obligation, agency, and accountability—each of which illustrates predictable pathologies created by the splitting off of the personal from the public realm.

Notes

1. Smith and Berg (1990) note that "Kierkegaard suggested that this myth deals with the dawning of consciousness symbolized as a descent from innocence, a *fall* into self-consciousness as it were, an awakening from a comfortable ignorance" (p. 48).

2. Just how much Jung owed to Immanuel Kant on this matter I am uncertain; but there is probably more than a coincidental similarity between Jung's use of antinomy and Kant's (1949, pp. 328-458) use of it in "The Antinomy of Pure Reason," Chapter 2 of the "Transcendental Dialectic" in the *Critique of Pure Reason*.

3. One reviewer of the manuscript of this book commented that the

> problem of self-reference could be brought to bear on the terms
> *man the maker* and *man the answerer*, for of course the term
> *man* here uses a "current definition" to reflect on what needs to
> be changed. Harmon does well in general with gendered usage
> (he and she, etc.)—but saying something about how one-sided

the term *man* is and indeed how masculine "rationality" is could bring added weight to his argument, though I could understand why this might be something it would take a lot of re-working to get into.

Since Niebuhr's book was written in the early 1960s, before gender sensitivity in English usage became an issue, I have chosen not to tinker with his use of *man* as synonymous with *human*, nor do I think that the reviewer would have expected me to do so. Nonetheless, she (or he) makes a useful point, one that I had originally intended to develop in a somewhat different form in a chapter (later deleted from the manuscript's original proposal because of limits placed on the size of the book) called "The Paradox of Rationality." Much of that chapter would have drawn from contemporary feminist critiques of rationality, logic, and related notions. Some flavor of the argument of that chapter can be gleaned from Andrea Nye's (1990) *Words of Power: A Feminist Reading of the History of Logic*, Carole Pateman's (1988) *The Sexual Contract*, and Camilla Stivers's (1993) *Gender Images in Public Administration*.

4. In slightly revised form, much of the remainder of this chapter and portions of Chapter 5 were published in "The Responsible Actor as Tortured Soul: The Case of Horatio Hornblower," in Henry D. Kass and Bayard L. Catron (Eds.), *Images and Identities in Public Administration* (pp. 151-180), Newbury Park, CA: Sage, 1990.

5. Two works by Charles Hampden-Turner, *Maps of the Mind* (1982) (especially pp. 178-180) and the Appendix to *Radical Man* (1971), should be credited as the chief sources of inspiration for the framework.

6. Quotations from *Hornblower and the Hotspur* here and elsewhere in the chapter are reprinted with permission of Little, Brown.

7. In *Being and Nothingness* (1956) Sartre introduces the notion of "bad faith" in Chapter 2 (pp. 47-70), which his English translator, Hazel E. Barnes, takes to mean:

> A lie to oneself within the unity of a single consciousness. Through bad faith a person seeks to escape the responsible freedom of Being-for-itself. Bad faith rests on a vacillation between transcendence and facticity which refuses to recognize either one for what it really is or to synthesize them. (p. 628)

8. The material from White (1990) appears in G. L. Wamsley et al., *Refounding public administration* (pp. 182-245), © Sage Publications, Newbury Park, CA. Used with permission.

9. Michael W. Jackson pointed out to me the comparison that readers are likely to draw between the Hornblower/Doughty episode and Herman Melville's (1948) *Billy Budd*. I prefer the Hornblower case, not only for its happier ending (at least for Doughty), but also for reasons that were chiefly intuitive until I read Jackson's correspondence to me on the matter, which I take the liberty of quoting from here:

> On responsibility . . . I think of Hannah Arendt's *The Life of the Mind* [1971] . . . . She argues for a responsibility to judge and for the judgement of responsibility, relying on Kant's aesthetics as a theoretical framework because it necessarily includes the participation of the observer. Weber thought the rule of judgement in

> a bureaucracy was determinative (apply the right rule and it
> determines the outcome). Against this Arendt argues that moral
> judgements (and these sometimes have to be made within a
> bureaucratic world) are reflective (requiring the judge to reflect
> upon context). . . . The antithesis to Hornblower is Captain Vere
> in *Billy Budd*, who follows determinative judgement, while ago-
> nising over it. His is a true agony since he lacks the inner subtlety
> and complexity attributed to Hornblower.

While I appreciate and agree with the distinction Jackson draws between
determinative and reflective judgment, I would add the caveats that Hornblower's
contriving Doughty's escape was determined mainly by his *feelings* of pity and
appreciation, and that his reflective judgment, which took place after the event,
produced in him an agony probably the equal of Captain Vere's.

   10. In noting the contemporary pervasiveness of narcissism, in contrast to the
principal psychopathologies of an earlier age, Lasch (1979) says that

> psychoanalysis, a therapy that grew out of experience with se-
> verely repressed and morally rigid individuals who needed to
> come to terms with a rigorous inner "censor," today finds itself
> confronted more and more often with a "chaotic and impulse-rid-
> den character." It must deal with patients who "act out" their
> conflicts instead of repressing or sublimating them. (p. 37)

5

The Paradox of Obligation

◈ As a condition of employment, public servants sign contracts specifying their formal duties and obligations. In
virtually all instances, they do so freely and voluntarily, but in the
bargain they give up certain rights, including, but not limited to,
avenues of private gain that are otherwise open to ordinary citizens. Public service constitutes a special kind of citizenship—a
public citizenship—that carries with it a burden of obligation not
shared, at least as directly and immediately, by others (Cooper,
1991). For public servants, that is, the balance of rights and
obligations enjoyed and struggled with by ordinary citizens is
weighted heavily toward the latter. In return for shouldering this
burden, however, public servants receive, in combinations that
vary according to individual circumstances and predilections,
both a degree of financial security and the satisfaction that, ideally,
attends the skilled performance of public duties.

During careers governed by these conditions of employment, public servants inevitably confront moral quandaries that fall into either of two general categories. The first involves conflicts between their public or official obligations, on the one hand, and their private commitments and aspirations, on the other. The second category includes conflicts between various competing official or otherwise "public" sources of obligation, for example, between laws or rules and orders from political or organizational superiors, or between either of these sources and professional codes of ethical conduct. According to the conventional—which is to say, the rationalist—conception of responsibility, proper judgments regarding conflicts of either sort have to do with determining which obligations should take precedence over others. In the first category, official obligations more often take priority over private commitments by virtue of the voluntary nature of the contract into which the public servant enters. For ordinary citizens, by contrast, private commitments and aspirations generally take priority, with obvious important exceptions, over the claims made by government, which is presumed to exist for their benefit and at their pleasure. Public servants do retain certain rights of citizenship, however, including the right to vote and to protection of their basic civil liberties. But to claim additional rights of ordinary citizenship, public servants must demonstrate that the exercise of those rights will not seriously compromise the skilled and faithful performance of their official duties.

Conflicts resulting from competing sources of moral obligation have been the principal topics of dispute between opposing viewpoints in the rationalist discourse on responsibility ever since Herman Finer (1940) and Carl J. Friedrich (1940) initiated the debate on the subject more than a half century ago. For the rationalists, both hard-core and soft-core alike, responsibility as an explicitly moral concept is synonymous with the idea of obligation, which is then institutionalized through structures of public accountability. More briefly, moral responsibility equals obligation, and *official* obligation equals accountability. Problems of responsibility, then, are construed as conflicts over which obligations have higher or more legitimate standing than others.

In the critique that follows I shall argue that rationalist responsibility's equation of morality with obligation is misconceived and therefore that debates within the rationalist discourse over which among various competing obligations may rightfully claim superiority is at best relevant to only a limited set of questions about responsible government. Moreover, given the way that rationalism construes the relation of individual persons, both ordinary citizens *and* public servants, to institutions of government, the idea of obligation is paradoxical in the vicious or schismogenic sense described in the previous chapter. That is, apparently unintended and unwanted consequences predictably and even inevitably flow from the logic of situations in which public servants try to fulfill their official obligations.

My intention, however, is not to discredit the idea of obligation, but to show both how the rationalist conception of it generates insoluble dilemmas and why obligation, however it is construed, is only one among many sources of moral guidance. The genesis of the critique may be found in Chapter 4, which noted that institutions of modern societies have produced a radically privatized individual whose personal aspirations and commitments have become split off from his or her public life. Personal responsibility can have no meaningful public expression; and responsibility as a generic concept can only mean accommodation to an external source of morality. The person's status as a moral agent as reflected by H. Richard Niebuhr's image of "man the maker" is thus subordinated in the rationalist account of responsibility to a dutiful and compliant impersonation of "man the answerer."

To provide a clearer idea of where the critique of obligation is headed, I shall include here a summary version of the paradox of obligation, which in subsequent pages will be expanded upon. The paradox of obligation holds that:

> **If, as rationalist responsibility assumes, public servants are free to choose but at the same time are obliged to act only as others authoritatively choose for them, then they are not, for all practical purposes, free. If, on the other hand, public servants do**

> choose freely, their actions may violate authorita-
> tive obligations, in which case their exercise of free
> choice is irresponsible.

In order for the paradox of obligation to command serious
attention it must enable us to explain real-world consequences
that, although unintended, are nonetheless predictable. The paradox of obligation, in other words, must be shown to be more than
simply a disembodied logically paradoxical *statement*; it must also
encapsulate the internal logic of real situations in which ostensibly
rational actions produce pathological consequences. Two pathologies in particular—bureaucratic opportunism and the reification
of obligations and authority—will be shown to be insoluble and,
in the latter instance, unrecognizable problems from the standpoint of rationalism's paradoxical conception of obligation. Finally, I will propose reframing the problem of obligation by depicting responsibility in antinomial relation with a conception of
freedom rooted in the notion of moral agency.

The Problem of Political Obligation

Practitioners of the so-called helping professions, such as coun-
seling, social work, and psychotherapy, sometimes remark only
half-jokingly that the best thing about advice is that it is hardly
ever taken. Basic instruction in these professions in fact typically
includes stern warnings against giving advice as a way to help
clients. One of the best proverbs about advice giving maintains that
it can have only three results, all of them bad: First, the advice will
probably be ignored, in which case both the giver and the receiver
will have wasted their time; second, although rarely, the advice
will be taken, but will turn out to be *bad* advice, in which case the
advice receiver can blame (hold responsible) the advice giver for
its consequences; or third, and rarer still, the advice will not only
be taken, but be found to be *good* (fitting or appropriate) advice, so
that thereafter when the receiver has a problem he or she will
request from the giver even more advice, thus conceding to the
giver the responsibility for living the receiver's life.

The rationalist discourse on responsibility, summarized in Chapter 3, essentially boils down to the giving of moral advice, albeit coupled with dire warnings of the consequences of not following it. As a special form of advice, the rationalist discourse is prone to many of the same pitfalls, at least by analogy, as giving personal advice. No matter how tightly reasoned its justification, and regardless of the weight of official authority that might sanction it, moral advice reminding people of their obligations almost invariably has a superficial and preachy quality. In view of the level of generality at which it is pitched, advice about official obligations typically fails, like advice more generally, to take account of the unique details of real-life situations that people experience.

Prior to the problem of the inappropriateness of particular nuggets of advice, however, is the broader question of why people should feel moved to consider moral advice about obligations at all. Rationalism confronts an insoluble predicament in finding an answer to this question in view of some crucial assumptions that it makes regarding individual motivation. Recalling arguments made in Chapter 4 that rationalism presupposes an atomistic, privatized individual driven by the motive of self-interest, it is this same individual whom rationalism expects to honor obligations and promises. For the privatized, self-interested individual, however, opportunism can be the only genuine motive for honoring obligations and promises, and for the same reason for dishonoring them when it appears expedient to do so. Later in the chapter I shall note how some contemporary exponents of rationalist responsibility try to get around this problem by asserting a second characteristic quality of the individual, namely, his or her essentially compliant nature. But rather than solving the problem of obligation by means of this strategy, the rationalists simply compound their own difficulties by inadvertently revealing an additional problem, that of the reification of obligations and authority.

In developing the first part of my argument I shall borrow freely from political philosopher Carole Pateman's (1985) critique of the idea of political obligation. Because Pateman is concerned with the relation of citizens to the state rather than with public servants to government, some interpretation of the relevance of her argument to our present concerns will need to be made. Pateman's general thesis is that obligation in the liberal democratic state, that is, a state that is rationalized in terms of the liberal contractarian philosophies of Thomas Hobbes and especially John Locke, poses an insoluble problem. In such theories, the obligations of citizens to the state are assumed to be voluntary, which is to say that they consist of moral commitments that are self-assumed and freely made, taking the form of individual agreements, choices, and promises. It is the voluntary nature of this obligation that is presumed to confer upon the liberal state its legitimacy and indeed defines it as democratic.

The idea of self-assumed obligation achieved prominence during the seventeenth century, a time when justifications for the state deriving from theories of divine right and patriarchy began to fall into disfavor, and modern market societies emerged. Commenting on the significance of obligation's elevation to prominence, Pateman explains that:

> Once the belief gained currency that individuals were not "naturally" arranged unequally and in subordination [to] one another, but, on the contrary, were "naturally" free and equal, some enormous questions emerged about their mutual relationships. In particular, questions began to be asked about the basis of their political relationships, about political authority and political obligation. The social contract theorists had to address themselves to these questions; most importantly, they had to find an answer to the fundamental political problem of *how and why any free and equal individual could legitimately be governed by anyone else at all.* (p. 13)

If, as the liberal view claimed, people are free and equal, then any obligations they may have toward the state must necessarily be self-assumed and arrived at through their own actions and judgments. This self-assumed quality of obligation is thus supposed to replace the idea of obedience, which was basic to liberal contract theory's immediate predecessors. To distinguish obligation from obedience, the former is assumed to be the equivalent of promising, which embodies the idea of commitments that are freely made and based on the individual's own considered judgment. Pateman argues, however, that the liberal theorists' version of obligation is far more akin to old-fashioned obedience than they realize, because as a practical matter it involves consent to a preexisting structure of political relationships. Its voluntary character is merely hypothetical rather than the product of actions that people actually will and negotiate. Moreover, the kind of obligation that is embodied in the passive notion of consent is a highly restricted kind of promising, namely, the promise to obey. Citing Jean-Jacques Rousseau's[1] critique of the liberal equation of obligation (to consent) with promising, Pateman argues that:

> A promise to obey is not merely one particular form that the social practice of promising can take; it is a very special and singular kind of promise. Promising . . . is important to liberal theory because it brings into being a relationship that, at one and the same time, is an expression of individual freedom and equality, yet commits individuals for the future. Promising also implies that individuals are capable of independent judgement and rational deliberation, and of evaluating and changing their own actions and relationships; promises may sometimes justifiably be broken. However, to promise to obey is to deny or to limit, to a greater or lesser degree, individuals' freedom and equality and their ability to exercise these capacities. To promise to obey is to state that, in certain areas, the person making the promise is no longer free to exercise her capacities and decide upon her own actions, and is no longer equal, but subordinate. (p. 19)

Pateman's quarrel is thus not with the idea of obligation itself, but with liberal contract theory's beliefs about how obligations are arrived at. Promises made in the course of actual social practices involving the free creation of new relationships, she says, provide a far more satisfying and plausible explanation of obligations in a democratic polity than do the hypothetical voluntary acts of isolated individuals, those whom liberal contract theorists believe would rationally consent to preexisting relationships mandated by the state. But liberal theorists compound the problem of their account of self-assumed obligation by depicting people as isolated individuals who, upon closer examination, have no rational reason at all for keeping their promises or honoring their obligations.

Consistent with the emotivist conception of the self criticized by
Alasdair MacIntyre (in Chapter 3), the rational individuals of
liberal theory are rational precisely insofar as they decide about
obligations, and indeed any other form of social commitment, prior
to and independently of relationship with others—informed only
by their isolated subjective point of view.

> The "natural morality" of [such an] abstractly conceived individ-
> ual is completely possessive, so that when a decision has to be
> made, for example whether or not to assume or fulfill an obliga-
> tion, the outcome will depend entirely upon the individual's
> subjective judgement of personal advantage and profit. (Pateman,
> 1985, p. 25)

The self-interest assumption also, of course, provides no reason to
believe that possessive individuals could regard promises of any
kind as binding.

Promising as a conceptual problem disappears, however, when it
is seen not as a discrete action taken by isolated individuals but as a
social practice that is intersubjectively negotiated and an integral part
of the social matrix in which people perceive possibilities for action.
Ideas such as promising and obligation are surely required in order
to have the most basic comprehension of what social life entails or
what it means to be a member of society. But liberal theory's individualist perspective is incapable of grasping the irreducibly social
character of promising, thus creating the problem of obligation that
it cannot solve. Pateman describes this insoluble problem as a
paradox that is created by liberalism's separation of obligation's
moral character from actual social practices, attempting instead to
locate it in an *a*social, abstracted individual.

> On the one hand, the use of "obligation" in . . . [liberal theory's]
> conceptual argument reduces individual choice to the acceptance
> or recognition of independently existing "oughts" and "rules" ("ob-
> ligations"); individuals are bound [by] but they do not create their
> obligations. On the other hand, abstract individualism focuses on
> individuals' capacity to create obligations, but it can say nothing
> about the rules and oughts. Individuals are superior to their obli-
> gations but their binding nature is incomprehensible. (p. 29)

How does this excursion into contractarian political theory, then, bear upon the obligations of public servants in democratic societies? In particular, does Pateman's critique of liberal contract theory apply by extension to the rationalist conception of responsibility? To show that it does, I am obliged to show that the rationalists discussed in Chapter 3 assume that individuals are of the isolated, abstracted kind presupposed by liberal theory and that they accept an interpretation of democracy as chiefly involving obligation as hypothetical voluntary consent as opposed to the free creation of social relationships.

Although neither John Burke (1986) nor Terry Cooper (1990) explicitly avows a commitment to abstracted individualism, it is nonetheless reasonable to infer a stance very close to it from the concerns that each expresses about the consequences that would— and, they assert, *do*—ensue when individuals are left to their own devices in making social and political judgments. As a hard-core rationalist, Burke (1986, p. 227) is especially dubious, frequently commenting that without the social safeguards that political authority provides, individual judgments will be dictated by personal values, which are by definition subjective, arbitrary, and motivated by selfish interests.[2] Cooper echoes the same concern, being only slightly less worried than Burke about the effects of such rampant emotivism, owing to his (Cooper's) greater optimism about the salutary influences of the state and its institutions in effectively socializing citizens and public servants. For both Burke and Cooper, however, the specter of anarchy fomented by the natural expression of individual wants and desires seems to simmer beneath the fragile mantle of state authority.

On the issue of consent, Burke is again more explicit than Cooper, although in the final analysis both may fairly be characterized as consent theorists. In the Appendix to *Bureaucratic Responsibility*, Burke spells out his reasons for basing his "democratic alternative" on the idea of consent. He argues that despite its limitations, consent, even if it is merely tacit, is preferable to its only practical alternatives, namely, obligations deriving from "professional" and "normative" sources or from "personal morality" (p. 227). From the standpoint of Pateman's critique, however, to argue about which of these sources of obligation have greater legitimacy than others is pointless. It makes no difference what levels of official sanction various kinds of obligation represent. Rather, what matters is whether particular obligations, regardless of which of Burke's categories they might fit, are both freely entered into and products of actual and mutually created relationships rather than hypothetical ones. The political legitimacy of particular obligations, in other words, depends on the nature of the actual social processes that produce them rather than the degree to which they accord with preexisting structures of authority or philosophical abstractions. Consent *itself,* rather than *which* social institution has the strongest claim to it, is the real problem; and the truly democratic alternative to consent is active participation by citizens in the free creation of political relationships.

Burke does acknowledge participation as desirable in a democracy, but chiefly as a *means* for obtaining consent, rather than as democracy's defining characteristic.

> Consent is perhaps the most central and justifiable way of creating a binding relationship between citizen and state, officeholder and office. . . . Not only does democratic participation give individuals the opportunity to consent to its politics, but participation itself may aid in the civic education of the individual, as many critics of contemporary democracy themselves recognize. (p. 234)

Why, however, would people value political participation, which is necessarily an *active* process, if its main purpose is to consent to preexisting political arrangements, which is by definition a *passive* process? Why be concerned, as Burke claims to be, with making government accountable to citizens if, as passive consenters, they have nothing actively to demand that government be accountable *for?* Why, in other words, should people freely participate in giving up their own freedom?

The answer, of course, is that free and rational individuals would not do so. Burke's confusion on this issue stems at least in part from some apparent uncertainty about where his loyalties lie: to the state or to the citizens who compose it. As a democrat, he has to give lip service to the latter; but his hypothetical and surely incongruous ideal of "perfectly consent-based politics" (p. 234) seems to suggest an unresolved ambivalence. To advocate participation chiefly as a *means* to obtain consent or indeed anything else is to instrumentalize the idea, and in so doing to assume the standpoint and interest of the state—prior to and independently of the interests of its citizens.[3]

Pateman is mainly concerned with the problem of consent as it pertains to the relation of citizens to the state. To show the relevance of her critique to the paradox of obligation, however, I not only have to show a general equivalence between the problem of consent for citizens and the problem of obligation for public servants, but also must anticipate the major exceptions to or qualifications of that equivalence that might be asserted. I believe that I have already met the first of these requirements by showing that the rationalist conception of responsibility in its unadulterated form is nothing more than a consent theory applied to public servants.

The second requirement can be met by imagining what a defense of Burke's consent theory would look like if he were to concede Pateman's arguments as they apply to citizens, but nevertheless claim that the situation of public servants is in some vital respect different. The most obvious difference is that unlike liberal contract theory, in which citizens' ostensibly self-assumed obligations are merely hypothetical, public servants actually *sign* their contracts; there is nothing hypothetical, therefore, about the way they assume their obligations. Moreover, having signed their contracts freely, they are morally bound to honor them; a promise is, after all, a promise.

But this only begs the question of why people should keep their promises. Why, in particular, should the isolated, abstracted individuals whom Burke seems to fear take their obligations seriously—even if those obligations are actually rather than hypothetically assumed? Unless public servants, as individuals, are somehow different in their fundamental character from ordinary citizens, there is no reason to believe that they would be any less likely than citizens to give vent to their emotivist impulses and pursue their selfish interests.[4]

The Pathologies of Obligation

In this section I shall use the countervailing principles framework introduced in Chapter 4 to frame the paradox of obligation. In the discussion that immediately follows (summarized in Figure 5.1), we see how the pathologies of bureaucratic opportunism and the reification of obligations and authority are natural consequences of the rationalists' splitting off the principles of obligation and freedom from one another, thereby creating a schismogenic paradox. Later in the chapter, the problem of obligation is reframed (as summarized in Figure 5.2) by construing obligations as actively created rather than passively accepted and by interpreting freedom as the reflective expression of moral agency rather than a synonym for the exercise of individual rights. Under this alternative formulation, obligation and freedom may be conceived in antinomial relation, thus making both comprehensible and tractable the pathologies of opportunism and reification.

Bureaucratic Opportunism. I have selected *opportunism* as the label for the public-servant equivalent of liberalism's possessive individual, in part because the word is so widely used in everyday conversations about "bureaucratic behavior" and because its ordinary connotation is general enough to cover a multitude of sins. It has the additional advantage of being theoretically "neutral": Observers representing different theoretical perspectives would probably all agree, first of all, that there is "such a thing" as opportunism, and they might also occasionally agree, at least in blatant cases, that particular actions of public servants merit the label. The rationalist and paradoxical views about obligation, however, differ markedly in how they construe the nature and origin of opportunism as well as in their strategies for dealing with it.

Just as liberalism assumes that individuals are naturally possessive, so too must rationalism assume opportunism to be a natural motive of public servants. And, therefore, just as liberalism cannot solve the problem of obligation owing to the presence of possessive citizens, rationalist responsibility cannot solve it because of the natural opportunism of public servants. "Rational" public servants would necessarily eye with cynicism ethical codes and moral advice about responsible conduct (including books on the subject) and would make decisions about whether or not to abide by it based on considerations of self-interest. For them, any notion of morality or ethics must itself seem incongruous. Finally, rationalism would also be incapable of appreciating the irony that compliance with official obligations may itself constitute a pernicious form of opportunism.

Burke and Cooper might well object that this interpretation vastly oversimplifies the conception of the individual that they presume in their theories. Each could argue, with some surface justification, that he has presented a far more balanced view of the individual than that found in Pateman's account of liberal theory's possessive individual. In particular, each could point to chapters discussing the "inner checks" of personal morality and the like, as well as to commentary on how social institutions are able to socialize and educate both public servants and citizens into willing acceptance of their obligations. But rather than providing a *balanced* conception of the individual, both Burke and Cooper try instead to have it both ways by assuming the existence of an individual who is alternately selfish *and* manipulable. Although it is certainly possible to depict individuals as having opposing aspects to their natures, some conceptual connection between them must be shown. In the absence of such a connection, *balancing* (or, to use Cooper's preferred word, *reconciling*) becomes a euphemism depicting an untenable compromise between two pathological extremes. Taken singly or in combination, these extremes provide neither a coherent conception of the individual nor much reason for optimism about the prospects for responsible government.

The Reification of Obligations and Authority. The reasons why rationalism cannot provide a satisfactory conceptual solution to the problem of opportunism help to explain the second half of the paradox of obligation, namely, that if individuals choose freely, their actions may violate their obligations, in which case their exercise of free choice is irresponsible. As I shall argue later in this chapter, the rationalists' conception of freedom is especially dubious because it fails to comprehend freedom's necessarily social

Principles	
Freedom: ◄──── split off from ────►	**Responsibility:**
The exercise of *rights* by self-interested individuals; rights are selectively denied to public servants as a condition of employment	The fulfillment of preexisting *obligations* by compliant individuals; obligations are passively consented to, rather than freely created and negotiated
Opportunism:	**Reification:**
The natural motive/activity of self-interested individuals; in the case of public servants opportunism is controllable through socialization, the threat of punishment or other sanctions, and the giving of moral advice	Incomprehensible as a general problem because public servants are conceived as compliant, rather than as active moral agents; extreme manifestations of reification are seen as "special cases" that are controllable by higher levels of authority
Pathologies	

Figure 5.1. The Paradox of Obligation as Generated by the Rationalist Conception of Responsibility and Freedom

character. Clarifying the reasons why freedom is a social concept enables the reframing of the idea of obligation promised in the introduction. For the present, however, my concern will be with the first half of the paradox of obligation and its connection with rationalism's alternative view of the individual as compliant and manipulable, rather than possessive and opportunistic.

Recall that the paradox of obligation begins with the statement that "If people are free to choose, but are at the same time obliged to act only as others choose for them, then they are not for all practical purposes free." This sentence clearly qualifies as a schis-mogenically paradoxical statement in view of the two contradic-tory injunctions that it includes. For the statement to be of practical use in illuminating actual situations, however, we need to see how its perverse logic is manifested in them.

In the case of the paradox of obligation, each of its two principal elements, freedom and responsibility, is split off from the other by being construed as in irreconcilable opposition. Their opposition is irreconcilable in the rationalist account by virtue of the two

mutually contradictory assumptions that it makes about the nature
of the individual: namely, that the individual is, on the one hand,
naturally possessive, self-interested, and opportunistic and, on the
other hand, compliant and manipulable. For such an individual,
freedom is the expression of the former set of characteristics and
responsibility the latter. In the section on opportunism, we saw
what happens when the rationalists' version of freedom is split off
from and displaces their version of obligation. In this section, I
shall explore the dynamics and consequences of this same generic
situation in reverse, that is, when obligation is split off from and
displaces freedom. I shall examine, in other words, what happens
when people lose consciousness of their status as moral agents
who freely choose and act, and instead come to regard official
obligations and the moral principles that legitimate them not only
as morally binding, but as actually compelling obedience. This is
commonly known as the problem of reification.

In Chapter 4, I discussed the pathology of principled thought as
a type of reification in which other people's beliefs are swallowed
whole rather than assimilated. Reifying principles, that is, using them
unreflexively, precludes the possibility of their playing a developmental role in mediating the relation between conscious thought
and unconscious energy. When this happens, the individual's sense
of agency is lost to conscious awareness, with the result that decisions
are compelled by principles rather than freely made. Responsibility
is lodged in principles, and subsequently in decisions that seem
ineluctably derived from them, rather than in the individual.

Reification more generally may be seen as an alienated mode
of consciousness in which people lose sight of their authorship of
the social world by apprehending "the products of human activity
as if they were something else than human products—such as
facts of nature, results of cosmic laws, or manifestations of divine
will" (Berger & Luckmann, 1967, p. 89). The reification of the social
world is made possible, and to a degree even inevitable, whenever
it is established and then thought of as an "objective reality,"
paradoxically existing apart from, so it seems, the ongoing human
production of it. Institutions and roles, because they appear to be
among the most objectively real of social artifacts, are especially

prone to reification, both by their inhabitants and by those whose lives are touched by them. As Berger and Luckmann describe it:

> The basic "recipe" for the reification of institutions is to bestow on them an ontological status independent of human activity and signification. . . . Through reification, the world of institutions appears to merge with the world of nature. It becomes necessity and fate, and is lived through as such happily or unhappily as the case may be.
>
> Roles may be reified in the same manner as institutions. The sector of self-consciousness that has been objectified in the role is then also apprehended as an inevitable fate, for which the individual may disclaim responsibility. The paradigmatic formula for this kind of reification is the statement "I have no choice in the matter, I have to act this way because of my position"—as husband, father, general, archbishop, chairman of the board, gangster, and hangman, as the case may be. This means that the reification of role narrows the subjective distance that the individual may establish between himself and his role-playing. The distance implied in all objectification remains, of course, but the distance brought about by disidentification shrinks to the vanishing point. (pp. 90-91)

Institutions and roles are bound by authority, which means that *their* reification also necessarily involves the reification of authority, including the official obligations that issue from it. When authority is reified, that is, when official obligations are interpreted as automatically compelling obedience, personal responsibility is disclaimed or simply lost to conscious awareness. Therefore, when authoritative obligations are reified, it would be inaccurate to say that people choose freely or decide on rational grounds to fulfill them, inasmuch as the possibility of consciously choosing whether or not to obey is precluded by a reified mode of consciousness.

Although the pathology of reified authority, and thus of reified obligation, finds its most grotesque expression in recent history in the case of Adolph Eichmann, it should be remembered that Hannah Arendt's (1977) analysis of his trial reveals the ordinariness, not of the terrible consequences of his acts, but of the mind-set that permitted him to act as he did. Eichmann did not decide, at least as we usually understand acts of deciding. To qualify as a meaningful act, a decision must presuppose both a self-conscious awareness of what one is doing and the availability of alternative courses of action from which to choose. To ignore the psychological impediments to self-aware choice makes impossible any meaningful distinction between the virtues of loyalty and accountability on the one hand and the pathology of blind obedience on the other.

Moreover, it is useless to assert consciously held moral values or principles of ethical conduct to countervail the reification of authority. Reification is by definition an unconscious process, which is likely to be reinforced rather than eliminated through attempts at persuasion through rational arguments about values and principles. These may occasionally have some *limited* value in countering the reification of authority, but only when they are understood self-reflexively, permitting people to comprehend their roles in producing, sustaining, and contesting authoritative relationships. The essential point, however, is that self-reflexivity, rather than rational thought and judgment, enables the *de*reification of authority and of the obligations that it seeks to enforce.

It is hard to imagine how rationalists might advise dealing with the reification of obligations, because their conceptual apparatus does not really permit them to comprehend the idea, much less regard it as a problem.[5] In the statement of the paradox, obligation's opposing idea is freedom, which must somehow be brought back into a countervailing relation with obligation in order to check the latter's reification. For the rationalists, however, freedom does not consist of the self-reflexive monitoring of personal agency that would permit this to happen, but it is instead the opportunistic pursuit of private ends. And developing programs of indoctrination for the purpose of socializing public servants *not* to reify their obligations, surely an ironic and even whimsical suggestion, could only compound the problem because by definition no one can possess a more highly reified consciousness than one who is "perfectly" socialized.

Public Obligations and Private Commitments

The concept of personal responsibility developed in Chapter 4, together with the section on reification just concluded, suggests that obligation, however it is conceived, is insufficient as an exclusive source of moral guidance. Here I want to focus upon one final concern about the problem of obligation, namely, the relative moral priority of public obligations and private commitments. In discussing this topic, however, it is important to bear in mind a crucial distinction, one that is almost always blurred in the rationalist discourse, between the meanings of *personal* and *private*. In Chapter 4 I argued that any comprehensive conception of responsibility must consider its personal character. It is necessary to do this in order to comprehend the meaning of moral agency, that is, the belief that people are able to choose freely, which in conjunction with obligation and accountability compose our commonsense understanding of responsibility.

To agree that moral agency is a defining element of responsibility is tantamount to insisting that the *personal* character of responsibility is an inherent feature of the word's dual meaning, rather than a *kind* or *category* of responsibility that may be paired with terms such as *public, institutional,* or *official.* Responsibility is irreducibly personal by virtue of people's status as agents of, as well as answerers for, their actions. Because all action involves the expression of human moral agency, it is therefore personal as it bears upon both public conduct and private activity. *Personal* is therefore not a synonym for *private*; and it is the latter word— which refers to the individual's intimate affections and projects of self-creation—rather than the former word that provides the opposing category for public. In view of the possessive, self-interested individual that rationalists assume to be virtually the sum total of personhood, however, it is not surprising that they both conflate the meanings of *personal* and *private*, and regard them, together, as being in dangerous opposition to public and its equivalents.

In Chapter 3 I criticized Terry Cooper's effort to, in his word, *balance* what he calls inner and outer controls, and John Burke's effort to *reconcile* bureaucracy with democracy. In the context within which each is used, balance and reconcile initially seem intended to convey the idea of unifying separate and opposing ideas that have co-equal status. For both of these authors, however, one of their pairs' two elements is actually superior to the other element, so that *balance,* as Cooper uses the word, cannot mean genuine unification, but rather the subordination of one element to the other. Similarly, *reconcile,* for Burke, does not mean unifying opposing principles under a higher one that encompasses both, but rationalizing one of those principles *in terms of* the other. *Balance* and *reconcile* are in effect euphemisms for the subordination of private projects and aspirations (which for Burke and Cooper are synonymous with personal responsibility) to public duties.

In weighing the relative priority of public servants' private commitments and aspirations against their public obligations, rationalism asserts that the latter take automatic priority over the former. That official priority and the right of the state to assert it, however, does not in itself necessarily constitute a moral impera-tive for the public servant; for it is not in the least inconsistent to argue that the state ought to try to enforce the obligations that public servants formally agree to honor, and at the same time to hold that the state, as a structure of preexisting relationships, is not the final arbiter of individual moral choice about the honoring of those obligations. To assume that individuals' moral choices must somehow be reconciled in terms of official obligations not only is the equivalent of denying their personal authorship, but also cannot account, as Pateman (1985) explains, for the social dynamic that characterizes relationships of obligation. Such rela-tionships, she says,

> depend upon, and arise from, the complex web of inter-subjective meanings and constitutive rules of social life, but they also tran-scend them. Individuals are not completely submerged in their rules, meanings and oughts, but are also superior to them, and use them as a necessary basis from which they judge, choose and act, and create and change their social relationships. People are com-mitted by, and responsible for, the relationships they have created. But they can also evaluate their past actions and try to make good unintended or unforeseen consequences; this is why it makes perfectly good sense to say "I have an obligation but I (now) see that I ought not to keep it." (pp. 29-30)

Pateman anticipates the objection that if people followed her suggestion, there would be nothing to prevent them from arbitrarily picking and choosing which obligations they would assume or refuse. In acknowledging this as a real problem like many other problems created by an uncertain social existence that need to be constantly struggled with, she also reminds us that from liberalism's "abstractly individualist viewpoint this problem appears to be insoluble" (p. 30). For the possessive individual of liberal theory, it will be recalled, there is no reason other than expedience to honor one's obligations.

Behind the rationalists' attempt to "unify" the private and public spheres by subordinating the former to the latter may lie a motive even more basic than that of social control on which their conception of responsibility is based. Such a motive could be described as a fear of contingency, an inability to accept that the world defies reduction to a grand system or a single explanatory principle. Richard Rorty (1989) has written that the dilemmas posed by the conflict between the public and private sides of our lives will always be with us and cannot be "resolved by appeal to some further, higher set of obligations which a philosophical tribunal might discover and apply" (p. 197). Even to attempt to do so would be to split off from and subordinate Niebuhr's man the maker to man the answerer, the person as moral agent from the person who is morally obligated. Even the word *obligation,* which Bernard Williams (1985, p. 173) has called a "peculiar institution" handed down from Christianity via Kant, is a loaded one in that it almost always has a *public* connotation. For that reason, I believe, Rorty does not speak of competing public and private obligations, but of public obligations on one side and "private affections and attempts at self-creation" (p. 194) on the other. This seems a more fitting way to divide the two spheres, especially recalling Horatio Hornblower's (Forester, 1962) decision to contrive the escape of his steward, Doughty. Hornblower was not torn between competing obligations, for he did not act out of a sense of obligation toward Doughty, but from feelings of pity and affection for him. Thus, to condemn *or* to praise Hornblower for the manner in which he weighed his obligations is to misunderstand both the reason for his action and to deny the paradoxical nature of responsibility.

	Principles	
Freedom: ←—— the reciprocal of ——→		**Responsibility:**
Both the "private" activity of self-creation, as well as the ongoing creation of relationships made possible by the person's status as a moral agent; obligations are freely made, but may be revised and transcended		The self-reflexive monitoring of action enabled by relationships with others; obligations are indispensable features of human communities, which naturally both enable and constrain the exercise of freedom
Opportunism:		**Reification:**
The pathological consequence of the breakdown of social relationships and human community; principal remedies consist in the strengthening of those relationships, whereas punishment and moral advice are regarded as worst-case options		The pathological consequence of passive consent to preexisting obligations such that personal authorship is lost to consciousness; principal remedies consist in fostering active and self-reflexive participation in the creation of obligations
	Pathologies	

Figure 5.2. The Idea of Obligation From a Reframed Conception of Responsibility and Freedom

Reframing the Problem of Obligation

Jean-Paul Sartre (1956) said that we are all "condemned to be free" (p. 553), and by virtue of that freedom we are condemned to bear the responsibility for our exercise of it. From the standpoint of the rationalist conception of responsibility, it is hard to imagine a statement more puzzling than this one. For, whereas Sartre asserts responsibility as the reciprocal of freedom, rationalists construe it as freedom's diametrical opposite. The two ideas are radically split off from one another, the former being expressed in people's compliant fulfillment of their obligations and the latter in their pursuit of private interests.[6]

Like the liberal theorists whom Carole Pateman criticizes, rationalists define freedom as the pursuit of private gain, which is defended through appeal to individual rights. A right is essentially a negative idea, a claim of protection against the infringement by the state or by other individuals upon people's pursuit of private gain or their unique projects of self-creation. The notion of individual rights is a cornerstone of both the economic libertarianism of the American political right wing and the civil libertarian left. Thus, in systems where a "rights-based ethic" (Sandel, 1984) dominates all other considerations, politics is conceived as a free-market process involving competition either among individual interests, which are usually defined in economic terms, or among opposing political ideals.

In recent years, however, the notion of individual rights has been subjected to a line of criticism—chiefly by those representing a communitarian viewpoint—that is the reciprocal of Pateman's critique of the liberal view of obligation. One representative of this view, David Schuman (1992), has argued that the liberal fixation on rights encourages in people a sense of isolation apart from their communities. This isolation generates a predictable pathology in which individuals assume a pugnacious posture toward their fellow citizens, resulting in a politics of separation, exclusion, and alienation. Communitarians urge us to consider that individual rights, as asserted by liberalism's right-wing *and* left-wing variants, can be sustained only if people feel intimately connected with the values and traditions of their communities, which provide a stable social context in which the exercise of individual rights is enabled in the first place. A commitment to the common good, even if it sometimes infringes upon the pursuit of certain private aims, is nevertheless necessary in order to counterbalance the overassertion of individual rights. Thus, the meaningful exercise of political freedom, to the communitarians, is necessarily a social rather than a solitary activity.

Despite their general agreement about the meaning of freedom, liberal contract theory and the rationalist conception of responsibility differ in their assessments of its importance to their theoretical projects. Because liberal theory, as a political theory, is mainly concerned with the relation of citizens to the state, it must grapple with the often opposing moral injunctions issuing from its particular conceptions of responsibility and freedom. In the rationalist discourse on responsibility, however, the subject of freedom as it pertains to public servants receives far less attention, and, indeed, seems oddly out of place. This lack of attention is predictable: From the rationalist standpoint, public servants voluntarily give up much of their freedom as ordinary citizens when, in contracting to perform public duties, they trade it for other benefits.

If the idea of freedom seems incongruous within the rationalist conception of responsibility, however, it is by virtue of its presumed equivalence with the notion of individual rights. If true, that equivalence of meaning would force the conclusion that freedom consists in the autonomous assertion of individual will that is apart from rather than in association with others. If freedom is instead construed as the exercise of moral agency within a context of social relationship, then the importance of rights may be put into a more balanced perspective by recognizing that not all constraints are unreasonable and that constraint itself is a precondition of freedom.

Moreover, freedom is not something that as individuals we ought to have granted to us, for as intentional moral agents we already have it, whether we realize it or not, as an inescapable fact of our personhood. As the expression of our moral agency and thus of our undeniable authorship, freedom is therefore intimately connected with responsibility, which consists in the self-reflexive awareness of agency; and whatever rights public servants may sacrifice in return for their employment, therefore, do not alter that fact. Freedom, as the expression of moral agency, thus has to be seen as an intrinsic aspect of public servants' responsibility, rather than subordinated to it or split off from it. In the absence of their genuine reconciliation, freedom's natural expression degenerates into opportunism (including opportunistic obedience), whereas responsibility's natural consequence is the reification of obligations and authority wherein the fact of moral agency has been lost to consciousness.

Conclusion

The principal arguments of this chapter are, first, that rationalism assumes overly restrictive meanings of the two words that are essential to the idea of obligation, namely, responsibility and freedom. Second, the paradox of obligation is created by the pairing of these two meanings, which stand in irreconcilable opposition. That opposition, in turn, predictably generates the pathologies of opportunism and reification from which there can be inferred no theoretical solution nor any plausible practical strategies for mitigating their effects.

In order to escape from the rationalist paradox of obligation, responsibility and freedom need to be understood as reciprocally related to one another rather than diametrically opposed. Although the basic elements of such a reframed understanding of obligation should already be evident from this and earlier chapters, the differences between it and the rationalist view of obligation come into sharper focus when we compare Figures 5.1 and 5.2.[7] Since Figures 5.1 and 5.2 mainly recapitulate the discussion presented thus far, I shall limit my comments to noting only a few crucial differences between them. First, in Figure 5.1, the characterization of opportunism and reification *as pathologies* does not necessarily follow from the meanings of freedom and responsibility that rationalism asserts. That is, there is no necessary reason to regard opportunism as a *perverse* expression of freedom in view of how the latter is construed in the rationalist view of obligation. Instead, opportunism is the natural expression of freedom, if freedom is both defined atomistically as the pursuit of self-interested aims and rationalized in terms of individual rights. Similarly, the reification of obligations cannot, for a consistent rationalist, be interpreted as a pathological expression of responsibility, if responsibility is defined as compliant consent to and fulfillment of obligations, which is itself a virtual formula for their reification.

This is not, of course, to say that rationalists, as sentient observers and interpreters of situations, are always incapable of recognizing particular manifestations of these pathologies when they occur. In order to do so, however, they must step outside their preferred frame of reference. Moreover, that frame of reference provides no useful guidance for mitigating the effects of those pathologies even when they are recognized. Recall that in Chapter 4 I noted that the pathological underside of a particular virtue or principle is manifested when the latter is split off from its counterpart, which has been lost sight of or has atrophied. It is the rediscovery and reassertion of the second, or countervailing, principle that provides the vital clue for inventing strategies to mitigate the pathological expression of the first. In view of the rationalist meanings of freedom and responsibility, however, it is difficult to see how either principle could be reasserted in order to perform this task. Freedom defined as the pursuit of self-interest provides no plausible counterbalance to reification, in part because interests may themselves be reified; and responsibility construed as passive consent cannot countervail opportunism, because possessive individuals have no evident motive to consent other than self-interest, which is itself indistinguishable from opportunism,

In the alternative framing of the problem of obligation depicted in Figure 5.2, opportunism and reification are construed as pathological precisely because the principle of which each is the "shadow" underside has been overasserted to the exclusion of its counterpart principle. Opportunism is thus interpreted, at least chiefly, as a consequence of the breakdown of community and social relationships, thus isolating people from one another and giving vent to the narcissistic and pugnacious assertion of their individual rights. Similarly, the reification of obligations is interpreted as the unconscious denial of the freedom enabled by moral agency by means of which people, including public servants, might otherwise freely and self-reflexively participate in making, revising, and transcending those obligations.

Rationalists appear reluctant to agree to such a conception of freedom and thus to its implication that public servants should be encouraged to participate actively in the ongoing creation of their obligations. That reluctance is understandable if the issue is whether such participation can be defended on the basis of individual rights. But from the alternative framing of the issue that I have proposed, the freedom of public servants that is expressed via that participation is not, at least chiefly, a matter of rights. Rather, freedom defined as the fact of moral agency is inseparable from and is the natural counterpart of responsibility, which is defined as the self-reflexive awareness of its exercise. It is certainly the case that freedom so conceived might pose a threat to the rationalists' overall aim of controlling public servants' behavior.

But if, as I argue in Chapter 7, such control is as a practical matter impossible, the rationalists would be well-advised to consider other alternatives.

Notes

1. If the villains in Pateman's critique are Locke and Hobbes, its hero is surely Rousseau. Rousseau, she says, is a *social* contract theorist, rather than a *liberal* contract theorist like Locke and Hobbes; and it is the distinction between a social and a liberal contract that is the point of contention rather than the idea of contract generically.

2. For example, Burke (1986) comments that "The danger of applying to substantive policy choices normative recommendations that reflect *only* [italics added] personal preferences is that it undermines the claims of reason and 'rightness' upon which philosophy stakes its claim of authority" (p. 228). (Quotations here and elsewhere reprinted by permission of the author and The Johns Hopkins University Press.) This single sentence is revealing in three ways that bear upon my argument in this chapter. First, as an emotivist Burke equates the idea of *normative* (but also substitute *moral* and its various synonyms) with *personal preference*, an equivalence of meaning that is possible only if morality is defined wholly independently of social relationship and historical association. Second, in highlighting *only* my intent was to draw attention to Burke's habit, throughout his book, of assuming that any one of the various sources of moral or political obligation that he discusses can—and in fact can *only*—be used to the exclusion of the others. He seems to have reified his categories in a way that obscures the commonsense truth that people are informed by sources of obligation and other bases of moral judgment at the same time, and that as both a practical and a theoretical matter there is no reason to believe that one of these sources should be seen as excluding or even necessarily diminishing the other. Finally, Burke's remark that philosophy stakes its authority on "claims to reason and 'rightness' " begs the question of whether, in the first place, philosophy can make any authoritative claims whatsoever (see Rorty, 1989); and even if it *could*, surely more precise and informative terms than reason and rightness would be required in order to make such an assertion comprehensible, much less, plausible.

3. To mention a final irony in the passage quoted above from *Bureaucratic Responsibility*, Burke (1986) ends the last sentence with an indicator of an endnote presumably identifying for readers either relevant citations of some of the "critics of contemporary democracy" to whom he refers, or providing further commentary on the subject of political participation. The endnote (on page 270), as it turns out, is a very brief one containing only two book citations, both by Carole Pateman, one of which is *The Problem of Political Obligation*. The endnote, however, includes no commentary on the possible implications of her book for his own position. This is an especially disappointing omission because Pateman's (1985) book constitutes a direct and thorough rebuttal to the kind of argument that Burke is trying to make. Thus the reader is left to wonder how Burke might have either defended his position in the light of Pateman's argument or constructed a countercritique of her position.

4. Although Cooper does not appear to believe that the fundamental character of civil servants differs from that of ordinary citizens, he does believe that the former might take seriously their obligations in and to a democratic society if a vigorous ethical citizenship were to be infused in the everyday workings of government. In *An Ethic of Citizenship for Public Administration,* Cooper urges that the obligations of public servants "to participate in the search for larger public interests" (p. 11) is a realistic possibility if *professionalism* is expanded beyond its narrow technical meaning to include, in the words of Bellah and his colleagues (1985), "the ethic of the calling. To change the conception of government from scientific management to center on ethical obligations and relationships is part of our task" (p. 212). Cooper urges that public administrators adopt these sentiments, saying that "If citizenship is the appropriate normative basis for the public administrative role, it can be argued that it is the high ethical view of citizenship . . . that should inform and shape the professional identity and role of public administrators" (p. 13).

5. This difficulty is evident in both Burke's and Cooper's books. Recall in Chapter 3 my criticism of Cooper's handling of the "Nuremberg defense" and the Eichmann case, both of which he treats as problems of mistaking a lower-order obligation for a higher-order one, rather than as illustrating the problem of reified obligations. Burke, on the other hand, dismisses the Eichmann case as being unrepresentative of the kinds of issues with which public servants in a democracy must deal.

6. Many contemporary formulations of liberalism, however, do not restrict the meaning of freedom to the maximization of private gain. Rorty's (1989) conception of liberalism, for example, is rooted firmly in the notion of social solidarity, an idea far removed from anything imaginable within the liberal contractarian tradition of Locke and Hobbes.

7. In reframing these terms we are not thereby enabled to *solve* the paradox, nor having reframed them can we infer solutions to problems of opportunism and reification that arise in actual situations. The expectation that a theory should be able to provide such solutions in fact generates its own paradox. Because solving a practical problem requires *taking* responsibility for its solution, to demand that a *theory* solve the problem is in effect to lodge responsibility in the theory, which constitutes a denial of personal responsibility; the theory becomes responsible, not the person who uses or is informed by it (White, 1973).

6

The Paradox of Agency

To inhabit . . . a radically imperfect form of social life is itself
a moral task which can be performed well or badly. One of the
best ways to assure that it will be performed badly is to refuse to
admit one's own involvement in radical moral imperfection and to
see this as a condition in others which justifies perpetual moral
indignation in oneself. Another equally good way is to use the
recognition of radical moral imperfection as a moral alibi to excuse
complacent satisfaction with the status quo. The first attitude is a
characteristic liberal vice, the second an equally characteristic
conservative vice.

—Alasdair MacIntyre (1983, p. 356)

The idea of responsibility is to be brought back from the
problems of specialized ethics, an "ought" that swings free in the
air, into that of lived life. Genuine responsibility exists only when
there is genuine responding.

—Martin Buber (1947, p. 16)

◈ TO *HOLD* PEOPLE responsible is to declare them blameworthy,
should their actions fall short of authoritative expectations.
With an important exception to be noted shortly, the rationalist
view of responsibility maintains that only individuals may be held
responsible because of the practical difficulty of dispensing sanctions
(and also rewards) to collectivities. This practical consideration

126

also has a moral aspect, as seen for example in Downie's (1991) assertion that "for there to be moral responsibility there must be *blameworthiness* regarding a morally faulty decision, and this can occur only at the individual level" (as paraphrased by May and Hoffman, 1991, p. 6). Most rationalists are therefore skeptical about the idea of collective responsibility because it portends the elimination of fault and by extension of blame and guilt. The aphorism that "if everyone is responsible, then no one is responsible" expresses the rationalist conviction that responsibility is an individual matter as well as the fear that effective social control would be imperiled unless responsibility is "pinpointed."

Insofar as the subject of blame dominates the rationalist discourse, responsibility becomes a virtual synonym for accountability. Accountability institutionalizes blame by making individuals liable for punishment or rewards, depending on whether their actions comply with authoritative standards of conduct or achieve authoritatively defined goals. From the standpoint of H. Richard Niebuhr's (1963) twin images of the responsible self, accountability as institutionalized blame corresponds to "man the answerer," but only in the passive sense of obedience to authority. The second image of "man the maker" is in a like manner reduced to an official precondition of blameworthiness, rather than, in Jean-Paul Sartre's (1956) phrase, an expression of individuals' "incontestable authorship" of their actions. Such authorship under the rationalist view is, as both a moral and a legal matter, the province of institutional authority.

Blaming implies, although only tacitly and unconsciously, a declaration of the blamer's innocence. That declaration of innocence is in turn often reciprocated by the recipient's own claim of innocence by, for example, an outright denial of guilt; providing a moral justification for an alleged offense; disputing the factual portrayal of the action assumed by the blamer; claiming an inability to control the events in question; or invoking, as did Eichmann and the Nuremberg defendants, the doctrine of *respondeat superior:* "Let the superior answer." That is, those who are blamed may, sometimes for plausible reasons, assert that they have been made scapegoats, although the blamers may with seemingly equal plausibility construe such denials of guilt as "passing the buck," or worse.

In the rationalist discourse on responsible government, scape-goating and buckpassing are familiar themes, but they are usually depicted as regrettable aberrations—or, to those who are more pessimistic, as evidence of people's inherent sinfulness—that may be made tractable through sterner vigilance and more careful specification of goals, policies, rules, ethical codes, and sanctions. From the standpoint of arguments presented in earlier chapters, however, scapegoating, buckpassing, and other pathologies associated with blaming are neither aberrations nor, at least necessarily, evidence of pervasive sinfulness, original or otherwise. Rather, they are the predictable results of the failure to grasp the irreducibly paradoxical relation between the opposing ideas embodied in the notion of responsibility and depicted by Niebuhr's twin images. The rationalist preoccupation with sin, construed as guilt, and the corresponding notion of moral innocence combine to produce the paradox of agency:

> **If individuals acknowledge, on the one hand, the personal authorship expressed through their exercise of moral agency, they are guilty by virtue of denying their ultimate answerability to others. On the other hand, the claim of moral innocence implied in the assertion of ultimate answerability to others can only be achieved by the individual's denial of moral agency.**

Such is the existential double bind created by the rationalist paradox of agency in which the opposing aspects of responsibility—making and answering—are split apart from one another. The paradox of agency is doubly paradoxical in view of the irreconcilable opposition that it generates not only internally between maker and answerer but also between the privatized individuals of the modern era that rationalism assumes and the collectivities of which they are therefore merely self-interested yet reluctant members. These two sets of oppositions are intimately related inasmuch as the former, the inner division between the dual images of the responsible self, is recapitulated in the public sphere as the radical separation of the individual from society.

Rationalism professes two opposing stances on the subject of agency. The first—the conservative variant—overasserts the individual by depicting him or her as the exclusive object of blameworthiness for irresponsible behavior. This allows collectivities to maintain an official posture of innocence of complicity in creating those conditions in response to which such behavior may be rational in a perverse but nonetheless real sense. Alternatively, but still within the rationalist tradition, proponents of contemporary entitlement liberalism are prone to hold individuals, especially members of groups that have historically been victimized, innocent of complicity in perpetuating their current plight, thus discouraging, ironically, their own exercise of personal agency.

The current debate between conservatives and liberals about the nature of responsibility, as well as the causes of *ir*responsibility, clearly warrants the rationalist label. Each side to the debate, that is, confronts the paradox of the other with simply an opposing paradox of its own. The project of this chapter is to show how that debate may be reframed by converting both schismogenic paradoxes of agency, the conservative and the liberal, into antinomial ones by reuniting making and answering, the individual and the collectivity. Key to accomplishing this task is challenging the rationalist conviction that the related notions of blame, fault, guilt, and innocence, seemingly indispensable words of our conventional moral vocabulary, are needed to comprehend what it means to act responsibly. Responsibility, I shall argue, is not chiefly a matter of making judgments about individual morality and ethics, as these are conventionally understood, but is instead deeply and systemically implicated in the matrix of social relationships and the dynamics of internal dialogue that enable and inform action. At the same time, however, I hope to make it clear that the possibility and the necessity of responsible individuals are in no way diminished, and in fact are enhanced, by recognizing responsibility's social, systemic nature. In order to make that argument plausible it will be necessary near the end of the chapter to reexamine a perennial and contentious issue in public administration and public life, namely, the proper role and exercise of institutional authority.

The Paradox of Agency
and the Overassertion of the Individual

More than any other myth of antiquity, Adam and Eve's fall from grace as symbolized by their expulsion from the Garden of Eden has been a subject of continuing reinterpretation in the light of an altered comprehension of the human predicament. Even in the modern era, during which time that predicament has been increasingly cast in secular terms, the idea of redemption, although expressed in and disguised by vocabularies seemingly far removed from the theological and the spiritual, nevertheless retains a powerful hold on the collective consciousness. The secular counterforce of atomistic individualism generated by modernism's two signature institutions, market capitalism and bureaucratic organization, has thus far failed to discourage completely the quest for redemption, although it has surely rendered it a difficult and ironic enterprise. Commenting on the modern influence of the first of these institutions, historian Garry Wills (1987) says:

> If the doctrine of the Fall entangles humans in each other's errors, the doctrine of the Market disentangles each fumbled attempt toward a final concatenated good. Modern capitalism lives by a counter-myth to the Fall of Man. . . . The earlier myth called for a repenting awareness of sin. The latter one calls for dutiful innocence and optimism. (p. 384)

If market capitalism lives by a countermyth to the doctrine of the Fall, then modern bureaucracy, as morally certified by the rationalist conception of responsibility, lives by a variant on that countermyth. In Chapter 4 I argued that rationalism seeks to restore innocence by denying the paradoxical quality of human existence. For Kierkegaard (1957), the false hope of restoring innocence is sustained only through ignorance, or, more precisely, through the disingenuous posture of ignorance, which amounts in Wills's terms to the countermyth denying the Fall's occurrence. Unlike capitalism, bureaucratic rationalism concedes that individuals are often sinful, that is, guilty of moral transgressions, although that sinfulness is interpreted as merely a temporary fall from grace. Redemption, which to rationalism is synonymous with the restoration of innocence, may be achieved through confessing sin and accepting punishment. Kierkegaard said that this view is mistaken, however, because it falsely equates redemption with a moral innocence lost irretrievably with the dawning of self-consciousness. If innocence is ignorance, he asked, then how can redemption be achieved through a state or posture of ignorance?

Together Kierkegaard and Wills offer complementary interpretations, not only of the meaning of the Fall in theological terms, but by extension of the "redemptive" implications of Niebuhr's images of the responsible self. Kierkegaard's belief that the myth of Genesis describes Man's "fall" into a state of self-consciousness brings to mind Niebuhr's first image of man the maker, the moral agent whose authorship of his or her actions is, by virtue of that self-consciousness, informed rather than innocently ignorant. And Wills's depiction of the Fall as "entangl[ing] humans in each other's errors" (p. 384) evokes Niebuhr's second image of man the answerer, whose moral agency, enabled by self-consciousness, is meaningless and indeed incomprehensible except for the existence of a moral community. Rationalist responsibility's inability to unite the opposing images of maker and answerer stems directly from its equation of responsibility with blame and its concomitant preoccupation with the recovery of innocence both by blamers and those who are blamed. Some of the pathologies generated by blaming in organizations are illustrated by the following brief episode recounted by Henry Kass (personal communication, November 1, 1994).

*   *   *   *   *

When I worked at an urban renewal agency several years ago, one of my fellow employees was instructed to determine the deterioration rate of some of our public housing units, a task for which he was singularly ill-prepared. He shouldn't have been assigned the task in the first place; but to make matters worse, no one offered to help him, and they probably would have felt put out if asked to do so. For his part, the employee was reluctant to admit his incompetence, fearing that such admission might hurt his career.

The upshot of the affair was a confrontation at a staff meeting at which the man's boss publicly held him accountable by shaming him into admitting to everyone present that he should have asked for help and reported his problems with the assignment. His boss then offered him "absolution" on the condition that he never again dissemble regarding his progress on a project. For his part, the employee said, in effect, that he had learned his lesson. With the employee's innocence restored, his boss intoned to us all that the issue had been settled as far as he was concerned.

Of course, little had in fact been settled. No training was provided to improve the employee's competence; and no effort was made to encourage cooperative effort on difficult problems in the future. Indeed, that the conditions for a replay of the same situation were still very much present was later borne out by the recurrence of similar incidents involving both this employee and others as well.

*   *   *   *   *

If blaming inevitably creates a schismogenic paradox, then the transformation of that paradox into an antinomial one requires that responsibility be redefined in a way that excludes the ideas of guilt and innocence and in so doing reestablishes the vital connection between Niebuhr's images. To accomplish this, a good place to start is to recall Chapter 2's initial discussion of the concept of agency. In particular, the idea of a "Davidsonian agent"—one whose actions may, according to at least one of his or her own true accounts, be described or redescribed as intentional—was proposed as a generic definition of agency. The idea of the David-sonian agent has the advantage of incorporating, at least prelimi-narily, the rationalist view of agency, namely, as a precondition of individual blameworthiness. But Davidson's (1980) description of the agent is also amenable to expansion and reinterpretation in a way that links the idea of intentionality, the defining element of agency, with that of answerability within a moral community, while at the same time preserving the notion of moral authorship implicit in man the maker.

Preserving the idea of moral authorship, rather than simply blameworthiness, in the concept of agency makes possible a conception of responsibility that does not require nor indeed permit claims to moral innocence either by the agent or by those to whom he or she is answerable. Peter A. French (1991) expands upon the idea of agency by saying that "A moral person, we should say, is a Davidsonian agent with the capacity to respond and responsively adjust to moral evaluation" (p. 143). To "respond and responsively adjust," it should be noted, are not the same as simply acknowledging one's errors and promising in the future to obey those to whom one is accountable in order to secure redemption. Indeed, being blamed or accused of moral transgression is more likely to evoke either the outright denial of guilt or other forms of defensiveness than to encourage responsive adjustment. This is also generally true of moralistic language, which focuses on the isolated acts of individuals rather than on their reflective dialogue within a community of other answerers.

The rationalist conception of responsibility seems incapable of breaking free of this moralistic individualism owing to its equation of responsible action with correct behavior defined in terms of disembodied principles, values, and standards deriving from sources external to the lived experience of the individual. Martin Buber's (1947) belief that "genuine responsibility exists only when there is genuine responding" (p. 16) requires an appreciation of the social and historical contexts within which possibilities for individual choice are perceived and acted upon. The mistake of rationalism is to suppose that a sense of moral agency, and thus personal responsibility, can be achieved by requiring individuals in isolation either to prove their innocence or concede their guilt. Rather than producing a Davidsonian agent with the capacity to respond to moral evaluation, the rationalist preoccupation with individual guilt and innocence is more likely to cause just the reverse, namely, disclaimers of responsibility in the form of buckpassing and scapegoating.

In explaining how the pathologies of buckpassing and scape-goating predictably result from the conservative rationalists' overassertion of the individual, we need to reconsider our prior endorsement of Sartre's notion of incontestable authorship as the defining element of agency. For if the individual's authorship of his or her actions is indeed as incontestable as a cursory reading of Sartre might seem to suggest, there would be no reason to quarrel with the rationalist equivalence of responsibility and individual blameworthiness. That is, if individuals are incontestably the sole agents of their actions, then responsibility cannot be lodged, even partially, elsewhere. Indeed, the very idea of shared responsibility seems to contradict not only the rationalist presumption of blameworthiness, but also the sense of individual moral agency that seems implicit in Sartre's definition of responsibility.

The idea of moral authorship, however, is not fatally compromised and is indeed accentuated by interpreting it in social or systemic terms. Moreover, the idea of individual agency as reflected in man the maker may be preserved while at the same time giving up the rationalist belief that the individual is the sole cause of his or her actions, which is otherwise necessary to sustain the view of responsibility as synonymous with blameworthiness. Individual causality and moral agency, in other words, are not necessarily equivalent ideas, and it is possible to preserve the latter while discarding the former.

To disconnect the idea of moral agency from the belief that individuals are the sole causes of their actions is to recognize that the idea of agency is itself paradoxical, involving a tension between the incontestability of the individual's moral authorship and the social context that both enables and constrains it. From the systemic view of social relations described below, the idea that individuals are the sole causes of their actions not only perpetuates the misguided equivalence of responsibility and blame, but also an inflated conception of the individual will that is unaffected by social relationships.

Composer and philosopher John Cage once explained why his teacher, the Zen philosopher D. T. Suzuki, objected to the idea of causality by noting that:

> When one [Suzuki] says that there is no cause and effect, what is
> meant is that there are an incalculable infinity of causes and effects,
> that in fact each and every thing in all of time and space is related
> to each and every other thing in all of time and space. (Quoted in
> Revill, 1992, pp. 112-113)

Among "things" Cage also included people, whose individual actions
are comprehensible only in a matrix of relationships. Therefore,
pinpointing the causes of discrete human actions is, even in
theory, impossible from the Zen perspective.

This insight has provided a cornerstone assumption of contemporary Western approaches to family psychotherapy (Bowen, 1978),
the treatment of alcoholism (Bepko, 1985), and organizational
studies (Framer, 1993; Weinberg, 1995). Sometimes grouped under
the heading of *family systems theory,* these therapeutic approaches
dispute the belief in individual and linear causality that underlies
the rationalist equivalence of blame and agency, and do so in a way
that exposes the paradoxes resulting from actions based on that
belief. Claudia Bepko, for example, notes that:

> One contribution of systems theory to the mental health field has
> been to remove our thinking about human behavior from the frame
> of causality. In systems terms it is more relevant to view complex
> human behavior from the perspective of interactive process than it
> is to attempt to identify a specific cause or "reason" for behavior
> that can be located with a specific individual. (p. 4)[1]

This paragraph appears early in Bepko's (1985) *The Responsibility Trap: A Blueprint for Treating the Alcoholic Family.* Although
at first glance it may seem far removed from concerns about
responsible government, the problem of alcoholism in fact provides a useful metaphor for analyzing the paradoxes generated by
blaming in a variety of contexts. Bepko's first clue concerning the
systemic nature of responsibility appears in her book's subtitle,
which refers to alcoholic *families.* These are not families in which
all members drink to excess. Rather, the excessive drinking of *one*
member is understandable from the standpoint of the tacit and
usually unconscious participation in its continuation by the family's other members.

The family systems approach to treating alcoholism, as well as pathologies in families and groups more generally, holds that alcoholism, as a systemic or circular process, "is both a cause and an effect of system changes that are or become dysfunctional" (p. 5). In particular:

> We make the assumption that alcoholism constitutes a sequence of interactional events which occur between the drinker and the alcohol, the drinker and himself, and the drinker and others. The physiological and psychological effects of alcohol, over time, set in motion changes that shift the way the drinker interacts with himself and with others in his environment. In turn, interaction with others shapes the way the drinker drinks. (p. 6)

The systemic character of alcoholism is evident both intrapsychically, that is, within the drinker, and interpersonally, with other family members. At each of these systemic levels, paradoxes are generated that are understandable within the framework supplied by the images of maker and answerer, providing insight into the social nature of human agency. In describing the paradox of alcoholism at the level of the individual's internal conversation with himself, Bepko draws from Gregory Bateson's (1972) pioneering work on alcoholism. According to Bateson, Bepko says, "the major flaw in the thinking of the alcoholic is a kind of pride—an assertion that one can change, control what one wants to control, . . . 'a repudiation of the proposition, I cannot' " (p. 8). She then summarizes the alcoholic's subjective experience in Bateson's terms:

> Joe A takes a drink.
> The drink enhances or diminishes some self-perception that reduces Joe's sense of disharmony with self or others.
> Joe takes another drink.
> The effect is intensified. Joe comes to feel that he can regulate his emotional status by taking a drink. He gains a false sense of his own power that enables him to feel differently about himself and to operate differently with others. (p. 8)

Paradoxically, however, Joe's drinking, which is intended to show that he is in control, soon thereafter leads to his loss of control:

> Over time, Joe denies or "forgets" that loss of control and continues
> to relate to alcohol in such a way that he feels he can regain his
> "empowered" self by "losing" it to the relationship with the alcohol.
> He feels equal to the alcohol because he still thinks that he is in
> control. The more he tries to be in control, the more he loses control
> to the alcohol. The more he periodically and intermittently loses
> control and experiences negative feedback about self in terms of
> the fact that he is out of control, the more he drinks to prove that
> he is in fact in control. Over time, the singular event of taking the
> drink becomes a sequence of events in which a fundamental shift
> occurs in Joe. (p. 8)

Translated into the terms introduced in this chapter, Joe's pride reflects his inflated belief in his "incontestable" authorship of his actions. For Joe to admit otherwise—to acknowledge that he cannot drink and still be in control—would be an intolerable admission of guilt. He feels that he can prove his innocence only by showing that he can be a "responsible drinker." Eventually and inevitably, however, his drinking becomes excessive, thus generating feelings of guilt that can be alleviated only by drinking even more.

The vicious circularity of alcoholism is also played out in the paradoxical dynamics of the alcoholic's family, where the central focus of the nondrinking members' actions is on adapting to the drinker's oscillations from sober to drunk states. Nondrinkers, that is, *re*act to the behavior of the drinker rather than act on the basis of their own needs in the situation. "Their self-perceptions become inextricably linked to the actions of the drinker, and their adaptive behaviors represent their own attempts to self-correct in the face of the feedback generated by the alcohol-affected person" (Bepko, 1985, p. 11). The behaviors of all members of the family are thus in an important sense irresponsible in view of Bepko's definition of self-responsibility "as the activity of meeting one's own physical and emotional needs in a way that is developmentally appropriate" (p. 18). Irresponsibility, then, involves actions that fail to meet those needs by being either *under*responsible in the sense of failing to act on one's own legitimate interests (while at the same time ignoring the interests of others) or *over*responsible by responding exclusively and excessively to the needs of the other at the expense of one's own needs.

In dysfunctional families, one member's overresponsibility is predictably reciprocated by the underresponsibility of the other(s). In alcoholic families, this usually begins with the drinker's attempt to maintain an idealized self-image as someone who is able to keep his drinking under control.

> Since an individual's "idealized" or inaccurate belief about self has typically been generated as a protection in response to feedback or communications from his original family system that are inconsistent, negative, of self-negating, pride is a self-corrective mechanism in itself that often requires the reinforcement and further self-correction of alcohol to be sustained.
>
> In response to the negative and self-negating feedback that the alcoholic usually transmits to others, all people in an alcoholic system tend to evolve adaptive, idealized images of themselves which are sometimes reinforced and sometimes attacked in their interaction with the alcoholic. As a result, the sense of self and behavior become pride-based, distorted, and corrective—in short, a mirror of the process that occurs for the alcoholic, but without the alcohol. (Bepko, 1985, p. 13)

The alcoholic's pride, together with the overresponsibility typically exhibited by other family members, ensures the continuation of his drinking. This is because people naturally want to maintain relationships that are symmetrical or equal. When other family members appear to exhibit self-control by, for example, drinking only in moderation, the drinker's pride requires him also to drink in moderation in order to exhibit an equal degree of self-control ("If others can control their drinking, so can I"), paradoxically guaranteeing "that he will lose control and thereby reestablish himself in a dependent, one-down position" (pp. 40-41).

Bepko describes relationships in which symmetrical interactions get out of control—leading to "runaway" and the breakdown of the system—as schismogenic (pp. 17-18). In schismogenic relationships, the breakdown of the system results from habitual covert attempts by any of the parties to assert a "one-up" position on the other(s). More fundamentally, however, the problem of alcoholism, like most other problems of system dysfunction, usually resists solutions that depend upon the autonomous exercise of individual will. The chief lesson of family systems theory, according to Orion White (1990), is that successful therapeutic interventions focus on the social processes of the system as a whole rather than on a single individual.

> All cause-effect relationships are mutual, hence any attempt at assertion of control produces a countervailing effect in the opposite direction. Therefore, only the overall, the *system itself,* can produce change in a given direction. . . . [Citing the example of Alcoholics Anonymous] as long as any party attempts to impose controls on the alcoholic, or the alcoholic attempts to assert personal will over the addiction, the problem continues. It is only when the alcoholic *submits,* by saying "I am an alcoholic," "I am not able to control alcohol," that the regulating processes of the AA group itself begin to bring the drinking behavior under control. . . . To the extent that ego, self-importance, or individualism can be moved past, so that the person can participate in the power of process, strong and effective action can be accomplished. (pp. 202-203)[2]

White's reference to the importance of social process rather than individual will as a curative force helps to make comprehensible perhaps the most cryptic of the eleven representative statements about responsibility introduced early in Chapter 2, namely, Mary Parker Follett's (1924) contention that:

> Empty will can no longer masquerade as a spiritual force. We can rely neither on facts nor . . . on our "strong will," but only on full acceptance of all the responsibility involved in our part in that unfolding life which is making both "facts" and ourselves. (p. 150)

From Follett's viewpoint, responsibility as the reflective exercise of moral agency is inseparable from participation in the social processes that reveal, in her phrase, "the law of the situation." As Harmon and Mayer (1986) interpret Follett on this matter,

> Responsibility, here, does not mean adherence to an objective standard of truth arrived at through abstract intellectual thought nor obligation to a superordinate source of authority. Rather, in the personal sense that Follett intends, it refers to the self-understanding and self-realization that individuals experience when they invest their emotional energies in collaborative endeavors. (p. 343)

The plausibility of Follett's argument in favor of personal investment in collaborative endeavors over intellectual thought is nicely illustrated in the award-winning film *Schindler's List*. Although we ordinarily think of responsible—and, perhaps especially, heroic—action as motivated by a priori moral principles that are then interpreted to fit particular situations, the case of Oskar Schindler supports an explanation much closer to Follett's. At the start of World War II, Schindler was a war profiteer (and remained so virtually until Germany's defeat in 1945). His efforts to shield his (primarily Jewish) workers from Nazi extermination was initially a practical expedient aimed at keeping his factories running. Schindler's transformation—his development of a sense of responsibility for the lives of his workers—only emerged as his personal association with them made vivid to him that his own fate, spiritually as well as materially, was intimately linked with theirs. His "responsive adjustment," therefore, was not to moral principles subsequently animated by his association with his workers, but to and with the workers themselves through which, in Follett's phrase, the law of the situation—his and their situation—was revealed.

From Follett's process perspective, then, responsive adjustment by individual agents involves not their acknowledgment of error or sin (followed by contrite obedience to authoritative edicts and standards), but their reflective awareness of the limits and possibilities of the exercise of agency within the communities of which they are members. Process, therefore, has not only a social dynamic, in the sense of describing interactions among people, but also, owing to its self-reflexive character, a critical psychological dimension as well. It is in terms of this psychological dimension—the standpoint of the unconscious in both its individual and collective aspects—that, as we shall see in the next two sections, buckpassing and scapegoating appear to be in a perverse sense rational responses to blaming.

Buckpassing as a "Rational" Response to Blame. Earlier in this chapter I noted five typical ways in which individuals claim innocence in response to being blamed:

1. The outright denial of guilt

2. Offering a moral justification for the action in question
3. Disputing the factual portrayal of events assumed by the blamer
4. Claiming an inability to control the events in question
5. Invoking the doctrine of *respondeat superior*

It should be noted at the outset that, depending on the particular contexts in which they are offered, all five responses could be persuasive to an impartial observer, in which case the label of buckpassing would be patently unfair. For example, the first kind of response, the outright denial of guilt, may be amply justified if blaming someone for an action was motivated by malice or resulted from mistaken identity. The accused, that is, may in the most literal and uncontroversial sense of the word be innocent. Regarding the second kind of response, the recipient of blame may actually be able to marshal a plausible moral argument, at least as plausible as that made by the accuser, to justify his or her alleged offense. In the third instance, the factual account of events asserted by the blamer may be legitimately disputable, a fact that should not be surprising in view of the ambiguity and controversy that often attend the collective interpretation of social facts. The fourth claim of innocence, that is, the assertion of an inability to control the events in question, may often appear eminently reasonable, especially in view of MacIntyre's (1984) argument, discussed later in Chapter 7, that the notion of bureaucratic control is a masquerade. Finally, the claim of innocence for having obeyed the order of a superior may just as reasonably be characterized as evidence of loyalty as of Eichmannism; depending on the context, it is at least an arguable point.

With the possible exception of cases of mistaken identity, the common denominator in these claims of innocence is that they are endlessly arguable, not only because of the myriad factual and ethical interpretations that both the accusers and the accused may place upon disputed incidents, but, more significantly, because each side to the controversy has an unconscious and sometimes a conscious interest in prolonging the argument. For, once blaming begins, both sides try to demonstrate their innocence in order to keep themselves from being, in Bateson's term, in a one-down position relative to the other. When blaming threatens the symmetry of a relationship, the party who finds himself or herself in jeopardy of being in a one-down position to the other must, in order to regain a position of equality in the relationship, devise strategies that will give the appearance of reestablishing that symmetry. Like the alcoholic who must prove both his moral innocence and his equal status with nondrinking family members by "controlling" his drinking, however, such strategies may take the form of avoidances and other means of self-deception, thus provoking the schismogenic cycle of blaming and denial between parties to the relationship.

The essential point here is that the cycle of blaming, counter-blaming, and justification, owing to its fundamental connection to the establishment or recovery of the individual's moral innocence, thereby assumes an unrealizable vision of personal redemption. This is then translated into the naive and futile hope that agents will responsively adjust to a community to which they are supposed to be answerable, but from which they are split apart by virtue of their claims to innocence. Whether failure to satisfy authoritative expectations is, in particular cases, legitimately excusable or evidence of buckpassing is nearly always debatable and therefore as a practical matter relatively unimportant. More important is that the agent's refusal or inability to responsively adjust to blame is predictable, as the case of Janet Cooke illustrates in the following section, to the extent that others in the relationship appear bent on establishing their own innocence.

Scapegoating as a "Rational" Motive for Blaming. Scapegoating, the reciprocal pathology of buckpassing, may be defined as the attribution of blame to an individual in order to shield the blamers (for example, other members of an institution) from their own complicity in creating the conditions in which irresponsible behavior may seem, albeit in a perverse manner, reasonable. Scapegoating is a "rational" act in the sense that its purpose is to protect the blamers' illusion of their (usually collective) innocence of that complicity. A vivid illustration of the pathology of scapegoating has been recounted by Cynthia McSwain and Orion White (1987) in their analysis of the case of *Washington Post* reporter Janet Cooke, whose Pulitzer Prize was awarded and then rescinded for an article, later determined to be partly fictitious, about an eight-year-old drug addict named "Jimmy." McSwain and White's summary of the facts of the case is worth quoting at length:[3]

> The facts of the situation were reported in the *Post* on April 19, 1981, in a lengthy analysis by Bill Green, the *Post's* ombudsman. Janet Cooke is a young black woman who was in her mid-twenties when she was hired by the *Post* on January 3, 1980, after a series of interviews initiated by editor Ben Bradlee upon receipt of a letter from Cooke asking for a job and citing her credentials. In this initial letter to Bradlee, Cooke said that she had graduated Phi Beta Kappa from Vassar in 1976. Bradlee was impressed by this, underlining this fact when he had her invited for interviews. In her interviews she was noted to be exceptionally bright, aggressive, ambitious, and attractive. Everyone liked and admired her and never bothered to check any of her background or references before she was hired.
>
> In her first nine months on the job, before the "Jimmy" story was published in September, she wrote 52 pieces for the *Post*. Her supervisors encouraged her, sensing that she was unusually talented. Although her rise to prominence was rapid, she seemed to be driven, insecure, and constantly defending her job as if uncertain that she was doing well enough.
>
> During an investigation into illegal drugs, her editors found mention in her notes of a young child addicted to heroin. They suggested she find him and write a story. She was unable to locate the child mentioned but several weeks later said she had found another, similar child and began the research that led to the story, "Jimmy's World." In order to have interviews with Jimmy and his family, Cooke and the *Post* editors agreed to guarantee anonymity. When presented with the story, her editors were fascinated. Her editors were Milton Coleman (district editor for the Metro section and her immediate supervisor), Bob Woodward (Metro editor), Howard Simons (managing editor for the *Post*), and Ben Bradlee. They sensed that it was a potentially explosive, front-page story. No one questioned her sources. No one asked for any real names. No one did any further verification.
>
> The story ran on the front page of the Sunday *Post* on September 28, 1980, and was an instant and controversial success. A search to locate the child was initiated immediately by the District of Columbia government. Officials acknowledged defeat 17 days later, abandoning the search, and publicly stating that they thought the story a fraud. Suspicions also emerged among Cooke's colleagues at the paper, individuals who thought it unlikely that she could have had such interviews and who also found her ignorant of relevant details.

Some of these suspicions were reported to the editorial staff; some were not. All were disregarded.

Cooke maintained the truth of her story and was not pressured for further confirmation by her editors, who indeed nominated the story for a Pulitzer Prize. On April 13, 1981, announcement was made of the Pulitzer award to Cooke. Discrepancies between the vita released by Cooke following the award and her original resume quickly surfaced, as did questions from Vassar officials who had no record of her graduation. Cooke falsely had claimed graduation from Vassar, study at the Sorbonne, fluency in four languages, and seven journalism awards. Under questioning by *Post* editors, Cooke admitted that her story was a composite. Jimmy did not exist. She was asked to resign and did, returning to her parents' home in Ohio. The Pulitzer award was withdrawn, and the *Post* undertook an explanatory investigation.

Two quotations from that investigation seem particularly significant. Ben Bradlee: "She was a one-in-a-million liar. . . . There is no system to protect you from a pathological liar and if you constructed it that way you'd never make a deadline." Bill Green, the ombudsman: "Hers was an aberration that grew in fertile ground." (pp. 426-427)

From the rationalist conception of responsibility, the Janet Cooke case seems clear-cut: She was incontestably the agent of her actions and as such was exclusively blameworthy for them. As synonymous with blame, responsibility according to the rationalist account is a finite quantity, which means that any acknowledgment by the blamers of their complicity, however inadvertent or retrospectively discovered it might be, must be steadfastly resisted because it would seem to diminish proportionally the level or amount of responsibility of the accused. Acknowledgment by the blamers of their complicity, in other words, would necessarily be viewed, in the Janet Cooke case, as "letting her off the hook." In fact, the notion of scapegoating would itself appear to be virtually incomprehensible from the rationalist standpoint, because it requires an admission, first, of the irreducibly systemic character of scapegoating and, second, of the unconscious aspects of irresponsible action by individuals that the systemic nature of scapegoating reveals.

To say that scapegoating is a systemic phenomenon requires some understanding not only of the systemic *causes* of irresponsible action by individuals but also of the *effect* of such action on other members of the system. McSwain and White describe Janet Cooke's action as tragic, both for her and for her colleagues, and that her treatment by her colleagues can properly be construed as scapegoating in that it represented an oblique attempt to minimize the effect of that tragedy on them. It needs to be stressed here that scapegoating, except in rare cases, only infrequently involves the blaming of someone who is in no way legitimately culpable of wrongdoing. McSwain and White note in this regard:

> Janet Cooke did lie and in a dangerous way. She, and we, know that what she did was a detriment to her personally, and we also know that to allow it to go unconsidered would be a detriment to us all and a further detriment to her. (p. 428)

The fact of her guilt in a formal sense, in other words, is not in question. What is in question is the systemic problem of complicity, however inadvertent, by other *Post* staff members in creating, in ombudsman Bill Green's phrase, the "fertile ground" in which Cooke's "aberrant" action grew.

In order to comprehend the problem of individually irresponsible action in systemic terms requires setting aside the rationalist preoccupation with blame and the pinpointing of responsibility in order

> to see responsibility for the case in terms of the human community of the *Post*. Cooke failed the *Post* and society generally, but the *Post* failed her by not confronting the matter in such a way that might have produced in her a maturational self-reflection. (McSwain & White, 1987, p. 428)

The meaning of responsibility implied by this statement is obviously quite different from mere blameworthiness. It more closely matches Bepko's definition of self-responsibility as "the activity of meeting one's own physical and emotional needs in a way that is developmentally appropriate" (p. 18). For such a revised conception of personal or self-responsibility to be comprehensible, however, there must be a fuller consideration of the role of other system members, especially those in positions of authority, in creating (or, alternatively, discouraging the creation of) the conditions under which those needs may be met in a developmentally appropriate manner. Personal development, which in a Kierkegaardian sense involves the ongoing process of coming to terms with the irretrievable loss of moral innocence, has an irreducibly social character and, as such, is always and continually affected by dealings with others who by the same token must struggle with their own loss of innocence. Only in the most superficial sense is that struggle waged at a conscious level of awareness, the level at which blaming is supposed to produce a responsive adjustment. Rather, irresponsibility of the sort shown by Janet Cooke reflects more significantly an unconscious avoidance of issues crucial to her developmental agenda. If organizations, such as the *Washington Post* in the Janet Cooke case, were to see their roles as promoting such agendas—and thus to see themselves as responsible for developing a sense of responsibility in their employees—their focus might well be on establishing

> the conditions . . . that will lead people to see that their greatest interest is in determining if lying, cheating, and stealing are occurring, *from the point of view of the conscious*. From this perspective—that is, that of the unconscious—these behaviors are all simply *avoidances, in one form or another, of facing the task of coming to terms with and integrating unconscious material*. Whether or not facts are misstated is an ambiguous and relatively unimportant matter to the unconscious. The central question in such instances concerns whether or not the ambiguity around the facts represents an ambivalence in facing some aspect of one's self and one's life. Willingness to proceed with such facing is what the Jungians call "the moral attitude," and this label indicates the only firm point of reference for morality: the register of individual development. (McSwain & White, 1987, p. 425)

This conception of a moral attitude must surely seem incongruous and even dangerous to rationalists, for whom the term *moral* characteristically describes actions that conform to institutional standards of correctness. *Morality*, in effect, is a virtual synonym for *innocence*, the absence of which, in both themselves and others, they find intolerable. McSwain and White's endorsement of Jung's "moral attitude" might seem, therefore, unduly permissive, an affront to the traditional values that conservative rationalists, especially, often claim that they honor. McSwain and White's reply, however, more truly represents the conservative values that they see as implicit in long-standing social practices of communities:

> Although our argument may seem unorthodox . . . , its conclusions are a part of commonly accepted folk wisdom. Personal development considerations are typically used as a guide for choice and action. People intuitively know that such issues are valid, and they live accordingly. At the day-to-day level we acknowledge the connection of moral choice and personal development and the centrality of unconscious factors in this process. (p. 430)

McSwain and White's analysis closely parallels Wills's interpretation of the Fall as inevitably entangling us in one another's sins. These are the sins, however, that rationalists, by virtue of their preference for blaming over healing, regard as purely individual matters. Blaming signifies the hidden fear of such entanglement, which in turn provides a virtual recipe for the breakdown of social relationship. In the terminology of the countervailing principles framework used in this book for framing the paradoxes of rationality, the blaming of individuals reflects a splitting off of individual agents from those to whom they are answerable, thus making the pathologies of buckpassing and scapegoating predict-·able and even inevitable consequences.

The Paradox of Agency and the Overassertion of the Collectivity

As predictable results of social processes generated by the blaming of individuals, buckpassing and scapegoating represent pathologies characteristic of contemporary conservatism's overassertion of the individual as the exclusive locus of responsibility. The individualism of contemporary conservatism, however, reflects an ironic reversal of the word's original meaning. In particular, conservative ideologies of the present day show a closer affinity with the classical liberalism (as represented by utilitarianism and laissez-faire economics) of the 18th and 19th centuries than with the traditional conservative view rooted in an ethic of shared responsibility and a commitment to, at most, gradual change.

By the same token, contemporary liberalism, as Robert Reich (1987) has suggested, experienced a similar although more recent transformation of meaning and political priorities. During the New Deal of the 1930s, governmental activism, a consistent hallmark of political liberalism throughout the twentieth century, was inspired and legitimated by an ethic of social solidarity captured, for example, by the phrase "We are all in the same boat" (p. 165). The wide public support for the New Deal derived from a shared conviction, articulated masterfully by Franklin Roosevelt, that each person's fate was entangled with everyone else's. The later decline in political liberalism's wide public support, Reich says, was occasioned by a significant but largely unnoticed reorientation of its political agenda, beginning in the 1950s and solidifying in the 1960s. Whereas the New Deal's social programs, such as Social Security, were typically *inclusive* in that everyone both relied upon and contributed to them, liberal programs of the postwar era became increasing *exclusive* in the sense that some people— "them"—relied upon the compassionate largess of others—"us."

The exclusivity of these later social programs was surely influenced by a growing public recognition of the injustice represented by the widest gap of any industrialized nation between the richest and the poorest segments of the population. "But the subsequent discovery of 'the poor,' " Reich says, "bifurcated the system. This discovery inspired antipoverty programs and eligibility formulas that sharply distinguished the needy from the rest of us" (p. 166). Reich goes on to note that this bifurcation placed an intolerable strain on the long-standing myth of a "Benevolent Community"—the principles of compassion and generosity that had united Americans during the social and economic strife of the Great Depression (and before)—that had traditionally been expressed chiefly in the private, voluntary acts of individuals and groups, rather than in government welfare programs. With the advent of government welfare on a massive scale, reaching its zenith in the Great Society programs of Lyndon Johnson's administration, the national consensus began to dissolve.

It is widely accepted that welfare does not work, but there is no alternative vision of public action that might. The Benevolent Community is bereft of any guiding philosophy for demarcating public and private responsibilities. As private individuals, we understand our obligations toward the poor; as citizens, we are frequently baffled, disappointed, and suspicious. (Reich, 1987, p. 168)

In this passage Reich equates responsibilities (evident in part by his use of the word's plural form) with obligations, which is to say, the moral basis of our answerability to others. But his own subsequent analysis, as well as that of others who have commented recently on the social and psychological effects of welfare and other entitlement programs, also points toward responsibility's other core meaning, namely, that of agency, which denotes the individual's authorship of his or her actions. In particular, Reich and other commentators on both the political left and right are increasingly dismayed by the *atrophy* of individual agency, a loss of a vital sense of personal responsibility, not only *to* others, but also *for* the shaping of the individual's own destiny.

In this section I shall argue that the atrophy of individual agency and the avoidance of individual accountability are predictable pathologies of entitlement liberalism's overassertion of the collectivity as the primary locus of responsibility. Both pathologies, that is, are predictable and paradoxical consequences of liberalism's equation of responsibility with blame. Entitlement liberalism radically if inadvertently splits off the notion of individual agency from answerability to others and thus, like its conservative counterpart, qualifies for the label of rationalist. Blame is shifted in liberal rationalism's account of responsibility from the individual to the collectivity; but, as a comparison of Figures 6.1 and 6.2 reveals, the hope of restoring moral innocence—the motive force of rationalism's quest for redemption—is still present, but in merely an altered form.

This is a crucial point to underscore at the outset of this discussion inasmuch as conservative rationalists will no doubt be tempted to interpret what follows as an implicit rebuttal to many of the arguments made earlier concerning the paradox of agency

	Principles	
Responsibility for (Individual Agency):	◄── split off from ──►	**Accountability to** (Individual Answerability):
Individual authority to act as an agent of an institution in the pursuance of its legally mandated goals; such agency is an official precondition of blameworthiness		Individual liability for blame and punishment (as well as entitlement to rewards); obedience and goal achievement are the means by which innocence is (re)established
Buckpassing:		**Scapegoating:**
Declaration of the individual's innocence by means of disclaiming either personal authorship or sufficient authority and resources to achieve the institution's goals		Attribution of blame to an individual in order to shield the institution from its complicity and thus protect its members' illusion of their collective innocence
	Pathologies	

Figure 6.1. The Conservative Paradox of Agency as Generated by the Overassertion of the Individual

	Principles	
Social Entitlement (Collective Agency):	◄── split off from ──►	**Social Responsibility** (Collective Answerability):
Entitlement of historically disadvantaged groups to compensation for past and present victimization		Responsibility of privileged groups to redress—through political, economic, and bureaucratic means—injustices resulting from historically caused inequalities
Atrophy of Individual Moral Agency:		**Avoidance of Individual Accountability:**
Asserting moral innocence through the claim of victim status, thus discouraging the exercise of personal authorship and responsibility		Perpetuating the illusion of victim innocence by relaxing standards and avoiding confrontation and candor needed for instilling a sense of personal answerability
	Pathologies	

Figure 6.2. The Liberal Paradox of Agency as Generated by the Overassertion of the Collectivity

generated by the overassertion of the individual. Similarly, entitlement liberals might also believe that the following critique of their own position is contradicted by the earlier critique of their conservative opponents. As I noted in Chapter 3, however, the reframing of debates often discloses, as it does in this case, a fundamental but heretofore hidden agreement on key assumptions held by long-standing adversaries. The agreement by liberals and conservatives alike that responsible government requires the designation of innocent and guilty parties far overshadows their disagreements, because it is the quest for innocence itself that creates both paradoxes of agency.

It is probably not too great an oversimplification to condense the chief tenets of entitlement liberalism into two reciprocal propositions. The first of these holds that certain groups—namely, those which through accidents of history have attained privileged social, political, and economic status—bear a moral responsibility to redress the injustices indicated by the gap between their own advantaged position and that of those who are less fortunate. The gap between the rich and the poor, between Reich's "us" and "them," constitutes prima facie evidence of the historical sins of the former, atonement for which may be at least partially achieved by giving back many of the riches and other benefits they do not entirely, if at all, deserve. In terms of Niebuhr's images of the responsible self, such privileged groups, having historically been the agents or makers of injustice, are now obliged to reverse roles by collectively accepting the burden of answering for it, thus conjoining the centuries-old doctrine of noblesse oblige with the more contemporary notion of psychological guilt. The reciprocal proposition of liberalism holds that historically disadvantaged groups, by virtue of their past and continuing victimization, are entitled to compensation for damages incurred. Here, too, a reversal of Niebuhr's images has taken place: as victims, disadvantaged groups now demand—and liberal members of privileged groups condescendingly allow them—to be "empowered" (as the currently fashionable word would have it), to act as agents, having paid their historical dues as mere answerers.

If this terse summary of entitlement liberalism's chief tenets seems cavalier, it is not because of any cynicism concerning the root sentiments that motivate them. Liberal theories of justice—most notably, perhaps, that of John Rawls (1971) of a generation ago—are typically motivated by the best of intentions, namely, a sincere commitment to human fairness, and also often show an astute appreciation of the historical causes of contemporary inequalities. The modern liberal agenda also includes, however, a subtext of attributed and acknowledged guilt that, coupled with claims to moral innocence, provides a vital clue as to why the liberal vision of equal justice is dimmer today than a generation ago. The dimness of that vision is far from accidental, for it is entitlement liberalism's promotion of the ideal of innocence that paradoxically produces just the reverse of its intended goal of equal justice.

The Atrophy of Individual Agency as a "Rational" Consequence of Collective Entitlement. To seek power and feel entitled to it, Shelby Steele writes, requires as a precondition a belief in one's own innocence. Innocence is a feeling of superiority over others, which inflates us and gives us a sense of power. In *The Content of Our Character,* his landmark book on race relations, Steele (1990) observes that an unarguable source of black innocence in America is the tragic history of black victimization at the hands of the white majority and that many of the political gains produced by the civil rights and, later, the black power movements capitalized on the admission by whites of their collective guilt in that role. Such admissions, of course, have been far from universal and, more important, they are almost always accompanied by feelings of ambivalence, both by whites who admit to their guilt and by those to whom such admissions are directed. People cannot tolerate feeling guilty for very long (although white liberals seem marginally more adept at it than conservatives) without longing for the restoration of their innocence. Steele cites President Reagan's public posture of color blindness in matters of race as an example of what many whites regard as a socially acceptable claim of *current* innocence that does not at the same time explicitly deny his, and therefore *their,* historical guilt. Blacks instinctively view even such qualified claims of innocence, however, as simply precursors of "a power move to be made against them. Reagan's pretense of innocence made him an adversary and made his quite reasonable message seem vindictive. You cannot be innocent of a man's problem and expect him to listen" (p. 9).

The dramatic political gains made by African Americans during the past few decades have been enabled largely by the assertion of victim power, the precondition for which is the posture of black innocence (and the claim of economic and political entitlements that now accompany it) against a sea of white guilt warranted by even the most superficial reading of U.S. history. Steele warns, however, that a heavy price is necessarily and paradoxically paid for such gains, namely, what I call here the atrophy of a sense of individual agency.

> Whatever gains this power brings in the short run through political action, it undermines in the long run. Social victims may be collectively entitled, but they are all too often individually demoralized. Because the social victim has been oppressed by society, he comes to feel that his individual life will be improved more by changes in society than by his own initiative. Without realizing it, he makes society rather than himself the agent of change. The power he finds in his victimization may lead him to collective action against society, but it also encourages passivity within the sphere of his personal life. (pp. 14-15)

Steele's reasoning about the increase of personal passivity thus highlights the bitter irony of two decades of "decline and demoralization" (p. 15) that have accompanied an era of otherwise impressive political advance. Blacks are often reluctant to examine this paradox, he says, because

> To admit this fully would cause us to lose the innocence we derive from our victimization. And we would jeopardize the entitlement we've always had to challenge society. We are in the odd and self-defeating position in which taking responsibility for bettering ourselves feels like a surrender to white power. (p. 15)

Throughout *The Content of Our Character*, Steele carefully avoids the vocabulary of blame and moral judgment, preferring instead the language of sympathetic interpretation of the crisis in American race relations, one in which he is nevertheless invested in the deepest and most personal way. His later contention that blacks and whites *share* responsibility for that crisis, for example, is not merely a tactic for finding a safe and politic middle ground in order to give the impression that blame and innocence should be equitably distributed; it is instead an assertion that responsibility in its truest sense, both individual and collective, is impossible so long as we insist on thinking and judging in such terms. Steele therefore is not, as some have claimed, a "black conservative," a peculiar label indeed for one whose book's title is a phrase from Martin Luther King's famous "I Have a Dream" speech. Rather, Steele's insistence on the importance of personal responsibility and initiative is motivated less by a need to establish individual blameworthiness than by a desire to show how the exercise of personal agency might be nourished. Neither, on the other hand, can he properly be called a liberal, at least an *entitlement* liberal, by virtue of his deep quarrel with the presumption of moral innocence that liberalism depends upon, which in turn inevitably atrophies the exercise of individual agency.

The relevance of *The Content of Our Character* extends beyond the crisis in race relations by supplying a metaphor for interpreting in a new light claims to victimhood made by members of virtually every category of Americans. Even some white males now vie for victim status by presenting themselves as products of dysfunctional families in order to trade in their historical role as oppressors for membership in the ranks of the oppressed. In the "culture of complaint," to borrow Robert Hughes's (1993) phrase, to be a victim now qualifies one for the status of hero. Rather than being used simply to illuminate the tragic undeniability of past oppression, lessons of history, which Steele has often been unfairly accused of forgetting, are trumpeted by victim groups in "complaining celebration" (Steele, 1990, p. 15) of their innocence in order to justify colluding in that oppression. By insisting upon remaining a victim, and a *heroic* one at that, one has a ready-made excuse for avoiding responsibility for the authorship of one's fate.

Liberals are not uniformly unaware, however, of the pitfalls of heroic complaint, and in its stead some have recently proposed therapeutic strategies for promoting self-esteem as a means for empowering those who have historically been oppressed (Steinem,

1992). If oppressors are ridden by historical pangs of guilt, the oppressed suffer from the companion malady of shame, a deep feeling of personal (but also class, racial, and ethnic) unworthiness, inferiority, and self-contempt. To promote the traditional liberal ideal of social justice and also to undo the historical effects of, among other things, the authoritarianism of patriarchy, the new therapeutic agenda of liberalism would consist of programs, although not necessarily in all cases government-sponsored, designed to enhance self-esteem and thus reverse the corrosive effects of crime, alcoholism, and drug abuse brought about by its absence.

In a searing critique of the liberal therapeutic model, Christopher Lasch (1992) argues that public policies and private initiatives that are based on it produce precisely the opposite of their intended effect. "Far from promoting self-respect," he says, such programs

> have created a nation of dependents. They have given rise to a cult of the victim in which entitlements are based on the display of accumulated injuries inflicted by an uncaring society. The politics of "compassion" degrades both the victims, by reducing them to objects of pity, and their would-be benefactors, who find it easier to pity their fellow citizens than to hold them up to impersonal standards, the attainment of which would make them respected. Compassion has become the human face of contempt.
>
> Democracy once meant opposition to every kind of double standard. Today we accept double standards—as always, a recipe for second-class citizenship—in the name of humanitarian concern. We hand out awards indiscriminately, hoping to give the recipients the illusion of accomplishment. Having given up attempts to raise the general level of competence, we are content to restrict it to the caring class, which arrogates to itself the job of looking out for everybody else. The professionalization of compassion does not make us a kinder, gentler nation. Instead it institutionalizes inequality, under the pretense that everyone is "special" in his own way. And since the pretense is transparent, the attempt to make people feel good about themselves only makes them cynical. "Caring" is no substitute for candor. (p. 34)[4]

Is therapy, however, simply by virtue of becoming intertwined with politics, necessarily reduced to a patronizing tactic for making people feel good about themselves? Although Lasch may be correct in arguing that therapy is no substitute for politics, the more important point is that therapy construed as feel-goodism is simply bad therapy, regardless of whether it is practiced in a private, face-to-face encounter or expanded into a larger programmatic strategy of personal development. If politics, rather than being seen simply as the grubby allocation of material benefits, is instead interpreted more hopefully as a vital means for contributing to the individual's maturation as a citizen, then it is by no means clear why therapeutic insights, in particular those that encourage candor and honest confrontation, might not prove to be valuable assets. Thus Peter Vaill's (1981) question about a closely related context also applies to politics: "If organizational life," he asks, "is neither a Renaissance city-state of stab-or-be-stabbed nor a hot tub of gemutlichkeit and positive strokes, what is it and how shall we live it with grace?" (p. 427). Both politics-as-usual and the new politics of self-esteem provide little help in finding the answer. A more promising approach might be to reconsider the meaning and role of shame as a possibly healthy ingredient not only for developing a realistic sense of personal agency—and, incidentally, of genuine self-esteem—but also for instilling a sense of personal accountability.

The Avoidance of Individual Accountability as a "Rational" Consequence of Social Responsibility. The paradoxes of agency are produced by the splitting off of Niebuhr's first image of the responsible self—that of maker, one who is responsible *for* the authorship of his or her actions—from the second image of answerer—one who is accountable *to* other members of a moral community. Because agency *for* and accountability *to* are complementary, the denial or neglect of one inevitably leads to the atrophy of the other. The previous section sought to explain why, when agency is construed chiefly as entitlement, the atrophy of individual agency, or under-responsibility, predictably follows. The overassertion of entitlement divorces agency from answerability to the constraints inherent in any social context, producing the illusion that freedom, the moral expression of agency, is synonymous with mere liberty—the right to do as one pleases.

Freedom is meaningless, however, in the absence of limitation and constraint because its exercise, that is, the assertion of personal will and mastery, requires the presence of obstacles to be overcome or at least struggled with. Freedom cannot simply be given and then enjoyed as if it were a leisure activity or a commodity to be consumed. Despite the best of intentions, entitlement liberals, who believe that they bear the responsibility for redressing the past and current injustices of which they see themselves as the historical agents, try to assuage their guilt by relaxing standards of excellence and refusing to confront irresponsibility when it appears—in short, by abrogating their authority. Demands for special entitlements, however capricious they might be, are automatically and condescendingly acceded to whenever they are uttered in the name of victim rights. To the innocent, requirements for accountability in the form of measuring up to authoritative standards are objected to as yet further evidence of oppression; and entitlement liberals, although with increasing reluctance, agree for fear that they will be accused of perpetuating even further the cycle of shame among those who have historically been victimized.

Shame has another, more hopeful side, however, that predates not only its current association with victimization and self-esteem, but the literature of contemporary psychology as well. Take, for example, the now almost archaic adjective *shameless,* which means "impudent or immodest; brazen . . . indicating a lack of pride or decency" (Morris, 1969, p. 1190). The capacity to experience shame, at least in the prepsychoanalytic sense that the meaning of shame*less* assumes, used to be regarded more positively as "evoking feelings of awe and reverence" (Lasch, 1992, p. 34) or, more prosaically, of simply not living up to standards set by oneself or others. Without discounting the destructive effects of shame that have been documented by its recent "rediscovery" in the psychological literature, other meanings of the word fare far better not only in that literature but also in anthropology, theology, and philosophy. In reviewing the "confounding variability" (p. 55) of the word, clinical psychologist Robert Karen (1992) divides shame into several categories, including *existential* shame, which

arises from suddenly seeing yourself as you really are—too preoc-
cupied with yourself to notice that your child is sinking, too
frightened of the opinion of others to stand up for someone you
love, too wrapped up in your bitterness to allow yourself or anyone
close to you to be happy. This kind of shame, although it reflects
negatively on the self, lacks the quality of hopeless deformity that
is associated with the shame wounds inflicted in childhood. (p. 58)[5]

Not only does shame, in the existential sense of seeing oneself
in new light, lack the crippling disaffirmation of self-worth associated with other categories of shame; the capacity to feel shame
of this kind also appears to be a vital element in the individual's
maturation. Orion White (1973) notes that, unlike guilt, which
tends to be destructive by virtue of its being simply the internali-
zation of others' blame and disapproval, shame in this more positive sense aids personal development by acting as a stimulus for
self-reflexive consideration of one's actions. Recalling arguments
made in Chapter 4, it is self-reflexivity that fosters personal responsibility in the sense of an awareness not only of the possibilities of
self-authorship but also of its realistic limits in institutional and
other social contexts. On this point, White (1990) observes that:

The core process of development . . . is reflexivity, or the continual process of struggling to assess and define the meaning of
what one is doing. Reflexivity necessitates, in turn, that an alternative viewpoint be present, there must be something to "come up
against." The creation of *subjective* meanings depends on the existence of *objective* meanings from which the person can initiate
the process of "reflexion." In this sense one can only define
oneself against society or in tension with the values its institutions
represent. . . .
    This reality produces the basic paradox of human development:
institutional rules must exist if we are to develop, and hence we all
have a stake in establishing, maintaining, and enforcing them. Yet
such rules are useful only as points of reference for how we are to
live. In other words, the rules are essential, but they are not to be
taken with ultimate seriousness. (p. 224)

It is authority that plays the fundamental role of managing the
paradoxes of personal development, of integrating the tensions
between making one's life and answering for it to others. White is

thus critical of liberal rationalism's emphasis on participative decision making in organizations (analogous to its abrogation of political authority in the name of victim "empowerment") when it is proposed as an *alternative* to authority. "Antiauthority ideologues," he says,

> often use the misbehavior of actual authority holders as an argument against authority itself. This is to make the same error as those who argue against participation on the grounds that it has in fact gone wrong so frequently as people have attempted to use it as a decision process. (p. 231)

But unlike conservative rationalists, White insists that the *responsible* use of authority does not involve, at least chiefly, the attribution of individual blame, but rather is the activity of helping subordinates to construct, "in a two-way, back-and-forth process" (p. 231), a factual picture of their behavior and of the context in which it has taken place. The individual's sense of accountability that emerges from this process thus is not rooted in the fear of blame and punishment, but gradually emerges from the learned conviction that systems of accountability, even if they may on occasion be knowingly breached or transcended by either oneself or others, ultimately serve his or her own long-term interests.[6] In the absence of that conviction the individual's efforts to avoid the constraints of authority will continue to appear rational.

Conclusion

The final task remaining in this chapter is to show how the images of making and answering, which in the rationalist conception of responsibility are split apart to produce the conservative and liberal paradoxes of agency, may be reunited. How, in other words, might the schismogenic division of those images created by rationalism's preoccupation with blame, guilt, and innocence be transformed into antinomial relation with one another? A good place to start is to recall the quotation from Martin Buber with which the chapter began. Buber (1947, p. 16) declared that the idea of responsibility should not be seen as "the province of specialized ethics, an 'ought' that swings free in the air," but that instead responsibility should be understood as "genuine responding" within the flow of "lived life." Responsible action, then, is necessarily *inter*action, an irreducibly social activity that is profoundly misunderstood when it is seen as synonymous with the making of ethical decisions by isolated individuals, as conventional approaches to ethics typically presuppose. "Responsible decision" is therefore an incongruous term inasmuch as the idea of decision itself is usually regarded as a discrete, isolable act performed by autonomous individuals.[7]

Niebuhr amplifies Buber's point by distinguishing the idea of responsibility from the two principal strands of Western moral philosophy—utilitarianism (teleology) and Kantianism (deontology)—both of which are chiefly concerned with problems of ethics rather than responsibility. As ethical systems, both begin with the question: "What should I do?" (p. 60). Utilitarianism translates this to mean "What is my goal, ideal, or telos?" (p. 60), thus defining ethics with reference to a previously decided "good." The Kantian tradition, by contrast, construes the question "What shall I do?" as meaning "What is the law and what is the first law of my life?" (p. 60), thereby subordinating consideration of the good to a concern with doing what is morally right, irrespective of the consequences that such a decision might produce. Both approaches agree that in principle it is possible to identify standards of correctness on the basis of which to make ethical decisions and also that those decisions may be made independently by individuals. Thus, despite their differences concerning the proper basis for making decisions, both sides agree that individuals' failure to decide according to whatever basis is selected provides a legitimate ground for blaming them. Blaming, then, is a natural consequence of both utilitarian and Kantian ethics.

Niebuhr, however, says that "no action taken as an atomic unit [a discrete act of an individual] is responsible" (p. 64). Responsibility involves action that is *fitting* or appropriate within particular social contexts rather than action that is correct from the standpoint of an abstract criterion of the good or the right. Niebuhr advises that the ethicist's question "What should I do?" should be preceded by the question "What is going on?" (p. 60). This is because responsible action, as interaction, involves continuous reciprocal interpretations of one another's intentions, questions, actions, and reactions. Responding, which is a defining feature of responsibility, is always based on such interpretations and, moreover, involves an anticipation of others' responses to our responses. Niebuhr refers to this as

> *accountability*—a word that is frequently defined by recourse to legal thinking but that has a more definite meaning, when we understand it as referring to part of the response pattern of our self-conduct. Our actions are responsible not only insofar as they are reactions to interpreted actions upon us but also insofar as they are made in anticipation of answers to our answers. An agent's action is like a statement in a dialogue. Such a statement not only seeks to meet, as it were, or to fit into, the previous statement to which it is an answer, but is made in anticipation of reply. It looks forward as well as backward; it anticipates objections, confirmations and corrections. It is made as part of a total conversation that leads forward and is to have meaning as a whole. (pp. 63-64)

As an integral feature of social discourse, accountability as Niebuhr (1963) defines it does not necessarily preclude the possibility of blaming. But he accentuates an aspect of accountability quite different from the rationalist view of it as a synonym for obedience, which separates answerability from moral authorship. Just as responsibility means mutual responding, Niebuhr is equally literal about the meaning of accountability as involving reciprocal accountings of one another's actions. These accountings, although they may include on occasion the language of justification, are more fundamentally *factual* accountings, that is, interpretations of contexts that are mutually constructed in order to find out both "what is going on" and what kinds of action seem "fitting" within those contexts.

The final component of Niebuhr's (1963) conception of responsibility—in addition to response, interpretation, and accountability—is *social solidarity*, which he defines as "a continuing discourse or interaction among beings forming a continuing society" (p. 65). Responsible action, as a process of social interaction, requires a stable scheme of interpretations in order that individual responses may be comprehensible to one another over time. Solidarity, then, is more than a fancy synonym for a feeling of togetherness. It is also an empirical precondition of responsible action in which the images of maker and answerer are reunited, and in which blaming is therefore a divisive element.

Notes

1. This and the quotations that follow are reprinted with the permission of The Free Press, a Division of Simon & Schuster, from *The Responsibility Trap: A Blueprint for Treating the Alcoholic Family*, by Claudia Bepko with Jo Ann Krestan. Copyright 1985 by Claudia Bepko with Joan Ann Krestan.

2. The material from White (1990) appears in G. L. Wamsley et al., *Refounding public administration* (pp. 182-245), © Sage Publications, Newbury Park, CA. Used with permission.

3. The material from McSwain and White (1987) appeared in *Administration & Society*, 18, 411-431. © Sage Publications, 1987. Used with permission.

4. This quotation is reprinted by permission of *The New Republic*.

5. This quotation is reprinted by permission of *The Atlantic Monthly*.

6. Mary Parker Follett (1924) captures the spirit of Niebuhr's description of responding by saying that:

> In human relations . . . this is obvious: I never react to you but to you plus me. "I" can never influence "you" because you have already influenced me; that is, in the very process of meeting, by the very process of meeting, we both become something different. . . . It is I plus the-interweaving-between-you-and-me meeting you plus the-interweaving-between-you-and-me, etc., etc. If we were doing it mathematically we should work it out to the *nth* power. This pregnant truth—that response is always to a relation, the relation between the response and that to which the response is being made . . . is the basic truth for all the social sciences. (pp. 62-63)

7. For further elaboration of this point, see Chapter 7's discussion of "The Contingency of 'Decision.'"

7

The Paradox of Accountability

◈ THIS CHAPTER CONSIDERS the paradox of the third core
meaning of responsibility introduced in Chapter 2. Like the
paradoxes of obligation and agency discussed in Chapters 5 and 6,
the paradox of accountability is produced by the splitting of H.
Richard Niebuhr's (1963) dual images of the responsible self:
maker and answerer. In particular, the rationalist conception of
accountability creates an insoluble moral dilemma in which public
servants, as answerable for achieving purposes decided upon by
others, may disclaim personal responsibility for them. Conversely,
by asserting their personal responsibility as makers of purposes,
public servants undermine the legal and political bases of their
answerability. Stated more formally, the paradox of accountability
holds that:

> If public servants are accountable solely for the effective achieve-
> ment of purposes mandated by political authority, then as mere
> instruments of that authority they bear no personal responsibility

as moral agents for the products of their actions. If, on the other
hand, public servants actively participate in determining public
purposes, their accountability is compromised and political authority is undermined.

In the rationalist conception of responsibility, accountability
assumes the prior existence of purposes spelled out in official
policies and programs. Because purposes can never be perfectly
achieved, however, rationalists employ measurable criteria—most
notably, of effectiveness and efficiency—to assess how well public
servants perform their jobs. Public servants are accountable, that
is, not simply for the legal and ethical misdeeds they or others
under their purview might commit, but also for the extent of their
success in achieving the purposes with which they are charged.
As "implementors," they may claim immunity from the contami-
nating effects of politics by asserting that the criteria of effectiveness and efficiency are value neutral and therefore apolitical. As
we have already seen from earlier chapters, however, opinion
within the rationalist camp is divided over the degree to which
public servants should be permitted a significant discretionary role
not only in interpreting policies during implementation, but also
in voicing their opinions about policies during their formulation.
Hard-core rationalists, it will be recalled, seek to minimize that
active voice, whereas soft-core rationalists are more tolerant of,
and in fact often explicitly encourage, public servants' participation in the dialogue over public purposes.

The initial task of this chapter is to sketch the contours of the
rationalist debate over the proper role of public servants in formulating public purposes. As in the two previous chapters, I will show
that embedded within that debate is an irreconcilable conflict
between hard-core and soft-core rationalism in which each side is
able to marshal crippling objections against the other. The primary
virtues expressed by each side, in other words, are also accompanied by predictable pathologies owing to the splitting of Niebuhr's
two images. The rationalist debate about accountability is thus
inherently paradoxical in the vicious or schismogenic sense; and
transforming that paradox into an antinomial one requires a reexamination of the central assumptions about the relation of purpose

and action that both branches of rationalism hold in common. Specifically, the current impasse results from their shared adherence to a series of conceptual dichotomies—between thought and action, values and facts, ends and means, and, finally, between politics and administration—in which the opposing elements in each dichotomy are assumed to be in irreconcilable opposition. The rationalist dichotomies not only create the moral dilemma stated in the paradox, but also both produce an empirical misunderstanding of organizational action and sustain the illusion that action is controllable via the exercise of expert authority.

Reframing the paradox of accountability requires a redescription of the generic problem of accountability that not only honors (when appropriate) the distinctions implied by rationalism's dichotomies but also captures the relatedness of their opposing ideas. Alasdair MacIntyre's (1984) analysis of practice provides a plausible basis for that redescription, which then sets the stage for an alternative conception of accountability that unites the various oppositions that rationalism splits apart. The chapter concludes with a proposal for transforming the functional relation between politics and administration so that dual attributes of the responsible self—making and answering—are reunited.

Political and Professional Responsibility

The combined legacies of Woodrow Wilson (1887/1941), Max Weber (1946), and Herbert Simon (1947/1976) provide the theoretical basis for the most familiar and influential conception of responsible action in American public administration discourse. Wilson's advocacy of the separation of politics (policy formulation) from administration (implementation) paralleled Weber's distinction between ends and means implied by the legal/technical mode of rationality embodied in the bureaucratic form of social organization. Drawing from logical positivism, Simon later provided an influential epistemological basis for Wilson's dichotomy by arguing for a radical analytical distinction between values and facts, with value judgments constituting the stuff of politics, and factual judgments comprising the domain of administration.

Organizationally, the separation of politics from administration dictates that administrators are hierarchically subordinate to elected representatives. That is, organizational arrangements, which usually approximate the bureaucratic form described by Weber, should be devised so that rewards (e.g., promotion, pay, job security) and penalties are dispensed in order to ensure that administrators comply with a policy's rules and intent. Their compliance defines whether administrators have acted in an accountable manner; and the letter and intent of a policy provide the basis on which administrators may be called to account for their actions or inaction. Political (or hierarchical) responsibility is thus synonymous with accountability, which, in addition to being enforceable through legal sanctions, also carries with it a moral imperative that is embedded both in the democratic ethos of the broader society and in the value system of public administrators.

An important parallel to the idea of accountability is the notion of efficiency. If, through legitimate political processes, value judgments about the proper ends of the state have been enacted into law, the responsibility of administrators is not simply to implement the law in a dutiful manner but to do so at the least possible cost. Efficiency, defined as the ratio of expenditures to results, is thus an instrumental value, and discretion by administrators is properly limited to judgments about the *means* (for Simon, "factual judgments") by which efficiency may be best achieved, not to the desirability of the ends themselves.

The emergence of the idea of professional responsibility was prompted by a recognition of the limitations of political accountability as a sufficient practical and normative guide for administrators. In its earliest form professional responsibility simply entailed the avoidance of wrongdoing, especially of action intended to reap personal or political gain. Such phrases as "the doctrine of neutral competence" (Sayre & Kaufman, 1960, p. 404) and "a passion for anonymity" (the title of Brownlow, 1958), for example, suggest an image of the administrator as a selfless professional who shuns the limelight in the course of dutiful service. From this view, professional and political responsibility are complementary: The virtues as well as the pathologies of each serve to reinforce the other.

By the early 1940s, however, the notion of the professional as a neutrally competent bureaucrat was challenged by a growing acknowledgment of the breakdown of the policy/administration dichotomy. The blurring of the distinction between policy making and implementation revealed that administration necessarily entailed discretionary judgments, not only about technical matters of effectiveness and efficiency, but also about values. The complexities of modern government, according to Carl J. Friedrich (1940), who championed this view, required that administrators be attentive to public opinion, as well as to professional expertise and ethics, in their interpretation of legislative intent. As we saw in Chapter 3, however, Friedrich was harshly rebuked on this point by Herman Finer (1940), who uncompromisingly insisted upon the subservience of administrators to their political masters. Administrators in democratic governments, he argued, must be held accountable for the implementation of the public will through "an arrangement of correction and punishment" (p. 248) enforced "to the most minute degree technically feasible" (p. 249).

Although Friedrich's position subsequently attracted more adherents than Finer's, the still unresolved dilemma first revealed by their debate illustrates how deeply the paradox of accountability is ingrained in the mainstream discourse on responsibility. Having at least temporarily carried the day, however, Friedrich's argument for increased administrative discretion in policy implementation opened the door for later, more activist conceptions of the administrator's role in the policy process. Beginning in the late 1960s and early 1970s, for example, two initially distinct but later convergent lines of argument were introduced into the public administration literature—one from humanistic psychology and the other from political philosophy—that threatened even more severely the purity of Finer's and Simon's hard-core conception of responsible administration. In including these two lines of argument under the category of professional responsibility, I am using the term in a very broad sense to describe viewpoints that try to legitimate substantial independence for civil servants in the discourse over public values and policies. Professionalism in the narrower sense of applying value-neutral managerial expertise in the interests of efficiency and effectiveness, in contrast, is perfectly consistent with hard-core rationalism's subordination of such expertise to political decisions about ends.

Using Herbert Simon as his principal target, psychologist Chris Argyris (1973) criticized what he called the "rational-man" theory of organization for neglecting recent contributions to behavioral science that he believed would add a vitally needed normative dimension to organizational research. Argyris shared Simon's concern for increasing organizational effectiveness, but he criticized rationalism's preoccupation with "descriptive research" for perpetuating the status quo and for uncritically accepting top management's definitions of organizational objectives. Disguised by the ostensibly value-free terminology of social science, rational organizational theory's commitment to explanation and prediction meant that its research agenda served the practical purposes of manipulation and control. "Once people follow the implications of descriptive generalizations," Argyris said, "they become normative" (p. 264). He found the normative bias of rational-man organization theory objectionable in view of his own commitment to organizations that foster opportunities for self-actualization and personal growth along lines suggested by the leading humanistic psychologist of the day, Abraham Maslow (1965, 1970). If, as Argyris argued, "the social science universe can be what we make it to be, then what is needed is a concept, a view, or an image of what the world ought to be" (p. 264). Organizations populated by people pursuing projects of individual self-actualization seemed to Argyris to fit such a preferred normative image, and he urged organizational researchers to include in their investigations the development of strategies to make that image a reality.

Several factors conspired to assure that Argyris's proposal, and others like it appearing in the public administration literature, developed only marginal support in the field. First, his argument did not address the issue of administrative accountability within democratic government. However appealing Maslow's notion of self-actualization might be on humanistic grounds, public administration traditionalists remained troubled by the unanswered question of to whom or to what self-actualizing administrators were to be held accountable. The notion of self-actualization was, sometimes awkwardly, associated with arguments for increased participation in decision making by public servants, prompting objections from hard-core rationalists, who saw such participation as undermining political accountability. Several years before the publication of Argyris's article, for example, Frederick Mosher (1968) warned of the dangers of participation by professional experts in the formulation of public purposes.

> There has already developed a great deal of collegial decision-making in many public agencies, particularly those which are largely controlled by single professional groups. But I would point out that *democracy within administration*, if carried to the full, raises a logical dilemma in its relation to *political democracy*. All public organizations are presumed to have been established and to operate for public purposes—i.e., purposes of the people. They are authorized, legitimated, empowered, and usually supported by authorities outside of themselves for broad purposes initially determined outside of themselves. To what extent, then, should "insiders," the officers and employees, be able to modify their purposes, their organizational arrangements, and their means of support? It is entirely possible that internal administrative democracy might run counter to the principles and objectives of political democracy in which the organizations of government are viewed as instruments of public purpose. (pp. 18-19)

By not engaging the related issues of self-actualization and participative management in overtly political terms, the humanists in organizational psychology were incapable of offering a satisfactory response to the traditionalists' misgivings about the possibility of reconciling them with requirements for public accountability. Beginning in the late 1960s and early 1970s, this issue *was* engaged by younger public administration academics, deeply affected by the political turmoil of the Vietnam war and the civil rights movement, who challenged the legitimacy of traditional American political democracy on which hard-core rationalism was based. In a volume titled *Toward a New Public Administration* (Marini, 1971), Todd LaPorte captured the spirit of the new dissenting view by declaring that:

> Our primary normative premise should be that *the purpose of public organization is the reduction of economic, social, and psychic suffering*

and the enhancement of life opportunities for those inside and outside the organization. Translated into more detailed sentiments, this statement means that public organizations should be assessed in terms of their effect on the production and distribution of material abundance in efforts to free all people from economic deprivation and want. Furthermore, it means that public organizations have a responsibility to enhance social justice by freeing their participants and the citizenry to decide their own way and by increasing the probability of shared political and social privilege. Finally, it means that the quality of personal encounter and increasing possibilities of personal growth should be elevated to major criteria of organizational assessment. (p. 32)

These strong sentiments, quite predictably, found little support among hard-core rationalists, who read them as a proposal for obliterating the already tenuous distinction between politics and administration. At risk was not only public administration's historical relation to politics, but the nature and legitimacy of politics itself. The New Public Administration and its allies, moreover, were on the whole better critics of politics and administration as then practiced than they were architects of a new politics with which their proposals for administrative reform might be compatible. The often nihilistic politics of the New Left offered little in the way of a vision of a new politics palatable to even the most radical of the New Public Administration scholars. Liberal political theorist John Rawls's (1971) neo-Kantian theory of "justice as fairness," however, influenced some of the dissident academics in the field, supporting the notion of a public administration based on a commitment to social equity and distributive justice (Frederickson, 1980; Hart, 1975). But, as the political volatility of the 1970s abated and as fiscal resources of governments at all levels became scarcer, the preoccupation with social equity soon gave way to more traditional public administration concerns with efficiency and effectiveness.

Two features of the debate over the proper limits on administrators' involvement in the normative definition of public purposes have special bearing on the paradox of accountability. First, during the decade of the 1970s, when the disagreement between the hard-core and soft-core rationalists was at its peak, debate between the two sides in the form of direct engagement with one another was seldom sustained. In part this was due to the infusion of peripheral issues, such as quarrels about epistemology and the nature and role of social science, that often obscured the debate over public purposes. Moreover, the debate was to a great extent an intergenerational one in which the younger scholars seemed bent on making their distinctive mark on the field largely at the expense of their elders, who in turn seemed alternately baffled by and contemptuous of the upstarts. In addition to its proposals for the radical reform of administration, the newer generation also frequently spoke in esoteric technical vocabularies (e.g., of hermeneutics, phenomenology, and critical theory), chiefly of European origin, that were foreign to the traditional language of American public administration. As a result, the possibility of a fruitful dialogue was lost.

The second and probably more important reason for the absence of sustained debate was that neither the hard-core nor the soft-core rationalists were able to provide satisfactory answers to the criticisms made by the other. Advocates of increased administrative involvement, for example, typically offered weak responses to Mosher's (1968, p. 18) argument that such "democracy within administration" (participative management) might well violate current political definitions of public purposes. Moreover, Mosher's concern that administrative discretion justified on the basis of professional expertise might undermine the tenets of political democracy was based not simply on abstract arguments about the collision of two distinct conceptions of democracy. The hidden power of the professions in both shaping public values and allocating political resources was already a very real concern for both the traditional and the more activist camps. The most prominent example of this line of argument was Theodore Lowi's (1969) influential critique of "interest group liberalism," in which he argued that powerful interests, including government experts, had steadily and invisibly usurped from Congress the responsibilities for articulating public purposes and translating them into national policy. The consequence of interest-group liberalism, Lowi said, was nothing less than the loss of popular sovereignty, which could be salvaged only if the Congress were to reassert its traditional role as formulator of national policy and shift back to itself the locus of public discourse about it. Lowi's solution, however, amounted to reestablishing the dichotomy between policy and administration, greatly oversimplifying the problem of administrative accountability by ignoring the inevitability of political judgments made in the name of administrative discretion. In granting to Congress the exclusive role of defining public purposes, his critics argued, his proposal would only drive underground, out of public view, the necessary involvement of public servants in the formation of national policy.

Critics of hard-core rationalism also found Herbert Simon's connection between the value/fact dichotomy and the politics/administration dichotomy to be a questionable ground on which to base the accountability of public servants. Simon asserted that the essence of politics lies in the authoritative determination of public values, which are operationalized as policies. Because values are inherently irrational owing to their emotivist origin, however, administrators are therefore expected to conscientiously and efficiently implement policies whose moral basis is inherently irrational to begin with—hardly an inspiring reason for administrators to honor their obligations. And assuming that administrators could muster the energy to do so, it would be at the cost of denying personal responsibility for the content and consequences of their actions.

Rationalism's Dichotomies as the Source of the Paradox

Although rationalists differ over public servants' proper role in the discourse about public purposes, their differences mask an underlying agreement that produces the paradox of accountability. Specifically, rationalists of all stripes regard purposes as preconceived *ends* that are decided upon prior to social processes, which are in turn conceived solely as the *means* for attaining ends. The dichotomy between means and ends is traceable to the rationalists' common commitment to three other dichotomies—between thinking and acting, values and facts, and politics and administration.

These dichotomies not only radically split apart the opposing elements in each pair of ideas, but also subordinate the latter to the former. Action, for example, is seen as either inconceivable or meaningless unless it is preceded by thought-based decisions; facts are seen as relevant only in the context of values that have been previously decided upon; and administration, as an instrumental activity, presupposes the prior determination of the purposes that it is supposed to achieve.

The paradox of accountability is a product of these dichotomies, each of which contains a pair of ideas analogous to Niebuhr's two images of the responsible self: maker and answerer. As we have already seen from the two previous chapters, the paradoxes of obligation and agency are created when making, or moral authorship, is split off from answering. The paradox of accountability is produced in much the same way inasmuch as rationalists believe that accountability can be achieved only if the activities of making and answering are separated from one another. The *making* of public purposes, that is, involves authoritatively deciding prior to and independently of administrative processes, which are construed merely as the means by which others *answer* for the purposes' attainment.

Hard-core rationalists argue that each of these two activities should be performed by a separate category of people, with elected officials performing the role of making purposes and public servants answering to them in their roles as implementors. In being denied the status of makers of public purposes, however, public servants can therefore also deny personal responsibility for the moral consequences of their actions. Soft-core rationalists, on the other hand, grant public servants the status of makers of public purposes, but in the process compromise their answerability (their accountability) to political authority.

The dichotomies that underlie the paradox of accountability not only produce an unresolvable moral dilemma but also lead to empirical misconceptions about the nature of human action itself. In the two sections that follow I shall explain, first, why the rationalists' account of action is flawed owing to the influence of its dichotomous thinking and, second, why, as a consequence, their conception of accountability as the equivalent of bureaucratic control is an empirical impossibility. At the conclusion of these two sections, it will be possible to reframe the paradox of accountability so as to reunite the activities of making and answering in a way that avoids the empirical misconceptions about action that rationalism has spawned.

The Contingency of "Decision"[1]

"Interesting philosophy," Richard Rorty (1989) writes, "is rarely an examination of the pros and cons of a thesis. Usually it is, implicitly or explicitly, a contest between an entrenched vocabulary which has become a nuisance and a half-formed new vocabulary which vaguely promises great things" (p. 9). In the absence of any "hard" conception of truth to settle the competing claims of rival vocabularies, the only honest recourse for philosophers, and, indeed, for the rest of us, is to take an ironic stance by admitting that any position, including our own, "can be made to look good or bad by being redescribed" (p. 73). Whether an entrenched vocabulary is more of a nuisance than a help is ultimately a practical question rather than one of discovering ahistorical truth. Dislodging entrenched vocabularies in the face of nagging practical questions is often difficult, however, owing to both the sheer force of the cognitive habits that prevent us from seeing our own "final vocabularies"[2] as the contingent products of history.

In rationalism's final vocabulary, no idea is more deeply entrenched than that of decision. Initially formalized by Herbert Simon (1947/1976) in *Administrative Behavior,* the decision[3] has become almost universally accepted as a morally neutral and empirically self-evident starting point for organizational analysis. Because it is so familiar in everyday speech, it may at first seem odd even to suggest that *decision* might be a controversial word. As it has assumed a more formal academic meaning, however, there is an important sense in which *rational decision* has become a redundant term. The reasons for this redundancy provide clues about why the contemporary meaning of decision is both empirically problematic and deeply implicated in the paradox of accountability.

The selection of the decision as the primary unit of organizational analysis presupposes a particular set of beliefs about the purposes of and relation between thought and action. Thought occurs first, or so our intuition and experience usually tell us, and its purpose is to decide. Action, then, follows from deciding, and its (action's) purpose is to achieve what has been previously decided. This commonsense summary, in which the decision is depicted as a sort of fulcrum between thought and action, is echoed in the first page of *Administrative Behavior*, where Simon notes that choice (or decision)[4] "prefaces all action," and that "It is with this problem—the process of choice which leads to action—that the present study is concerned" (p. 1). In the following paragraph, he affirms the rationalist faith in the possibility of truth by saying that "a general theory of administration must include principles of organization that will insure correct decision-making, just as it must include principles that will ensure effective action" (p. 1).

The search for these principles, and indeed the assumption that they are out there awaiting discovery, underwrites what has become, in the decades since the publication of *Administrative Behavior*, the overall project of mainstream decision-making and policy-making theory. Setting the stage for his own critique of the theoretical mainstream, James G. March, one of Simon's early coauthors (March & Simon, 1958), summarizes its chief tenets:

> Human beings make choices. If done properly, choices are made by evaluating alternatives in terms of goals on the basis of information currently available. The alternative that is most attractive in terms of the goals is chosen. The process of making choices can be improved by using the technology of choice. Through the paraphernalia of modern techniques, we can improve the quality of the search for alternatives, the quality of information, and the quality of the analysis used to evaluate alternatives. Although actual choice may fall short of this ideal in various ways, it is an attractive model of how choices should be made by individuals, organizations, and social systems. (March, 1976, p. 69)

March then lists three assumptions underlying the mainstream view:

1. The preexistence of purpose
2. The necessity of consistency, which he describes as "a cultural and theoretical virtue"
3. The primacy of rationality, "a procedure for deciding what is correct behavior by relating consequences [of action] systematically to objectives" (pp. 69-70)

In most of the mainstream literature, it is the third assumption—the "systematic" quality by which consequences and objectives are related—that defines decisions as rational. There is a more elementary sense, however, in which the idea of decision—with or without being preceded by adjectives such as *systematic, effective,* or *efficient*—qualifies as rational: namely, as a consciously calculative mental act of individuals. Although the decision is often soft-pedaled as merely a methodological starting point, the belief that the decision conceptually separates and then links thought and action instrumentalizes action by depicting it as a means for attaining preexistent ends or purposes. It is the idea of preexistent purpose, the first assumption that March cites, rather than the systematic quality of the means by which action is related to them, that defines decision as rational in this more basic sense.

My intention here is to challenge rationalism's virtually automatic acceptance of decision analysis by arguing for a radical revision of the sequence of thought/decision/action that it presupposes. In support of this idea, March claims that it may be more sensible to "treat action as a way of creating interesting goals" (p. 75) than as a means for attaining goals that have already been decided upon. Contrary to the rationalist tenet that "goal development and choice are independent behaviorally," he says:

> It seems to me perfectly obvious that a description that assumes [that] goals come first and action comes later is frequently radically wrong. Human choice behavior is at least as much a process for discovering goals as acting upon them. Although it is true enough that goals and decisions are "conceptually" distinct, that is simply a statement of the [rationalists'] theory. It is not a defense of it. (p. 72)

In view of this description of the relation between goals and action, the question arises as to what sort of alternative to the rational model of organizing might follow from it. March's colleague and frequent coauthor, Johan Olsen (1976), describes organization as

> a collection of choices looking for problems; issues and feelings looking for decisions-in-process through which they can be mediated; . . . solutions looking for questions; . . . [and] a set of procedures by which participants arrive at an interpretation of what they (and others) are doing, and who they are. (p. 84)[5]

His label for this description of organization is the "artifactual (or non-decision) model," in which unconscious and "quasi-mechanical" aspects of behavior lead to organizational outcomes that are often unintended consequences of social processes, having a dynamic independent of the consciously held purposes of the participants.

> "Decision" in these models is a *post factum* construct produced by participants or onlookers. Events happen, and if they are afterwards described in a systematic fashion as decisions, it expresses more man's ability to form *post factum* theories of his own behavior than his ability to make goal oriented decisions through established structures and processes. (p. 83)[6]

If, as Olsen and March suggest, thought and action are mutually constitutive elements of organizational processes, we are left with a quite different understanding of what a decision is, as well as an altered understanding of its importance in organizational analysis. Rather than seeing decisions as the central aspects of organizational life around which all other considerations revolve, we would instead regard them as temporary and artificial stoppages of social processes. Although the language of decision analysis may sometimes prove practical, decisions are chiefly *post factum* objectifications of fluid and unpredictable processes. Put another way, decision is an *idea* by means of which we make some sense of the flow of our actions in order to "freeze" them and hold them up for inspection, often discovering in retrospect what we intended to do.

This alternative to decision-based analysis suggests a redescription of the chief issues involved in achieving administrative accountability and controlling administrative discretion. Rationalists believe that accountability may be achieved by applying tests of effectiveness and efficiency to link value commitments (policy objectives) with factual knowledge (expertise) relevant to their attainment. Problems of accountability, then, stem either from disagreements and misinterpretations concerning values that the policy is intended to realize, from lack of expertise needed for achieving them, or from negligence of duty and outright disobedience. Accordingly, solutions to such problems consist in either authoritatively resolving those disagreements (for example, by clarifying legislative intent), developing more reliable technical knowledge, or enforcing stricter controls on the performance of official duties. Discretion involves judgments about the application of technical knowledge in exceptional cases not covered by the standardized rules of implementation. Finally, acceptable discretionary actions are those judged to be consistent with the policy's objectives.

How, then, does this critique of the decision suggest altering the rationalist view of accountability and discretion? First, if the relation between ends and means is as fluid as March and Olsen suggest, then the relation between the values informing the selection of ends and the facts bearing on the selection of the means to attain them must be conceded to be fluid as well. Although we are accustomed to thinking of values as relevant to ends and facts as relevant to means, the preceding analysis suggests that moral justification and empirical description are fused with one another. In support of this notion, Harold Garfinkel (1967) has claimed, for example, that our moral investment in our factual understanding of situations is even stronger than our moral investment in our values. We not only *justify* our actions on moral grounds but also *describe* them in ways to which we are deeply, though unconsciously, morally committed. Our commitment is not primarily to values as somehow dissociated from neutral facts, but instead to what we regard as normal in terms of our own factual knowledge of situations and our belief that others share that same knowledge. Conflict, which rationalists typically interpret as resulting from disagreements over ends or values, is more likely, from Garfinkel's view, mainly to involve contested versions of the factual circumstances of the situation, of "what is going on here."

Rationalists are thus likely to misinterpret "irresponsible" conduct as evidence of disagreement about, lack of commitment to, or ignorance of the values embodied by a policy or rule. In other words, the problem will be seen as one either of deciding about "what we ought to do" or of making sure that someone else acts as he or she ought to. If, however, as Garfinkel suggests, cognition itself is a moral act, irresponsible conduct is more likely to involve contested or ambiguous factual accounts in which people are nevertheless morally invested. Clarifying values and ends or threatening the use of sanctions in order to control behavior, therefore, will probably be of less help than negotiating contested descriptions of situations in which participants have deeply held and conflicting commitments.

Within this altered view of accountability, effectiveness is transformed from an instrumental criterion for determining whether a particular means has achieved a predefined end to an assessment of the appropriateness of action in situations that are both morally and factually ambiguous. The meaning of policy itself also changes from a literal statement of "ends to be achieved" (and values realized) to a symbolic statement of purpose that authoritatively enables and constrains action. As symbolic statements, policies should be taken seriously but should not, and strictly speaking cannot, be taken literally. This redescription of action also affects how administrative discretion is viewed. Rationalists maintain that discretion involves a straightforward normative question of how much latitude public servants *should* be permitted in implementing policy. From what I have argued here, however, discretion is subsidiary to public servants' ongoing and unavoidable interpretation of policies in applying them to particular cases.

The fuller implications of this critique for reframing the paradox of accountability will become evident later when I consider Alasdair MacIntyre's discussion of social practices. As we have seen here, the rationalist view of decision, by radically separating the activities of making and answering, is the source of the moral dilemma embodied in the paradox. MacIntyre's notion of practices, in which goods or ends are conceived as internal to and continually transformed by the cooperative activity, provides an avenue for reuniting making and answering, enabling a revised conception of accountability that avoids the rationalist dilemma. Before proceeding to that discussion, however, I shall consider MacIntyre's arguments concerning why, as a practical matter, the rationalist project of achieving accountability by means of bureaucratic control is itself an impossibility.

The Masquerade of Effectiveness and Control

In common usage, responsibility refers to the human struggle to reconcile moral agency with accountability. Agency denotes consciousness of freedom's often unpredictable exercise, whereas accountability refers to our answerability to others. Accountability's more contemporary organizational meaning, however, has been expanded to include not only public servants' answerability for their *own* deeds and misdeeds, but also their responsibility for ensuring the accountability of others. In their roles as managers, that is, public servants are responsible for implementing policies or achieving organizational objectives on the presumption that they will be able to control the actions of their subordinates. This used to mean that managers could achieve such control by promising rewards or threatening punishments in order to exact subordinates' compliance. But as management theory and practice have more recently aspired to scientific status, and as the complexities of organizational life have revealed rewards and punishments as overly simplistic means for control, managers' claim to legitimate authority has shifted. The moral and legal language of duty and obligation has been supplemented, even largely replaced, by the technical language of organizational effectiveness. The responsible manager is now the *effective* manager—someone who is accountable for his or her subordinates by virtue of possessing technical expertise enabling manipulative control over them.

Alasdair MacIntyre has lodged two compelling objections against the idea of managerial effectiveness, the first on moral grounds and the second having to do with whether, as an empirical matter, effectiveness of the kind envisioned by the rationalists is even possible. Regarding the first of these objections, MacIntyre disputes the public servant's claim to moral neutrality as an effective implementor of the public will. The belief that effectiveness and, by extension, efficiency are morally neutral is itself based on the doubtful belief that "means" may be evaluated separately from the ends they are intended to produce. MacIntyre says, for example, that we are

> unaccustomed to think of effectiveness as a distinctively *moral* concept, to be classed with such concepts as those of rights or utility. Managers themselves and most writers about management conceive of themselves as morally neutral characters whose skills enable them to derive the most efficient means of achieving whatever end is proposed. Whether a given manager is effective or not is on the dominant view a quite different question from that of the morality of the ends which his effectiveness serves or fails to serve. Nonetheless there are strong grounds for rejecting the claim that effectiveness is a morally neutral value. For the whole concept of effectiveness is . . . inseparable from a mode of human existence in which the contrivance of means is in central part the manipulation of human beings into compliant patterns of behavior; and it is by appeal to his own effectiveness in this respect that the manager claims authority within the manipulative mode. (p. 74)[7]

Suppose, however, that we set aside MacIntyre's qualms that the idea of effectiveness is morally pernicious and focus instead on his argument that bureaucratic control via effective management is impossible to begin with. The justification of managerial authority based on expertise enabling manipulative control, he states, is nothing more than a moral fiction derived from the claim—mirroring a similar claim made by the natural sciences—that the manipulation of subordinates' behavior is enabled by the manager's knowledge of predictive, law-like generalizations concerning it. If the conditions required for law-like explanation could be met, then in theory it would be possible for managers to predict with some precision the consequences of acting from a knowledge of those laws, thereby allowing them to control subordinates' behavior—by, literally, *making* them accountable—and thereby ensure organizational effectiveness. If, however, there are compelling logical rather than simply methodological reasons for doubting the possibility of such predictive power, then the manager's claim to expert authority as a means to achieve accountability through effective performance collapses.

Drawing on Machiavelli's notion of *Fortuna*—the idea that no matter how good our generalizations, we may one day be confronted by unpredicted and unpredictable counterexamples—MacIntyre describes several reasons why human behavior is systematically unpredictable and why *Fortuna* is thus an inherent feature of social life. Two of those reasons are considered here, the first being what MacIntyre calls "the indefinite reflexivity of game-theoretic situations" (p. 97). To the extent that organizational relations are characterized, as they often are, by transactions among people with differing stakes in the outcomes but bound by common rules, each person will calculate his or her actions at least partly on a prediction of what the other will do. The other's actions will also be based not only on similar sorts of predictions, but also on predictions of the other's predictions, ad infinitum. Anyone having a passing acquaintance with stud poker can readily appreciate that

> at each stage each of us will simultaneously be trying to render himself or herself unpredictable by the other; and each of us will also be relying on the knowledge that the other will be trying to make himself or herself unpredictable in forming his or her own predictions. (p. 97)[8]

Unpredictability will be further increased by the absence of perfect knowledge, because each participant has an interest in maximizing the imperfection of the other's knowledge. More important, however, unpredictability is guaranteed because in complex organizations *several* games are being played at the same time, the rules and even the existence of which may be only dimly perceived by the participants. Thus, "not one game is being played, but several, and, if the game metaphor may be stretched further, the problem about real life is that moving one's knight to QB3 may always be replied to with a lob across the net" (p. 98).

The second and perhaps more important barrier to predictability, MacIntyre says, is pure contingency. Trivial accidents or omissions ("For want of a nail the shoe was lost . . . ") and the improbable connections between seemingly remote events[9] defy explanation in terms of law-like generalizations. The standard view of the scientific method on which the modern notion of effectiveness is based has long been uneasy with historical contingencies, whose unique occurrences cannot be reduced to law-like explanation. The idea of contingency underlies, for example, the recent emergence of so-called chaos theory (Gleick, 1987), as well as natural scientist Stephen Jay Gould's (1989) reinterpretation of "the 'pageant' of evolution as a staggeringly improbable series of events, sensible enough in retrospect and subject to rigorous explanation, but utterly unpredictable and quite unrepeatable" (p. 14). And in the contemporary literature of organizational theory, Herbert Kaufman (1991) has concluded upon reviewing the research on organizational change and effectiveness that the survival or demise of organizations is chiefly a matter of luck.

Because omnipresent *Fortuna* guarantees that unpredictable counterexamples will foil any effort to derive law-like generalizations, "we should not be surprised or disappointed that the generalizations and maxims of the best social science share certain characteristics of their predecessors—proverbs of folk societies, the generalizations of jurists, the maxims of Machiavelli" (MacIntyre, 1984, p. 105). This would seem to dilute considerably the force of Simon's criticism of the "Principles of Administration," propounded in the 1930s by Gulick and Urwick (1937), as constituting nothing more than proverbs.[10] I shall not be concerned here with whether Gulick and Urwick's "principles" are *wise* proverbs, but would only note that if MacIntyre is right, then the products of the more rigorously scientific methods of analysis that Simon advocates in their stead will surely be just as susceptible to the same kinds of counterexamples that he deplores in Gulick and Urwick's proverbs.

The final irony is that even if managers were able to eliminate or limit these sources of unpredictability within their organizations, such actions would be incompatible with dealing sensibly in the face of the unpredictable environments they are committed to changing. This is because organizational success (that is, effectiveness in a broader sense of the word) requires continuous innovation, adjustment, and problem- and goal-redefinition that are directly at odds with controlling and making predictable subordinates' behavior in order to achieve predefined goals (Vaill, 1989). Thus,

> Attempts to monitor what every subordinate is doing all the time tend to be counter-productive; attempts to make the activity of others predictable necessarily routinize, suppress intelligence and flexibility and turn the energies of subordinates to frustrating the projects of at least some of their superiors. (MacIntyre, 1984, p. 106)

Being otherwise sensible people, rationalists such as Simon have been alert to the perils of pursuing the rationality project too far or too narrowly. What has not been duly appreciated, however, is that, in conceding its limitations, both the rationalist claim to legitimate authority based on the predictive power of social science and the wisdom of trying to achieve accountability by means of that power are fatally compromised. Accountability under these circumstances loses most of its practical and moral relevance, becoming instead a fetish, something demanded both of managers and their subordinates in the absence of stable knowledge of what they ought to be accountable *for*. From this analysis it follows that:

> The notion of social control embodied in the notion of expertise is indeed a masquerade. Our social order is in a very literal sense out of our, and indeed anyone's, control. No one is or could be in charge. . . . The realm of managerial expertise is one in which what purport to be objectively-grounded claims function in fact as expressions of arbitrary, but disguised, will and preference. (MacIntyre, 1984, p. 107)

In sustaining the illusion of control and therefore of accountability, managers are called upon to enact a skillful dramatic imitation of it, leading MacIntyre to conclude that "It is histrionic success which gives power and authority in our culture. The most effective bureaucrat is the best actor" (p. 107).

Reframing the Paradox of Accountability

It will be recalled that the paradox of accountability holds that:

If public servants are accountable solely for the effective achievement of purposes mandated by political authority, then as mere instruments of that authority they bear no personal responsibility as moral agents for the products of their actions. If, on the other hand, public servants actively participate in determining public purposes, their accountability is compromised and political authority is undermined.

The paradox of accountability is stated in the vocabulary of moral discourse typically used by philosophers and public administration academics who have written on the subject. The preceding analysis, however, has been devoted as much to exposing the factual impossibility of achieving the kind of accountability that rationalists hope for as to criticizing their moral beliefs about it. They might object, therefore, that I have blurred a crucial distinction between empirical and normative analysis, and at the very least, reproach me for not having been careful enough in separating these two lines of argument. The distinction between the empirical and the normative, however, derives from the dichotomies—between value and fact, ends and means, and thought and action—that create the paradox of accountability in the first place. Although it is often true that these opposing pairs of terms may illuminate fruitful *distinctions*, it is the rationalists' insistence upon treating them as *dichotomies* embodying irreconcilable oppositions that gets them into trouble. Not all distinctions should be construed as dichotomies.

Figure 7.1 summarizes the consequences of rationalism's splitting apart the activities of making and answering, thus creating the paradox of accountability. The pathologies produced by that splitting—the atrophy of personal responsibility and political authority—are not only predictable but also incapable of being mitigated by the assertion of a countervailing or opposing principle. The reframed conception of the paradox that follows acknowledges the tensions

Principles

Political Responsibility ◄— split off from —► **Professional Responsibility**
(Hard-Core Rationalism):   **(Soft-Core Rationalism):**

By virtue of their nonelected status, public servants, as *answerers*, are accountable for the effective implementation of purposes mandated by legitimate political authority; implementation is achieved by means of technical expertise and professional knowledge that is morally neutral about purposes	By virtue of their professional expertise, experience, and standards of ethical conduct, public servants, as *makers*, play a legitimate role, not only in achieving public purposes, but also in formulating them

Atrophy of	**Atrophy of**
Personal Responsibility:	**Political Authority:**
In being *denied* status as makers of public purposes, public servants can therefore also deny personal responsibility for the consequences of their actions; if public servants are accountable only for the achievement of purposes defined by others, the moral consequences of their manipulative control through "effective" management are lost to consciousness	In being *granted* status as makers of public purposes, public servants, as professionals, become answerable only to themselves, thus undermining political authority and public accountability; "professional responsibility" becomes a euphemism for the covert manipulation of the political processes by which public purposes are determined

Pathologies

Figure 7.1. The Rationalist Paradox of Accountability

between making and answering; but by conceiving of accountability as an ongoing dialogue of the sort described by Niebuhr (and
discussed in Chapter 3), answering for action is inseparable from
the social production of the purposes served by it. The unification
of making and answering depicted in Figure 7.2 is implied by
the similar unity between thought and action suggested earlier
in the critique of rational decision. In order for such an alternative conception of accountability to be plausible, however, we
need a clearer understanding of how the creation of purposes is
affected by the internal dynamics of social processes.

Principles

Political Responsibility (Facilitating Practices):	← the reciprocal of →	Professional Responsibility (Participating in Practices):
Enabled by knowledge made available by politics, public servants as *answerers* are accountable to citizens by providing resources to aid them in creating social practices that are fitting for the unique life projects; as facilitators of those practices, public servants are personally responsible to citizens directly, viewing policy goals and objectives chiefly as legitimate constraints		Within constraints imposed by political authority, public servants as *makers* are held accountable for their actions through a continuing dialogue with citizens, colleagues, and elected officials; because goods are internal to the practices that they themselves create, public servants are personally responsible for the products of their actions

Atrophy of Professional Responsibility:	Atrophy of Public (External) Accountability:
Facilitating citizen practices may degenerate into a paternalistic or inappropriately personalized posture toward them, or violate legitimate political and other external constraints; chief remedies consist in the assertion of professional detachment, knowledge, and experience	Professional practices may produce internal goods satisfying only at the level of the organization; chief remedies consist in expanding dialogue beyond organizational boundaries to take fuller account of political knowledge and practices of citizens

Pathologies

Figure 7.2. Reframing the Paradox of Accountability

MacIntyre and Practices. To be a public servant, it is commonly said, is to be a practitioner of the science (or art, depending on one's point of view) of managing in government organizations. According to the rationalist version of what practitioners do, *practice* denotes the essentially technical activity of applying morally neutral expertise as the means for achieving authoritative ends. But what if practice were construed so that means and ends are inseparable in both a factual and a moral sense? And what would be the implications for the problem of accountability deriving from such an alternative view? Drawing upon Aristotle as his

chief source of inspiration, MacIntyre sets out to answer the first
of these questions in his discussion of practice as a formal concept.
Practice, he says, refers to

> any coherent and complex form of socially established cooperative
> human activity through which goods internal to that form of activ-
> ity are realized in the course of trying to achieve those standards of
> excellence which are appropriate to, and partially definitive of, that
> form of activity, with the result that human powers to achieve
> excellence, and human conceptions of the ends and goods in-
> volved, are systematically extended. (p. 187)[11]

Some of the key terms in this definition quite obviously require
explication, not just to make it intelligible to readers untutored in
philosophy but also to illustrate the differences between MacIntyre's
and the rationalists' conceptions of practice. To begin with, as a
"coherent and complex" activity, a practice involves more than
simply doing something; in addition, the activity must be undertaken within a form or structure that has developed over time. And
because it is a *cooperative* activity, a practice is not just the exercise
of a skill or the application of knowledge in isolation. "Throwing
a football with skill," for example, is not a practice, "but the game
of football is" (p. 187).

So far there is little in this description of a practice with which
rationalists are likely to disagree. Important differences appear,
however, when we examine MacIntyre's stipulation that practices
involve a form of activity in which "the goods internal to" the
activity itself "are realized in the course of trying to achieve those
standards of excellence which are appropriate to . . . that form of
activity." An *internal good*, in this context, has a dual meaning,
referring simultaneously to both the enjoyment of the activity itself
and the enjoyment of having performed the activity successfully.
Thus it seems reasonable to interpret the notion of an internal good
as falling roughly in between coach Vince Lombardi's callous
claim that "Winning isn't everything, it's the *only* thing" and the
fatuous aphorism that "It's not whether you win or lose, but how
you play the game."

From the standpoint of the game metaphor, trying one's best to
win is inseparable from conforming to the rules and standards

defining what excellent practices are. At the same time, however, the *end* of winning cannot be "the only thing" if it is pursued independently of an enjoyment of the excellence of the *means* by which winning is sought. The desire to win, that is, must be "internal to" the standards of excellence that define what winning entails. A young child who tries to win at chess—by cheating or even by playing well—solely in order to receive a reward of candy, for example, is not engaged in the *practice* of playing chess. To qualify as a practice, playing chess requires that the child try "to excel in whatever way the game of chess demands" (MacIntyre, 1984, p. 188), provided that he or she accepts the authority of standards and judgments of others who are similarly engaged in that same practice.

MacIntyre's linkage of practices with internal goods thus undermines two core rationalist beliefs about the relation between ends and means, and, by extension, of values and facts. First, he contends that a means, including the factual knowledge relevant to its exercise, has an inescapably moral component because it would not exist except for the presence of ends or values in whose service it is employed. Second, and conversely, ends served by practices are transformed by the practices themselves. And because practice is necessarily a social activity, the ends in whose service a particular practice is engaged in are themselves social products, which therefore can be judged only in terms of the social context within which they are produced. Notice how this view of the relation of ends to means avoids the modernist dilemma, discussed in Chapter 3, of having to decide about ends on either of two mutually unsatisfactory grounds: emotivism or abstract principle. On each of these grounds, decisions about ends are presumed to be made by isolated individuals choosing independently of others, thus reducing subsequent relations with them to the instrumental status of means.

In view of the interpenetration of ends and means in MacIntyre's account of practices, the idea that ends, or definitions of the good, are chiefly the products of conscious *decisions* appears dubious for reasons very much like those discussed earlier in this chapter. His conception of a practice also suggests that *processes* should not be construed as a synonym for *means*. Strictly speaking, the latter word has an instrumental connotation that presumes a logical separation between deciding and doing that does not square with MacIntyre's view of how practices are engaged in. When social processes are construed simply as means, the former are misunderstood as *procedures* that are temporally separated from decisions about the good and are thus stripped of their moral content. The vocabulary of "means and ends," it would appear, is therefore ill-suited for comprehending the moral (as opposed to the merely instrumental) nature of practices, suggesting that *the good* (or *goods*) and *process* would be a more felicitous pairing of terms.

If the moral nature of practice were not already clear enough, consider MacIntyre's (1984) definition of *virtue* as an intrinsic feature of it. "*A virtue,*" he says, "*is an acquired human quality the possession and exercise of which tends to enable us to achieve those goods which are internal to practices and the lack of which effectively prevents us from achieving any such good*" (p. 191). To be virtuous, then, is to subordinate ourselves to the social processes, that is, to relationships with others, within which practices are undertaken. In those relationships

> we have to listen carefully to what we are told about our own inadequacies and to reply with the same carefulness for the facts. In other words we have to accept as necessary components of any practice with internal goods and standards of excellence the virtues of justice, courage and honesty. For not to accept these . . . so far bars us from achieving the standards of excellence or the goods internal to the practice that it renders the practice pointless except as a device for achieving external goods. (p. 191)

The means-ends vocabulary of rationalism, however, necessarily regards *all* goods (as ends) as external; the very idea of an internal good is incomprehensible within such a vocabulary. As external goods, ends are purely emotivist in their origin from the rationalists' standpoint. By extension, actions taken to achieve ends must be accounted for strictly in terms of them, largely for fear that the same emotivist and therefore selfish impulses that rationalism assumes produce such ends would subsequently influence the actions of those who are charged with achieving them. However, if ends—which is to say, internal goods—are continually

transformed by practices, then the rationalist view of accountability ironically prevents practices from occurring for at least two
reasons. First, by imposing an artificial stability on definitions of
the good, efforts to control by means of accountability sanctions
dampen, if they do not prohibit altogether, the continuing transformation of the good that practices, in MacIntyre's sense of the
word, would otherwise enable. That is, accountability as rationalists conceive of it impedes organizational flexibility by disassoci-
ating learning and feedback from the processes through which the
good is simultaneously defined, redefined, and achieved (Schön,
1983). Second, by separating the moral evaluation of the good from
those processes, virtue is relegated to a synonym for passive
compliance in the achievement of external goods rather than
construed as a necessary ingredient of practice itself.[12]

Accountability as Dialogue. Chapter 6 concluded with H. Richard
Niebuhr's definition of accountability as a pattern of mutual interpretation and response producing action *fitting* the situation at
hand, rather than corresponding to an abstract criterion of the good
or a concrete and stable end. There is an obvious affinity between
Niebuhr's view of accountability and MacIntyre's account of practices in that each regards cooperative action as continually altering
ends. Although rationalists might concede some limited merit to
such a view, they could find it tolerable only if it does not violate
requirements of bureaucratic and legal accountability. Practices
and internal goods, that is, may be appropriate at the *micro*level of
day-to-day administration, but they have little or no bearing on the
authoritative relation of politics to administration. It is in the
former arena, according to the rationalists, where public purposes
are supposed to be defined in democratic governments; and in
view of the authoritative relation between the two arenas, public
policies *must* be conceived as means for achieving external rather
than internal goods.

Extending MacIntyre's idea of practice beyond the internal
processes of administration, therefore, requires an altered view of
the relation between politics and administration that, while preserving a functional distinction between them, does not at the
same time depend upon the conceptual dichotomies that have

created the paradox of accountability. Consistent with this objective, Orion White (1976) has argued that politics and administration may be seen as functioning according to two fundamentally different sets of principles. Politics, operating at a macro level, involves judgments about the "authoritative allocation of values"—enacted in the form of policies and programs—on the assumption that there is "an objectively discernible *problem that must be solved*" (p. 65). Typically, the benefits ultimately to be achieved are defined in terms of economic variables and measured by methods such as cost-benefit analysis, which means that those benefits are conceived as external rather than internal goods.

Although the role of administration implied by this conception of politics would appear to be a purely technical one, White notes that administration, as well as the mode of analysis most appropriate for it, is more fruitfully and realistically conceived quite differently. Administration, he says, should be seen as proceeding "from the idea of *opportunity to be realized*" in which the emphasis is "on *emergent action*—action that arises from a process of acting *first*, then assessing (learning), then acting, then assessing, and so on" (p. 65). The emergent character of administration, which demands flexibility and continuous innovation in implementation, often collides with the authoritative and often inflexible judgments embodied in policies. To reconcile their competing requirements a changed conception of politics is needed in addition to a changed conception of administration.

Under the current functional division of politics and administration, White says, the social role of the former is typically denigrated by adherents to macroanalysis, who reduce "political processes to a form of institutional economics" and exhibit "a condescending liberalism implicit in the view that politics amounts to government by administrative regulation" (p. 67). By limiting its own role to distributing external goods and regulating citizens' activities, politics thus precludes, in MacIntyre's sense, the possibility of practice and the creation of internal goods. As a result, administration, which could otherwise be a vital arena of practice, is reduced to a merely technical activity in which "professional responsibility is substituted for the idea of personal responsibility as the core concept of social relationships" (p. 68).

White proposes an alternative conception of politics having three principal functions:

1. Warnings and other statements that define the risks and opportunities that face the citizen in his or her everyday life
2. Actions of positive law that either create clearcut or nondiscretionary prohibitions on the behavior of the citizen . . . or create opportunities that are otherwise not available to the citizen
3. Programs that aid the citizen who wishes to find aid in making life readjustments that would not otherwise be possible—that is, for those who seek help in choosing a different set of risks and opportunities (p. 69)

How, then, would such a conception of politics foster practices in which goods are internal to cooperative activity? And how, in view of the answer to this question, can the paradox of accountability be reframed? Regarding the first of these questions, the three functions of politics may together be interpreted as providing the conditions within which practices and the creation of internal goods are appropriately enabled and constrained. Constraint, which should be distinguished from the rationalist notion of positive control through sanctions and subtler manipulative means, is evident in White's second function of politics, which acknowledges the legitimate role of politics in placing limits upon the kinds of social practices that the polity is willing to tolerate. Politics in this sense serves a valuable *negative* function of "thrashing out what people can agree ought not to be done" (Biller, 1973, p. 37). Beyond the establishment of legitimate constraints, however, the remaining functions of politics would chiefly provide enabling conditions for practices. Because one of the most important of these conditions is knowledge, politics—or "public science," as White terms it—is

an essentially symbolic process of the utmost importance to the maintenance of the social order. For as public science politics is the process through which the *risks and opportunities* of the everyday life of the citizen are defined and presented to him as the basis for the choices out of which he must make the meaning of his daily existence. (p. 68)

Public programs, by implication, would be conceived as providing the resources not otherwise available to the citizen "to aid
in making life readjustments," augmented by a clearer knowledge
of the "risks and opportunities" entailed in making them. By
emphasizing the creation of knowledge (which must always be
regarded as tentative or provisional in any event) over definitive
judgments expressed in the form of goals and objectives, we would
expect that public policies and programs would be based on
expectations that are at the same time both humbler and more
respectful of the unique and varied practices they are intended to
enable. As Robert Biller (1979) has noted in this regard,

> Recognizing that policies on complex aggregated information are
> always "wrong" with respect to the preferences of every person to
> whom they are applied, . . . you would expect that we would con-
> centrate on *limiting* the force of such policies to the specification
> of minima or "floors" made necessary by our joint understanding.
> (p. 154)

If Biller is right we should not be surprised by the irony that the
greater the "effectiveness" with which policy objectives are achieved
in a collective sense, the less appropriate they will be for enabling
particular practices.

This reformulation of the relation of politics and administration
does not entail as much a formal or structural alteration of government as a changed understanding of what is appropriate and
possible within it. Moreover, it is flexible enough to accommodate
two different conceptions of accountability relevant to public
servants. In discussing these, however, it is important to bear in
mind their differences in order to grasp their proper relation to one
another. First, in its role of creating "clearcut and nondiscretionary
prohibitions on the behavior of citizens," politics establishes the
authoritative constraints that public servants, in *their* roles as
enablers of citizens' practices, are legally bound not to violate.
Public servants are thus accountable to political authority in the
sense of being legitimately constrained by it. Viewing politics in
terms of this negative function, we would expect to hear less public
posturing by both politicians and citizens about "holding bureaucrats accountable" for the effective achievement of policy goals.

For reasons discussed earlier in this chapter, the idea of bureaucratic control implied by this notion of accountability is largely illusory and, as the two previous chapters have argued, generates predictable pathologies often far worse than the cure it promises. Thus, demands for clearer goals and stricter penalties for failing to achieve them would no longer be the automatic solutions of choice whenever problems of administration are experienced; instead, problems would be more accurately viewed as symptoms of frustration that beg a more ingenious definition of the problem.

The first kind of accountability, that of legal and political constraint, partially sets the context within which the second operates. The second kind of accountability builds upon the redescription of the relation of thought and action suggested earlier in my critique of rational decision. It also closely resembles Niebuhr's definition of accountability as a dialogue involving the mutual interpretation of people's actions in the process of cooperatively discovering what sorts of practices are worth engaging in. Within this conception of accountability, the role of the public servant is to be alert to the legal and political constraints on those practices; to make available relevant political knowledge to those engaged in practices; and, perhaps most important of all, to facilitate practice itself. That role, which is both authoritative and enabling, pertains to public servants' relations with citizens who wish or require aid in redefining their life projects as well as to relations with colleagues in creating and sustaining worthwhile organizational practices.

As Figure 7.2 illustrates, the reframing of the paradox is accomplished by viewing the relation between its opposing elements as reciprocal and mutually reinforcing rather than as dichotomous and contradictory. First, and most obviously, the relation of ends and means—or more precisely the substitution of these terms with *goods* and *processes*—is changed in order to emphasize that the moral nature of the former derives "internally" from the quality of social relationships in the latter. Insofar as goods are internal to social process, public servants cannot be accountable for their realization without at the same time being personally responsible both *for* their content and *to* others with whom they are engaged in creating them. Second, the rationalists' separation of thought (and judgment) from action is replaced by an appreciation of the emergent character of social action in which accountability is evident in the public servant's commitment and even submission to the social processes that are constitutive of practices.

Third, although a functional distinction is maintained between politics and administration that honors the legitimate authoritative role of politics, the possibilities for cooperation between these two spheres are enhanced by a revised understanding of their principal functions. If, in addition to its authoritative role in defining social constraints, politics were conceived as the public process for generating knowledge enabling citizens to assess the risks and opportunities confronting them, then it would likely seem far less controlling. Such a role is possible, however, insofar as politics— and the kinds of macro policy analysis that inform it—drop their official pretensions to truth and conclusive judgment.

> By *not claiming* that the products of macro analysis are the basis for *judgments*, these products can become more useful as a basis for action in the public policy process, for . . . [they] would no longer be seen as threats, but rather as information. (White, 1976, p. 70)

And, for *their* part, public servants, as intimately engaged in practices with both citizens and one another (as well as through continuing dialogue with political actors), would be less susceptible to charges of technocratic despotism—the tyranny of the clerks—that hard-core rationalists such as Herman Finer have rightly feared.

The preceding discussion should not be interpreted as an attempt to eliminate the paradox of accountability, but instead should be reframed so that each of its opposing principles might countervail the pathologies to which the other is prone. As Figure 7.2 shows, the atrophy of professional responsibility and public accountability in the reframed paradox may result from practices of the kind that MacIntyre describes. Such practices, that is, are no less immune to pathologies than other forms of social activity. In the reframed paradox, however, those pathologies may be manageable if accountability is construed chiefly as a process of dialogue rather than as passive compliance in the face of anticipated reward or punishment. The atrophy of professional responsibility, as reflected, for example, in a paternalistic or inappropriately personalized posture toward citizens, may be mitigated by public servants' accountability, in the form of ongoing dialogue, to (and with) fellow professionals and elected officials. And the atrophy of public accountability, evident in the professional isolation and perceived arrogance that may accompany the exercise of expert judgment, may be countervailed by expanding dialogue beyond organizational boundaries to take fuller account of political knowledge and citizens practices.

Conclusion

Whatever originality the argument of this chapter may claim should be tempered by acknowledging that others have anticipated its key elements. The chapter began by explaining how the rationalist conception of accountability derived from a particular set of beliefs about how public purposes are and ought to be determined, namely, as preconceived ends decided on the basis of either selfish interest or abstract moral principle. The alternative view presented here was initially stimulated by an insight, now more than a half century old, of Mary Parker Follett (1924), who argued that preconceived purposes neither do nor can provide an acceptable foundation for accountability. In distinguishing between "preconceived and actual purpose," Follett said that by assuming the existence of the former we make two serious errors:

> We try to substitute an intellectualistic purpose for that involved in the situation, or, when the purpose appears from out of activity, we think, by some strange mental legerdemain, that that was the purpose which had been actuating us all along. (p. 82)

Instead, she held,

> Activity always does more than embody purpose, it evolves it. With the general acceptance of this fact, part of our legal and political science will have to be rewritten. All history which jumps from one dramatic moment to another falsifies the situation; history must [instead] be viewed as continuously evolving relation. (p. 83)

Decisions about purposes are much like dramatic moments of history; they *appear* to be important and real because the moral and methodological commitments of rationalism sustain such an illusion. If, however, purposes are understood as emerging from social relationships, then the accountability of action would be determined not mainly through reference to preconceived purposes, but in terms of the relational contexts within which purposes emerge. In conceiving of purposes this way, Follett implicitly understood the paradox of accountability, as well as the wisdom of Niebuhr's plea for unifying the final and most basic opposition that rationalism splits apart, namely, the dual images—maker and answerer—of the responsible self.

Notes

1. In slightly revised form this section was published in Harmon, 1989a.
2. Rorty (1989) defines a "final vocabulary" as the

> set of words which [people] employ to justify their actions, their beliefs, and their lives. These are the words in which we formulate praise of our friends and contempt for our enemies, our long-term projects, our deepest self-doubts and our highest hopes. . . .
>
> It is "final" in the sense that if doubt is cast on the worth of these words, their user has no noncircular argumentative recourse. (p. 73)

3. More technically, in Simon's treatment the decision *premise* is the primary unit of analysis, although this qualification does not seriously affect the force of the critique of the decision that appears in the following pages.
4. Simon (1976) uses *choice* and *decision* interchangeably (p. 4).
5. This model originally appeared in Cohen, March, and Olsen, 1972.
6. Olsen (1976) says that, in addition to reflecting the particular interests of the researcher, the choice of an appropriate model should be determined by the empirical "nature of the organizational situation" (p. 83). Nondecision (artifactual) models are best suited to those cases characterized by ambiguity, complexity, and change both in the definition of the situation and of the values held by the participants in it.

There is an important qualification, however, that should be added to Olsen's advice. It is no doubt true that our intuitive reading of *one* organizational situation might seem, superficially, to match one model better than another, whereas our reading of another situation might suggest a different model as more appropriate for its analysis. But if there is no such thing as a fact without a prior (at least rudimentary) theory that permits its observation, it would seem to follow that the facts composing the "nature of the organizational situation" cannot be empirically ascertained in the absence of some prior theoretical commitment. Theoretical models are not simply tools for analyzing situations whose factual character is self-evident, but they also affect the manner in which those situations are "factually" described. Moreover, virtually any theoretical model may be used to analyze any situation, and often the most incongruous matches produce the most interesting results. Because the idea of rational decision is so deeply entrenched in people's commonsense understanding of organizations, the selection of the rational model will in most instances be all but guaranteed unless a more novel alternative is consciously chosen.

7. This and other quotations from MacIntyre, 1984, are reprinted by permission of the University of Notre Dame Press.

8. However, as Geoffrey Vickers once observed (in conversation with Bayard L. Catron), there is an important sense in which the reverse is also true. "People are often predictable," he said, "because they are concerned to be," not because they are caused to be predictable by virtue of being controlled by others.

9. MacIntyre (1984) notes that J. B. Bury once suggested

> that the cause of the foundation of the Roman Empire was the length of Cleopatra's nose: had her features not been perfectly proportioned, Mark Antony would not have been entranced; had he not been entranced he would not have allied himself with Egypt against Octavian; had he not made that alliance, the battle of Actium would not have been fought—and so on. (p. 99)

10. For the record these principles/proverbs include:

> 1) Administrative efficiency is increased by a specialization of the task among the group. 2) Administrative efficiency is increased by arranging the members of the group in a determinate hierarchy of authority. 3) Administrative efficiency is increased by limiting the span of control at any point in the hierarchy to a small number. 4) Administrative efficiency is increased by grouping the workers, for purposes of control, according to (a) purpose, (b) process, (c) clientele, or (d) place. (Simon, 1976, pp. 20-21)

11. In view of MacIntyre's earlier arguments on the impossibility of bureaucratic control, the question arises as to whether or in what sense managing qualifies as a practice under his definition. Broadly construed, his definition can probably accommodate managing, although managing might also be usefully conceived as the process of *facilitating* practice.

12. MacIntyre's description of the role that virtue plays in practices challenges not only the rationalist dichotomy between ends and means, but also the value/fact dichotomy that provides its epistemological basis. On this point he states

> that many of the explanatory projects of the modern social science, a methodological canon of which is the separation of "the facts" . . . from all evaluation, are bound to fail. For the fact that someone was or failed to be courageous or just cannot be recognized as "a fact" by those who accept that methodological canon. (p. 199)

8

Conclusion

Rationalism and the Paradox of Courage

◆ THE ISOLATION of the discourse on responsible government from other vocabularies was identified in Chapter 1 as the chief reason for its moral barrenness and practical naiveté. Stripping away the barriers separating these vocabularies makes responsibility's irreducibly paradoxical nature evident and reveals the futility of rationalism's quest for moral purity and innocence. Because paradox is a—perhaps *the*—cardinal attribute of responsibility, the task of discourse on the subject must therefore be to identify the sources of confusion and struggle that attend our loss of innocence rather than to proffer advice about how to reclaim it.

Despite their artful camouflage in the technical jargon of bureaucratic control, the rationalist paradoxes of obligation, agency, and accountability mirror the generic contradictions of the human predicament that Sören Kierkegaard described. In view of these unresolvable contradictions I have deliberately avoided any attempt either to adjudicate disputes about the proper assignment of responsibility or to identify standards of proper conduct for public servants. The paradoxical character of responsibility, which precludes equating it with one—or indeed any—version of acting correctly, prohibits such strategies of argumentation, as well as moral exhortation and advice giving. This is not, in other words, a book on ethics, of either the "high road" kind, which John Rohr (1978) describes as rooted in moral philosophy and cultural and political tradition, or the "low road" sort, which merely specifies legal sanctions against public servants for actions that are or might be perceived as self-serving.

Although I regard none of these omissions as liabilities, some comment is in order concerning the ironic nature of the continuing attractiveness of such strategies, and even their perceived necessity, not only to rationalist theorists but also to public servants who seek moral guidance from them. The irony consists in the simultaneous belief that objective criteria of responsible action must in principle exist, coupled with skepticism about and even outright rejection of particular criteria whenever anyone actually proposes some. "Relativism" in the abstract, that is, is regarded as intolerable while in everyday practice its necessity is conceded and even embraced. Richard Rorty (1991) captures this irony nicely in the following tongue-in-cheek account of a meeting of philosophers who finally admit that the rationalists are, after all, correct.

> Imagine . . . that a few years from now you open your copy of the *New York Times* and read that the philosophers, in convention assembled, have unanimously agreed that values are objective, science rational, truth a matter of correspondence to reality, and so on. Recent breakthroughs in semantics and meta-ethics, the report goes on, have caused the last remaining noncognitivists in ethics to recant. Similar breakthroughs in philosophy of science have led [Thomas] Kuhn formally to abjure his claim that there is no theory-independent way to reconstruct statements about what is "really there." All the new fuzzies have repudiated all their former views. By way of making amends for the intellectual confusion which the

philosophical profession has recently caused, the philosophers have adopted a short, crisp set of standards of rationality and morality. Next year the convention is expected to adopt the report of the committee charged with formulating a standard of aesthetic taste.

Surely the public reaction to this would not be "Saved!" but rather "Who on earth do these philosophers think they *are*?" It is one of the best things about the intellectual life we Western liberals lead that this *would* be our reaction. No matter how much we moan about the disorder and confusion of the current philosophical scene, about the treason of the clerks, we do not really want things any other way. (pp. 43-44)

Nor, in fact, do most public servants, especially when it is their own rather than others' actions that are involved. Although appealing in the abstract, principles and criteria, especially when taken as absolutes that may be applied without interpretation and modification, typically miss the mark by failing to account for the paradoxes of daily life. Such principles and criteria, so it sometimes seems, are more appropriately reserved for others, especially those whose actions evoke our disapprobation, or as normative guides for institutional reform. It is a virtual truism, however, that the reform of institutions cannot as a practical matter ignore without peril its effect upon the actions of individuals. This is especially true when reform is seen as synonymous with programmatic initiatives that seek to, in Weber's sense of the word, "rationalize" institutional relationships. The pathologies of the sort produced by the paradoxes described in the three preceding chapters are predictable precisely because they fail to discern the vital connections between the personal and the institutional level.

Moreover, even when attention is focused exclusively at an institutional or *macro* level of analysis, the paradoxical nature of reform is still evident in the predictable emergence of powerful counterforces thwarting apparently rational strategies to improve organizational performance. Albert O. Hirschman (1970) explains why this happens in his classic study of organizational decline and recovery, *Exit, Voice, and Loyalty*. He notes how two basic strategies for repairing lapses of organizational performance, each apparently sensible in its own right and necessary for the effective operation of the other, may also paradoxically work at cross purposes. *Exit,* which captures the essence of the idea of economic competition, describes the actions of dissatisfied customers or members to switch their allegiances by buying from or joining *another* organization, the effect of which is to signal their discontent to their current organization's leadership. *Voice,* Hirschman's abbreviated term for politics, is "defined as any attempt at all to change, rather than escape [exit] from, an objectionable state of affairs" (p. 30). The effectiveness of both exit and voice depends upon the presence of incentives for the leadership of an organization to take seriously expressions of discontent by either of these two means—incentives that, as Hirschman explains, are not always present.

Voice, for example, is unlikely to be taken seriously unless it is preceded by or accompanied by the *threat* of exit, whereas exit may send too ambiguous a signal of discontent to be comprehended by the organization's leadership without the clarification that only voice can provide. The presence of an effective exit alternative, moreover, paradoxically tends "to *atrophy the development of the art of voice*" (p. 43), because the easier it is for customer-members to exit an organization, the less they will be inclined to expend their energies working within the system to improve it. The atrophy of voice is especially problematic when, as is often the case, people who are most skillful in exercising voice—those whom Hirschman calls *quality-conscious consumers*—are also those for whom exit is easiest. One consequence of this is the deterioration of public institutions, an example of which is the quality of public school education. When public schools begin to deteriorate, he says, quality-conscious parents are usually the first to exit by sending their children to private schools. The possibly constructive signal that this action sends to the public schools, however, is canceled out by the loss "of those customer-members who would be most motivated and determined to put up a fight against the deterioration if they did not have the alternative of the private schools" (p. 46).

The more general point illustrated by this as well as other examples that Hirschman cites is that the paradoxical relation of exit and voice precludes the possibility of a stable and optimal combination of these two kinds of strategies. Hirschman (1970) claims his analysis

> *cannot* yield . . . a firm prescription for some optimal mix of exit or voice, nor does it wish to accredit the notion that each institution requires its own mix that could be gradually approached by trial and error. At any one point of time, it is possible to say that there is a deficiency of one or the other of our two mechanisms; but it is very unlikely that one could specify a most efficient mix of the two that would be stable over time. The reason is simple: *each recovery mechanism is itself subject to . . . forces of decay.* (p. 124)

Although *Exit, Voice, and Loyalty* does not explicitly address problems of responsible government, it illustrates why the moral advice that rationalists offer is bound to backfire when it ignores the paradoxically opposed incentives for and against following it. In Chapter 4 I explained the reasons for this by showing why the idea of responsibility is itself irreducibly paradoxical, and in Chapters 5, 6, and 7 by examining three vicious, or schismogenic, paradoxes in which particular pathologies predictably result from the rationalists' exclusive association of responsibility with blame and obedience.

Contradiction and opposition, as embodied both in schismogenic and antinomial paradoxes, are not merely aberrations that occasionally intrude upon an otherwise orderly and rational world, but are defining features, both empirically and morally, of the individual's inner experience and of the outer world of social and institutional relations. Paradoxes are empirical in the sense that they enable a kind of prediction and explanation of which rational, linear analysis is incapable; and they are moral because they frame the tensions between the individual's unique quest for self-creation and his or her commitments to others in a moral community. For much the same reason that there can be no stable and optimal mix between the institutional mechanisms that foster exit and voice, so also there can be no unassailable criteria for determining when the impulse for individual self-creation should supersede, or alternatively give way to, one's answerability to others. To insist upon such criteria, and thus to believe the false promises of institutional stability and individual moral purity they offer, is

itself an act of irresponsibility because it shifts the locus of responsibility wholly outside the individual, thus destroying the dialectic between Niebuhr's images, maker and answerer.

To act *practically* in the face of paradox is to reject any strict
distinction between the factual and the moral. Factual under-
standings of social life always presuppose categories of moral
appraisal, while moral judgment is inevitably limited, but also
enabled, by factual assessments of their meaning and their likely
success or failure, however fluid and contingent those assessments
might be. As Thomas McCollough (1991) has put it,

> Moral judgments are not simply "emotive," expressions of how
> people feel, but cognitive claims about how things are, that is, moral
> knowledge. In this regard, moral judgments are similar to scientific
> judgments. Both represent our considered beliefs about reality and
> are subject to critical testing in experience and by others. (p. 11)

So conceived, then, practical action is virtually indistinguishable from responsible action, which struggles to unify the polarities—
between the factual and the moral, the personal and the institutional,
making and answering—that rationalism, out of deep-seated fears
of contingency, uncertainty, and perhaps most of all of genuine
human contact, persists in splitting apart. Such fears are often
disguised by the charge of relativism against any moral viewpoint
that questions rationalism's abstract insistence on absolutes. Relativism, however, is dangerous chiefly insofar as it depicts the
rampant emotivism of isolated, atomistic individuals (including
public servants) acting independently, unanchored by the bonds
of a moral community within which the inevitable paradoxes of
inner experience and social life must and can only be honestly
confronted. Acknowledging paradox, then, does not force an acceptance of relativism, at least as it is typically construed, but
instead views community and relationship as more reliable guides
for responsible action than the abstractions of rationalism's moral
absolutism.

Seen in this light, many of the controversies surrounding proposals for administrative reform assume a very different meaning
and significance. The merits of decentralization, for example,

would from this alternative view be seen as lying not in the creation of smaller-scale structures of accountability whose purpose is to make easier the pinpointing of blame (usually of individuals), but in fostering conditions that permit more intimate and flexible contexts for creatively resolving differences. And administrative discretion would no longer be construed as the action of autonomous individuals informed by abstract considerations of rights and duties, but as an intrinsic feature of practices, described earlier by Alasdair MacIntyre (1984), undertaken by members of a moral community engaged in mutual interpretation and mutual responding. Practices—of the kind that produce what MacIntyre calls internal goods—and moral community are each the reciprocal of the other: Practices, collectively, are the constitutive elements of a moral community, while such a community in turn creates the contexts that enable practices.

The linkage of practices with the managing of paradox suggests a unique opportunity for revitalizing the role of public administration—far more so than for politics, either as the latter is conventionally defined or as redefined at the conclusion of Chapter 7. It is by no means absurd, by way of illustrating the point, to suggest that were Aristotle (MacIntyre's chief source of inspiration for *After Virtue*) writing today, he would be more an administrative theorist than a political theorist. The reasons are not hard to understand. The sheer scale of modern political systems, as measured by population and geographical size even at state and local levels, makes proposals for transforming politics into a vital arena of practice seem highly improbable, reflecting a nostalgic and futile hope for a return to the small-scale politics of intimate association that Aristotle envisioned. Political arenas are restricted in this regard not only by their size but also by their responsibility for authoritatively defining the "nondiscretionary prohibitions" (White, 1976, p. 69) on the behavior of citizens and public servants. These prohibitions, by defining the limits of administrative and citizen discretion and cooperation, appropriately constrain practices, but they cannot in and of themselves generate the kinds of practices through which internal goods are produced and the paradoxical relation between making and answering is managed on an ongoing basis. Rather, it is administration, where the association between citizens and government is more immediate, where the more fruitful possibilities lie for creating and sustaining practices that link citizens to government in a moral community. Some hint of these possibilities can be gleaned from the *Report of the National Performance Review* (Gore, 1993), which recommends that citizens be empowered, government decentralized, and public servants freed from the shackles of overregulation and micromanagement by the Congress. Then, however, the report undermines those very possibilities by offering, with no evident awareness of irony or contradiction, conventional rationalist solutions. Citizens are reduced to the status of mere "customers" to be satisfied, and public servants are still to be held individually accountable—presumably through the same bureaucratic means of reward and punishment that have historically produced the schismogenic paradoxes described in the three preceding chapters.

The view of responsibility offered in this book forces the recognition that, whatever benefits it might offer, the rational reform of government institutions is no substitute for, and in fact may well prevent, strengthening the communal bonds that form the substance of the institutions themselves. Rational reform in the guise of technical fixes and the more precise pinpointing of blame and accountability is not only inadequate for this task, but as earlier chapters have shown, may unwittingly contribute to unraveling the moral fabric of the very institutions that it seeks to mend. Such reform implicitly makes the liberal presumption of a world populated by autonomous individuals, whose presence it paradoxically both cherishes and fears.

> By imagining a world in which individuals can be autonomous not only from institutions but from each other, [the classical liberal view] has forgotten that autonomy, valuable as it is in itself, is only one virtue among others and that without such virtues as responsibility and care, which can be exercised only through institutions, autonomy itself becomes . . . an empty form without substance. (Bellah et al., 1991, p. 12)

Rationalism's flawed view of institutions is thus directly traceable to its impoverished conception of the human self entrapped in the irreconcilable contradiction of being at the same time both selfish and manipulable. If Eugene Schlossberger (1992) is correct in claiming that "Any satisfying account of moral responsibility must accord with a satisfying theory of personal identity" (p. 22), then surely the rationalist conception of responsibility must be adjudged a failure both morally and empirically. By denying the paradoxical antinomy of responsible making and answering, rationalist responsibility's radically divided images of the self produce and sustain the vicious paradoxes—of obligation, agency, accountability, and finally of courage—for which there is no realistic prospect of resolution nor even honest struggle.

* * * * *

On an intelligence mission in the Caribbean, Horatio Hornblower faced the dilemma of having to choose between obeying an order forbidding his ship to engage enemy vessels and disobeying that order so as to prevent—although this seemed to be only a remote possibility—a disaster for British interests that the order, issued many months earlier, could not have foreseen (Forester, 1958). Hankering for action in any event, Hornblower chose the latter course, which as luck would have it vindicated his hunch, and later rationalized his action in his own mind by the maxim that it was better to get into trouble for doing something than for doing nothing.

* * * * *

Whether he was reckless but lucky or courageous and shrewd is a question that troubled Hornblower far more than it puzzles readers of his exploits, who are usually willing to grant him the benefit of the doubt. Hornblower took his promises and obligations seriously, especially as the latter were spelled out in official orders stamped by the seal of the Admiralty. But he also regarded the oath of duty by which he felt morally bound in much the same way that Benjamin Freedman (1982) urges us to consider promising—as still leaving us "free to tinker with the moral web in which we live, leaving us free to create our own moral contradiction" (p. 67). Thus the most compelling objection against the rationalist conception of responsibility is its presumption that, for public servants, no such tinkering should be allowed; and worse, that academics, pundits, and official ethical tribunals have both the wisdom and the rightful prerogative to do their tinkering for them. Although it is true that public servants freely sign contracts promising to fulfill official obligations, such contracts cannot begin to anticipate the varied and subtle meanings of responsibility as they emerge in the often mundane details of everyday life. Contracts can specify only the penalties for the grossest violation of official obligations and the technicalities that define minimal compliance with them. Within these few official constraints, contracts and even obligations more generally can provide only limited moral and practical guidance for public servants as they struggle to act responsibly in an organizational world characterized by ambiguity and doubt. To equate responsibility solely with obligation and blame is to hold out a false promise that moral certainty and moral purity are possible in such a world. But even if they *were* possible, their attainment would have the ironic effect of eliminating the necessity and the possibility of courage, whose exercise requires the presence of doubt. Thus in its paradoxical quest for certainty and control rationalism merely creates yet another paradox: the paradox of courage.

> The paradox of courage is that courageous action, the willingness to speak one's mind and to act in accordance with it, is courageous only when it is undertaken in the presence of doubt and uncertainty. Without doubt, there is no courage. Without ambiguity, imperfection, and anxiety, the acts of speaking, influencing, and giving direction cannot be courageous, because one is free of the uncertainty that gives courage its meaning. (Smith & Berg, 1990, p. 133)

References

Arendt, H. (1958). *The human condition*. Chicago: University of Chicago Press.

Arendt, H. (1971). *The life of the mind*. San Diego: Harcourt Brace Jovanovich.

Arendt, H. (1977). *Eichmann in Jerusalem: A report on the banality of evil*. New York: Penguin.

Argyris, C. (1973). Some limits of rational man organization theory. *Public Administration Review, 33*, 253-267.

Aristotle. (1962). *Nicomachean ethics* (M. Ostwald, Trans.). New York: Macmillan.

Baier, K. (1986). Moral, legal, and social responsibility. In H. Curlter (Ed.), *Shame, responsibility, and the corporation* (pp. 185-195). New York: Haven.

Bateson, G. (1972). *Steps to an ecology of mind*. New York: Ballantine.

Bellah, R. N., Madsen, R., Sullivan, W. M., Swidler, A., & Tipton, S. M. (1985). *Habits of the heart*. Berkeley: University of California Press.

Bellah, R. N., Madsen, R., Sullivan, W. M., Swidler, A., & Tipton, S. M. (1991). *The good society*. New York: Knopf.

Bepko, C. (1985). *The responsibility trap: A blueprint for treating the alcoholic family*. New York: Free Press.

Berger, P. L., & Luckmann, T. (1967). *The social construction of reality*. New York: Doubleday.

Biller, R. P. (1973). Converting knowledge into action: Toward a postindustrial society. In J. S. Jun & W. B. Storm (Eds.), *Tomorrow's organizations: Challenges and strategies* (pp. 35-40). Glenview, IL: Scott, Foresman.

Biller, R. P. (1979). Toward public administration rather than an administration of publics: Strategies of accountable disaggregation to achieve human scale and efficacy, and live within the natural limits of intelligence and other scarce resources. In R. Clayton & W. B. Storm (Eds.), *Agenda for public administration* (pp. 151-172). Los Angeles: University of Southern California Press.

Bowen, M. (1978). *Family therapy in clinical practice.* New York: Jason Aronson.

Brownlow, L. (1958). *A passion for anonymity.* Chicago: University of Chicago Press.

Buber, M. (1947). *Between man and man.* London: Kegan Paul.

Burke, J. P. (1986). *Bureaucratic responsibility.* Baltimore: The Johns Hopkins University Press.

Cohen, M. D., March, J. G., & Olsen, J. (1972). The garbage can model of organizational choice. *Administrative Science Quarterly, 17*(1), 1-25.

Cooper, T. L. (1990). *The responsible administrator: An approach to ethics for the administrative role* (3rd ed.). San Francisco: Jossey-Bass.

Cooper, T. L. (1991). *An ethic of citizenship for public administration.* Englewood Cliffs, NJ: Prentice Hall.

Davidson, D. (1980). Mental events. In N. Block (Ed.), *Readings in philosophy of psychology* (pp. 107-119). Cambridge, MA: Harvard University Press.

Downie, R. S. (1991). Collective responsibility (a reply to Cooper). In L. May & S. Hoffman (Eds.), *Collective responsibility: Five decades of debate in theoretical and applied ethics* (pp. 47-51). Savage, MD: Rowman & Littlefield.

Dworkin, G. (Ed.). (1970). *Determinism, free will, and moral responsibility.* Englewood Cliffs, NJ: Prentice Hall.

Finer, H. (1940). Administrative responsibility in democratic government. In C. J. Friedrich (Ed.), *Public policy* (pp. 247-275). Cambridge, MA: Harvard University Press.

Follett, M. P. (1924). *Creative experience.* New York: Longmans, Green.

Forester, C. S. (1958). *Admiral Hornblower in the West Indies.* Boston: Little, Brown.

Forester, C. S. (1962). *Hornblower and the Hotspur.* Boston: Little, Brown.

Framer, B. (1993). *A psychoanalytic approach to organizational decline: Bowen theory as a tool for organizational analysis.* Unpublished doctoral dissertation, Virginia Polytechnic Institute and State University.

Frankfurt, H. G. (1991). Alternative possibilities and moral responsibility. In P. A. French (Ed.), *The spectrum of responsibility* (pp. 102-111). New York: St. Martin's.

Frederickson, H. G. (1980). *New public administration.* University: University of Alabama Press.

Freedman, B. (1982). A meta-ethics for professional morality. In B. Baumrin & B. Freedman (Eds.), *Moral responsibility and the professions* (pp. 61-79). New York: Haven.

French, P. A. (1991). Fishing the red herrings out of the sea of moral responsibility. In P. A. French (Ed.), *The spectrum of responsibility* (pp. 129-143). New York: St. Martin's.

French, P. A. (1992). *Responsibility matters.* Lawrence: University Press of Kansas.

Friedrich, C. J. (1935). Responsible government service under the American Constitution, Monograph No. 7. In C. J. Friedrich & others, *Problems of the American public service.* New York: McGraw-Hill.

Friedrich, C. J. (1940). Public policy and the nature of administrative responsibility. In C. J. Friedrich (Ed.), *Public policy* (pp. 221-245). Cambridge, MA: Harvard University Press.

Garfinkel, H. (1967). *Studies in ethnomethodology.* Englewood Cliffs, NJ: Prentice Hall.

Gleick, J. (1987). *Chaos: Making a new science.* New York: Penguin.

Goodnow, F. J. (1900). *Politics and administration.* New York: Macmillan.

Gore, A. (1993). *Creating government that works better and costs less: Report of the national performance review.* Washington, DC: U.S. Government Printing Office.

Gould, S. J. (1989). *Wonderful life: The Burgess shale and the nature of history.* New York: Norton.

Gulick, L., & Urwick, L. (1937). *Papers on the science of administration.* New York: Institute of Public Administration.

Hampden-Turner, C. (1971). *Radical man.* Garden City, NY: Doubleday.

Hampden-Turner, C. (1982). *Maps of the mind: Charts and concepts of the mind and its labyrinths.* New York: Collier.

Harmon, M. M. (1989a). "Decision" and "action" as contrasting perspectives in organization theory. *Public Administration Review, 49,* 144-150.

Harmon, M. M. (1989b). The Simon/Waldo debate: A review and update. *Public Administration Quarterly, 12,* 437-451.

Harmon, M. M. (1990). The responsible actor as tortured soul: The case of Horatio Hornblower. In H. D. Kass & B. L. Catron (Eds.), *Images and identities in public administration* (pp. 151-180). Newbury Park, CA: Sage.

Harmon, M. M., & Mayer, R. T. (1986). *Organization theory for public administration.* Boston: Little, Brown.

Hart, D. K. (1975). Social justice, equity, and public administration. *Public Administration Review, 34,* 3-11.

Harvey, J. (1974, Summer). The Abilene paradox: The management of agreement. *Organizational Dynamics, 3,* 63-80.

Herman, S. M., & Korenich, M. (1977). *Authentic management: A gestalt orientation to organizations and their development.* Reading, MA: Addison-Wesley.

Hesse, H. (1957). *Siddhartha* (H. Rosner, Trans.). New York: New Directions.

Hirschman, A. O. (1970). *Exit, voice, and loyalty.* Cambridge, MA: Harvard University Press.

Hughes, P., & Brecht, G. (1975). *Vicious circles and infinity.* New York: Penguin.

Hughes, R. (1993). *Culture of complaint: The fraying of America.* New York: Oxford.

Jung, C. G. (1958). *Answer to Job.* Princeton, NJ: Princeton University Press.

Jung, C. G. (1977). Introduction to the religious and psychological problems of alchemy. *Collected works of C. G. Jung:* Vol. 12 (Vollingen Series XX). Princeton, NJ: Princeton University Press.

Kant, I. (1949). *Critique of pure reason* (F. M. Müller, Trans.). New York: Macmillan.

Karen, R. (1992, February). Shame. *The Atlantic Monthly,* 40-70.

Kaufman, A. S. (1967). Responsibility, moral and legal. In P. Edwards (Ed.), *The encyclopedia of philosophy* (pp. 183-188). New York: Macmillan.

Kaufman, H. (1991). *Time, chance, and organization: Natural selection in a perilous environment* (2nd ed.). Chatham, NJ: Chatham House.

Kelman, H. C., & Hamilton, V. L. (1989). *Crimes of obedience: Toward a social psychology of authority and responsibility.* New Haven, CT: Yale University Press.

Kierkegaard, S. (1957). *The concept of dread* (W. Lowrie, Trans.). Princeton, NJ: Princeton University Press. (Original work published 1844)

LaPorte, T. R. (1971). The recovery of relevance in the study of public organization. In F. Marini (Ed.), *Toward a new public administration: The Minnowbrook perspective* (pp. 17-48). Scranton, PA: Chandler.

Lasch, C. (1979). *The culture of narcissism.* London: Norton.

Lasch, C. (1992, August 10). For shame: Why Americans should be wary of self-esteem. *The New Republic*, 29-34.

Lowi, T. (1969). *The end of liberalism*. New York: Norton.

MacIntyre, A. (1983). Why are the problems of business ethics insoluble? In B. Baumrin & B. Freedman (Eds.), *Moral responsibility and the professions* (pp. 350-359). New York: Haven.

MacIntyre, A. (1984). *After virtue: A study in moral theory* (2nd ed.). Notre Dame, IN: Notre Dame University Press.

Mackie, J. L. (1977). *Ethics: Inventing right and wrong*. Harmondsworth, UK: Penguin.

March, J. G., & Simon, H. A. (1958). *Organizations*. New York: John Wiley.

March, J. G. (1976). The technology of foolishness. In J. G. March & J. Olsen (Eds.), *Ambiguity and choice in organizations* (pp. 69-81). Bergen, Norway: Universitetsforlaget.

Marini, F. (Ed.) (1971). *Toward a new public administration: The Minnowbrook perspective*. Scranton, PA: Chandler.

Maslow, A. H. (1965). *Eupsychian management*. Homewood, IL: Irwin.

Maslow, A. H. (1970). *Motivation and personality*. New York: Harper & Row.

May, L., & Hoffman, S. (Eds.). (1991). *Collective responsibility: Five decades of debate in theoretical and applied ethics*. Savage, MD: Rowman & Littlefield.

May, R. (1991). *The cry for myth*. New York: Norton.

McCollough, T. E. (1991). *The moral imagination and public life: Raising the ethical question*. Chatham, NJ: Chatham House.

McKeon, R. (1957). The development and the significance of the concept of responsibility. *Revue Internationale de Philosophie, 11*, 3-32.

McSwain, C. J. (1985, March). *A structuralist perspective on organizational ethos*. Paper presented at the annual meeting of the American Society for Public Administration, Indianapolis, IN.

McSwain, C. J., & White, O. F. (1987). The case for lying, cheating, and stealing: Personal development as ethical guidance for managers. *Administration & Society, 18*, 411-431.

Melville, H. (1948). *Billy Budd*. Cambridge, MA: Harvard University Press.

Milgram, S. (1974). *Obedience to authority: An experimental view*. New York: Harper & Row.

Morris, W. (Ed.). *The American heritage dictionary of the English language*. (1969). Boston: American Heritage and Houghton Mifflin.

Mosher, F. C. (1968). *Democracy and the public service*. New York: Oxford University Press.

Niebuhr, H. R. (1963). *The responsible self: An essay in Christian moral philosophy*. New York: Harper & Row.

Nye, A. (1990). *Words of power: A feminist reading of the history of logic*. New York: Routledge.

Olsen, J. (1976). Choice in an organized anarchy. In J. G. March & J. Olsen (Eds.), *Ambiguity and choice in organizations* (pp. 82-139). Bergen, Norway: Universitetsforlaget.

Pateman, C. (1985). *The problem of political obligation*. Berkeley: University of California Press.

Pateman, C. (1988). *The sexual contract*. Cambridge: Polity.

Phillips, N. (1994a, May 24). Former Exxon chief revises story on spill. *Washington Post*, p. A3.

Phillips, N. (1994b, June 14). Exxon found reckless in Alaska spill. *Washington Post*, p. A3.

Quinn, R. E. (1988). *Beyond rational management: Mastering the paradoxes and competing demands of high performance*. San Francisco: Jossey-Bass.

Rank, O. (1978). *Will therapy*. New York: Norton. (Original work published 1936)

Rawls, J. (1971). *A theory of justice*. Cambridge, MA: Harvard University Press.

Reich, R. B. (1987). *Tales of a new America*. New York: Times Books.

Revill, D. (1992). *The roaring silence: John Cage: A life*. New York: Arcade.

Rohr, J. A. (1978). *Ethics for bureaucrats: An essay on law and values*. New York: Marcel Dekker.

Rorty, R. (1989). *Contingency, irony, and solidarity*. New York: Cambridge University Press.

Rorty, R. (1991). *Objectivity, relativism, and truth*. New York: Cambridge University Press.

Sandel, M. J. (1984, May 7). Morality and the liberal ideal. *The New Republic*, 15-17.

Sartre, J. P. (1956). *Being and nothingness: An essay on phenomenological ontology* (H. E. Barnes, Trans.). New York: Philosophical Library.

Sayre, W., & Kaufman, H. (1960). *Governing New York City*. New York: Norton.

Schlossberger, E. (1992). *Moral responsibility and persons*. Philadelphia: Temple University Press.

Schön, D. A. (1983). Organizational learning. In G. Morgan (Ed.), *Beyond method: Strategies for social research* (pp. 114-128). Beverly Hills, CA: Sage.

Schuman, D. (1992, April 1). Our fixation on rights is dysfunctional and deranged. *The Chronicle of Higher Education*, p. B1-2.

Simon, H. A. (1946). The proverbs of public administration. *Public Administration Review, 6*, 53-67.

Simon, H. A. (1952). Development of theory of democratic administration: Replies and comments. *American Political Science Review, 46*, 494-496.

Simon, H. A. (1976). *Administrative behavior: A study of decision-making processes in administrative organization* (3rd ed.). New York: Free Press. (Original work published 1947)

Smith, K. K., & Berg, D. N. (1990). *Paradoxes of group life: Understanding conflict, paralysis, and movement in group dynamics*. San Francisco: Jossey-Bass.

Steele, S. (1990). *The content of our character: A new vision of race in America*. New York: St. Martin's.

Steinem, G. (1992). *Revolution from within: A book of self-esteem*. Boston: Little, Brown.

Stent, G. S. (1978). *Paradoxes of progress*. Chicago: University of Chicago Press.

Stivers, C. (1993). *Gender images in public administration: Legitimacy and the administrative state*. Newbury Park, CA: Sage.

Stone, D. (1988). *Policy paradox and political reason*. Glenview, IL: Scott-Foresman.

Trusted, J. (1984). *Free will and responsibility*. New York: Oxford University Press.

Vaill, P. B. (1981). Review of S. A. Culbert & J. J. McDonough, *The invisible war. The Journal of Applied Behavioral Science, 17*, 425-427.

Vaill, P. B. (1989). *Managing as a performing art*. San Francisco: Jossey-Bass.

Waldo, D. W. (1952a). Development of theory of democratic administration. *American Political Science Review, 46*, 81-103.

Waldo, D. W. (1952b). Development of theory of democratic administration: Replies and comments. *American Political Science Review, 46,* 501-503.

Waldo, D. W. (1984). *The administrative state: A study of the political theory of American public administration* (2nd ed.). New York: Holmes & Meier. (Original work published 1948)

Weber, M. (1946). Politics as a vocation. In H. H. Gerth & C. Wright Mills (Eds. & Trans.), *From Max Weber: Essays in sociology* (pp. 77-128). New York: Oxford.

Weinberg, L. (in press). Seeing through organization: Exploring the constitutive quality of social relations. *Administration & Society.*

White, O. F. (1973). The concept of administrative praxis. *The Journal of Comparative Administration, 5,* 55-86.

White, O. F. (1976). Macro and micro approaches to policy analysis—Notes toward a synthesis. In P. M. Gregg (Ed.), *Problems of theory in policy analysis* (pp. 63-76). Lexington, MA: Heath.

White, O. F. (1990). Reframing the authority-participation debate. In G. L. Wamsley, C. T. Goodsell, J. A. Rohr, P. Kronenberg, O. F. White, J. Wolf, & C. Stivers, *Refounding public administration* (pp. 182-245). Newbury Park, CA: Sage.

Whitmont, E. (1982). *Return of the goddess.* New York: Crossroad.

Williams, B. (1985). *Ethics and the limits of philosophy.* Cambridge, MA: Harvard University Press.

Wills, G. (1987). *Reagan's America: Innocents at home.* New York: Doubleday.

Wilson, W. (1941). The study of administration. *Political Science Quarterly, 66,* 481-506. (Reprinted from 1887, June)

Index

About the Author

Michael M. Harmon is Professor of Public Administration at the George Washington University, where he has taught since 1970. He previously taught at the University of Southern California and the Federal Executive Institute and served as an organizational development specialist at the U.S. Agency for International Development. Since 1970, he also has been a visiting professor at universities in Beijing, China; Ottawa, Canada; and Sydney, Australia. He is the author of *Action Theory for Public Administration* (1981) and coauthor, with Richard T. Mayer, of *Organization Theory for Public Administration (1986)*. Numbered among his heroes are Mary Parker Follett and Horatio Hornblower.